Narrative and Stylistic Pat
the Films of Stanley Kub

García Mainar's critical study of the work of Stanley Kubrick offers both a formal analysis of his films based on style and narrative pattern, and a theoretical, postmodernist approach to ideas presented in the films. García Mainar is particularly concerned with analyzing the relevance of spectacle in Kubrick's films, seeing it as a disruptive mechanism that can call into question the value and necessity of communication. He identifies different kinds of spectacle in the films, and proceeds to a detailed examination of these different forms in *2001: A Space Odyssey, Barry Lyndon,* and *Full Metal Jacket.*

Luis M. García Mainar teaches English at the University of Zaragoza, Spain.

European Studies in American Literature and Culture

Edited by Reingard M. Nischik (*Constance*)

LUIS M. GARCÍA MAINAR

NARRATIVE AND STYLISTIC PATTERNS
IN THE FILMS OF

STANLEY KUBRICK

CAMDEN HOUSE

First published 1999 by Camden House.
Reprinted in paperback 2000.

Camden House is an imprint of Boydell & Brewer Inc.
PO Box 41026, Rochester, NY 14604–4126 USA
and of Boydell & Brewer Limited
PO Box 9, Woodbridge, Suffolk IP12 3DF, UK

ISBN
Cloth: 1–57113–264–3
Paperback 1–57113–265–1

Library of Congress Cataloging-in-Publication Data
García Mainar, Luis M.
    Narrative and stylistic patterns in the films of Stanley Kubrick /
Luis M. García Mainar.
        p.   cm. – (European Studies in American literature and
culture)
    Includes bibliographical references and index.
    ISBN: cloth 1–57113–264–3; paperback 1–57113–265–1 (both alk. paper)
    1. Kubrick, Stanley – Criticism and interpretation. I. Title.
II. Series.
PN1998.3.K83G37   1999
791.43'0233'092—DC21   98–32423
                           CIP

A catalogue record for this title is available from the British Library.

This publication is printed on acid-free paper.
Printed in the United States of America

Para Santos y María

Contents

Acknowledgments

I AM DEEPLY GRATEFUL TO A NUMBER OF people who have made this book possible. The lecturers in the doctoral courses I took from 1991 to 1993 have probably contributed whatever strengths my argument may have. I am, therefore, indebted to Francisco Collado Rodríguez, Chantal Cornut-Gentille D'Arcy, Celestino Deleyto Alcalá, José Angel García Landa, and Susana Onega Jaén, all of them from the University of Zaragoza. I am also grateful to María Delgado, Peter Evans, from Queen Mary and Westfield College (University of London), and Vickie Olsen, from the University of the Basque country, for their help in collecting bibliographical material both in Britain and the United States. Part of the present work would not have been written without their generous aid. Finally, my deepest thanks go to my doctoral supervisor, Celestino Deleyto, whose criticism, support, and resilience have markedly contributed to the completion of this task.

Technical and Critical Terms

crosscutting: editing technique of alternating shots of two lines of action, suggesting the interrelation between them.

diegetic: from the narratological concept of diegesis; used to refer to the world of a film's story; even to the events that are presumed to have occurred.

dissolve: editing device consisting in the gradual replacement of one shot by a second shot that is slowly superimposed until it becomes completely visible and the previous shot disappears.

extradiegetic: used to refer to all the material and all the effects absent from a film's story but provided by the text, such as the opening credit-titles.

fade: editing device in which a shot gradually darkens as the screen goes black or a shot gradually appears as a dark screen brightens.

match on action: editing cut that places two takes of the same action together, making it seem to continue uninterrupted.

mise-en-abyme: notion of the mirroring image which reduplicates the text that contains it. Useful metafictional concept.

shot/reverse shot: two shots edited together, alternating characters in a conversation situation. The classic version of the device tends to show the two characters for approximately the same length of time. The device may be altered by self-consciously withholding one of the two shots.

syuzhet: Russian formalist concept denoting the actual arrangement and presentation of events in a narrative.

three-point lighting: classical Hollywood lighting method that uses three light sources in order to create depth and enhance characters' features.

tracking shot: shot in which the camera moves through space parallel to the ground.

Introduction

THE ORIGIN OF THIS BOOK CAN BE TRACED back to my first research in the study of cinema under the new perspective offered by critical theories. The discovery of serious studies and analyses of cinematographic texts led me to appreciate theories that attempted the close analysis of formal structures as a method of discussing the originality and value of the text. Formalist approaches such as the ones led by the French critics Jean-Pierre Oudart and Jean-Louis Baudry; British critics, including Stephen Heath and the *Screen* contributors; and the re-elaboration of formalism attempted by David Bordwell aroused my interest in and enthusiasm for the analysis of cinema.

The second starting point for this work was the filmography of Stanley Kubrick, a thematically heterogeneous group of films that had discouraged the critics. The result was that there were not many books devoted to the analysis of Kubrick's art, and none of those few attempted the kind of study I wanted to undertake. A few books had appeared in the seventies and early eighties, featuring analyses that seemed to draw on the explicatory trend of film studies. These works were Alexander Walker's *Stanley Kubrick Directs* and Norman Kagan's *The Cinema of Stanley Kubrick*, both published in 1972, together with Gene D. Phillips's *Stanley Kubrick: A Film Odyssey*, published in 1975. The eighties saw the appearance of Michel Ciment's *Kubrick* (1983), Thomas Allen Nelson's *Kubrick: Inside a Film Artist's Maze* (1982), and Robert Philip Kolker's *A Cinema of Loneliness* (1988), which includes a chapter devoted to Kubrick's filmography. All of these books try to explain how Kubrick's films work and the meanings they produce. They use stylistic and narrative analysis to propose a consistent use of formal parameters that they interpret as indicative of a homogeneous ideological project. The search for such parameters is based on the hypothesis that all of his films revolve around the same themes. In short, this kind of analysis is mainly based on stylistic aspects that lead to the evaluation of the cinematographic quality of the films and is highly influenced by the idea of the auteur who produced a coherent oeuvre.

In the second half of the eighties Kubrick seemed to be rediscovered by the critics, as reflected in the many articles written in those years and in the early 1990s. It was then Kubrick's modernity that was mainly analyzed and advocated by criticism. Rainer Rother's "Das Kunstwerk als Konstruktionsaufgabe" (1989) seems to be the first example of criticism that was to concentrate on the connections of Kubrick's work with the new sensibility of postmodernism. The nineties have seen the publication of a great number of articles that have tended to select those films that seem to approximate the main issues of postmodernist thought. The films that have most often become the object of study have been *2001: A Space Odyssey* and *Full Metal Jacket*, since they clearly include reflections on, respectively, the difficulty of obtaining knowledge and current gender discourses. Finally, a book was published in 1994, in which a return to the study of the stylistic and narrative patterns of Kubrick's films was formulated: Mario Falsetto's *Stanley Kubrick: A Narrative and Stylistic Analysis.*

These various works have sketched two main paths in the study of Kubrick's cinema: a formalist one based on the analysis of style and narrative patterning, and a completely symptomatic[1] study that draws on the different interpretive cues present in the films and that generally leads the critic to postmodernist issues. There was no major study that attempted to establish links between a formalist analysis and the postmodernist ideas the films might suggest. Such a work is badly needed if we are to escape, on the one hand, from the mere evaluation that stems from stylistic analyses, and, on the other, from a consideration of postmodernist issues that at times seems completely disconnected from the films. This book will attempt to bridge the gap between structure and ideology.

The last few years have witnessed the flourishing of poststructuralist critical tendencies. Deconstruction and feminist theories have flooded the field of cinema studies with analyses that attempt a symptomatic reading of all kinds of cinematographic texts. Analyses of this kind have been defended on the grounds that they provide interesting accounts of the ways in which cinema works, and that this fresh reinterpretation of the filmic experience is precisely that at which criticism should aim. While I basically agree with this notion, I have a problem with it. These poststructuralist readings are original and interesting, but they pay too much attention to their own theoretical basis and too little to the actual text they are supposed to teach us to appreciate. Most of the time these complex theoretical analyses alienate the reader from an attempt better

---

[1] By the study of symptomatic meaning I refer, following David Bordwell, to the set of meanings the film may divulge "involuntarily," a kind of meaning that can be traced to the artist's obsessions or to economic, political, or ideological processes (1989, 8–9).

to understand the films. The critics defend the relevance of their studies, mainly, on the basis of the success of the theoretical advance they propose, using the films merely as illustrations of their ideas and failing to make a close study of them. The feeling of alienation experienced by the reader of these works results from their failure to connect the theoretical points with the structures and themes of the films.

It was in this context that this work was undertaken, as an approach where the theory should not be allowed to muffle the voice of the texts. Also, drawing conclusions from a close analysis of the most basic stylistic patterns could help define the kind of narrative form that governed the texts. Later, the relevant aspects could be dissected, which, in the case of the films subjected to analysis, were focalization and metaphor. This analysis of narrative form suggested conclusions that allowed the redefinition of some aspects of narration: in this case, the elements of style were redefined as they were affected by the notion of auto-focalization. And from this redefinition the conclusions were applied to broader issues, such as the main concerns of poststructuralism. This process, which would gradually ascend from the elements of the text, would allow one to connect theoretical aspects with basic elements of structure, tracing theoretical aspects to their "physical" manifestation. This procedure produces a critical system that stands a better chance of helping viewers improve their appreciation of the texts.

The application of conclusions from this process to the analysis of individual films would again help to combine formal and theoretical considerations. This combination would provide a richer appreciation of similarities and differences between films, which would become the basis of more complex considerations that might bring back the joy of rediscovering cinema under a new light.

I also wanted to analyze the relevance of spectacle as a narrative mechanism and its influence on style, a discussion I had started in my research on *Dr. Strangelove* (1991). Was spectacle part of the strategies of mainstream cinema? Was it not so persuasive and common to different styles and genres that the possibility of its belonging to the classical code should be seriously studied? The book is an attempt to formulate an answer to the concern with the relationship between spectacle and the precepts of deconstruction. Since spectacle seems to provide the possibility of disruption of the code entertained by deconstruction, it would be instructive to study the ways in which spectacle may contribute to an analysis of deconstruction. The dead-end posed by deconstruction with respect to art, which is typical of all poststructuralisms and postmodernist attitudes, needed exploration. If communication is impossible because language is a play of signifiers unable to provide a coherent meaning, what is the use of studying texts critically? We will never learn to appreciate them better if they are submerged in the impossibility of conveying meaning.

Another advantage of the attempt to combine structuralism and poststructuralisms was that such an analysis would bring the critic into closer contact with the mechanisms that produce meaning, thereby allowing a better scrutiny of the basic elements that contribute to the establishment of the ideology of the text. An analysis that tries to connect the final meaning with its origin allows the critic to trace the origin of the ideology back to the ways in which such an ideology has been modeled. This analysis can be used to deconstruct the text's "final meaning," or at least the claims of its inevitability.

The work of Stanley Kubrick was chosen because he is one of the few "auteurs" in contemporary cinema; therefore, one could expect from him a relatively coherent filmography. This coherence would facilitate the study of similarities and differences among his films, providing a perceivable core of structures and contents on which to elaborate any future conclusions. Since he was an American filmmaker living in Britain, the kind of cinema he had produced could be studied as a re-elaboration of classical cinema at the hands of one of its "rebellious" children who had grown apart. His status as an independent filmmaker who produced his own films seemed to secure a certain different view on the phenomenon of cinema, so tightly controlled by the American industry where the director is only one element in the complex production of films by big studios. Besides, Kubrick had not made a film since 1987, and one could wonder if it might be as a result of the conclusions about cinema that he had reached in his most recent experiences.[2]

Kubrick's films are difficult tasks for the critics, some of whom have been baffled by the novelty of a cinema they do not understand or accept, while others have hailed him as one of the few directors who can be labeled an artist. In both cases his cinema has been described as highly mysterious and ambiguous, which, for some critics, is a characteristic of his modernity. For Rainer Rother, Kubrick's films are attempts to prove his conviction that events are open to free interpretations, reflecting on the possibilities of cinematic narration in the film and within a story (1989, 387). Kubrick has acknowledged that his main goals when making a film are subtlety and an oblique treatment of themes:

---

[2] This period of inactivity has come to an end, since he has just completed *Eyes Wide Shut*, a psycho-thriller starring Tom Cruise and Nicole Kidman.

I think that for a movie or a play to say anything really truthful about life, it has to do so very obliquely, so as to avoid all pat conclusions and neatly tied-up ideas. The point of view it is conveying has to be completely entwined with a sense of life as it is, and has to be got across through a subtle injection into the audience's consciousness. Ideas which are valid and truthful are so multi-faceted that they don't yield themselves to frontal assault. The ideas have to be discovered by the audience, and their thrill in making the discovery makes those ideas all the more powerful. You use the audience's thrill of surprise and discovery to reinforce your ideas, rather than reinforce them artificially through plot points or phoney drama or phoney stage dynamics put in to power them across (Kubrick 1960/1961, 14).

He wanted to develop an ambiguous visual style:

Once you are dealing on a nonverbal level, ambiguity is unavoidable. But it's the ambiguity of all art, of a fine piece of music or a painting. "Explaining" works of art contributes nothing but a superficial "cultural" value which has no value except for critics and teachers who have to earn a living (quoted in Joseph Gelmis, 1970, 303–304).

The facts that this ambiguity is accompanied by narrative forms that, although eccentric, are still akin to those of mainstream cinema, and that the films rely on the effects of spectacle, make Kubrick's work particularly interesting. It offers a mixture of traditional codes and novelty that seems to fit the mixed critical mode with which this study proposes to experiment. Besides, the awareness shown by the director of the processes at work in his films promises a high degree of reflection on the mechanisms of cinema to be found in the texts.

This book will begin with the elaboration of a poetics of Kubrick's style, that is, the specific ways in which editing, cinematographic properties, mise-en-scène, and sound work in his films. In this first part the effects of the stylistic options chosen by the films will be studied, mainly the overall tendency to favor the construction of an external position for the viewer. The patterns of focalization exploit the films' capacity to present the visual material as too spectacular or mysterious for the viewer to identify with it. The viewer is asked to decodify the text by spotting metaphorical meanings, a reading that places viewers in an external position from which they can attempt a coherent comprehension of the film.[3]

---

[3] This external position posited for the viewer separates the films from the usual identification strategies of mainstream cinema and will be considered a mark of Kubrick's "modernity."

The kind of focalization used by Kubrick's films also tends to emphasize the purely visual side of cinema. The iconic status of cinematographic language is constantly claimed by these films. Consequently, the capacity of the icon both to convey meaning and to disseminate it will also be the object of scrutiny. The ways in which the icon can modify our understanding of the rhetorical structures created by Kubrick's cinema through style will be analyzed. This study will attempt to link the potentialities of the icon with the narrativity-antinarrativity debate that has pervaded poststructuralist discussions of ideology, the role of women, and the workings of languages.

The second part of this study will concentrate on the application of the conclusions reached in the first part, on the influence of the icon on style, to one example of poststructuralism: deconstruction. It will briefly study the tenets of deconstruction in order to suggest a theoretical alternative to its apparent skepticism about the capacity of language to signify. It will use the analysis of the three films by Kubrick mentioned above to explore how the concepts suggested by the study of the icon can help us to discern a new analytic realm. In this new dimension the critic will be allowed to enjoy the richness of the cinematographic text. The conceptual advance produced by the theoretical consideration of the icon will lead to a position from which the tenets of deconstruction will be criticized. The liberation from the constraints of one of the paradigmatic theoretical systems of poststructuralism might open the door to a new criticism that would focus on the details of the text rather than on a complex theoretical world disconnected from the experience of viewing.

The method followed in this work will be initially based on David Bordwell's study of cinema (1988), which mixes constructivist theories, Russian formalism, and structuralism. This framework will be complemented by diverse sources that represent the various kinds of poststructuralisms. The two poststructuralist tendencies on which the book will mostly focus will draw on the work of Laura Mulvey, Jane Flax, and Kaja Silverman in the case of studies of gender difference, and on Jacques Derrida, Roland Barthes, and John M. Ellis in the case of deconstruction.

Among the many narratological approaches that have been applied to the study of literary works, Mieke Bal's *Narratology* (1985) seems most useful for my attempt to analyze film. As all narratological accounts do, Bal divides the narrative work into several levels with varying degrees of abstraction. *Fabula* is the most abstract level, which comprises the collection of logically and chronologically related events that happen to entities Bal calls actors. The *story* is a reworking of the fabula material, which now appears with specifically temporal and spatial cues and is presented from a certain point of view. The *text* is the final structured whole, in which the narrative is related by an agent. The level of the fabula includes abstract, indefinite notions about events, actors, time, and location. The story is a step forward in the definition of these notions: events are arranged temporally and spatially, actors are transformed into characters, and the events are presented from a specific point of view through the activity of focalization. The text is the realm of narrators, of agents who "tell" the events.

Bal's account of narrative levels is particularly useful in our study of cinema, because she stresses the nature of focalization as a perceptual activity of selection of information. The connections established between the act of vision and focalization make this an appropriate model for the cinematic medium, where the appearance of the different parts of material offered to the viewer is usually motivated by the gaze of a character. The distinction between story and text, between the organization of events and their final presentation, however, poses some problems when we attempt to apply it to cinema. The close relationship in films between the mechanisms of representation, which offer a strong impression of reality, and the reality represented makes it difficult to differentiate two levels where, according to Bal, one is the actual presentation (text) and the other the organization of the represented (story).

The nature of cinema seems to demand a division into just two levels, since story and text are proximate in filmic narratives. Although Bal's description of focalization as a perceptual activity is certainly useful, its three-level division makes us turn our attention toward other accounts of narratology applied to literature that would seem more suitable to cinema. Gérard Genette, in his *Narrative Discourse: An Essay in Method* (1980), proposes a division into story, narrative, and narrating, where the last two are to be placed at the same level — the former designating the signifier, discourse, or narrative text, and the latter the narrative action (27). Genette's decision to place narrative and narrating at the same level seems to acknowledge the intimate relationship between the organization of material in a narrative and the action of representing such material. He still maintains the distinction between these two, however, as his model stems from the analysis of literary works. Seymour Chatman's *Story and Discourse* (1978) claims to be a study of narratology applicable to both literary and cinematic works. He proposes two levels, called story and discourse, or the levels of content and expression, respectively. Story contains the events plus the characters and the settings; discourse is the level of order and selection that lead to the final presentation of the events.

Chatman's model is similar to the models proposed by the Russian formalists and represents a step toward another proposal that was also influenced by the formalists. David Bordwell's *Narration in the Fiction Film* (1988) takes up this basic distinction between what is represented and its representation and adopts the Russian formalist concepts of fabula and *syuzhet*. The fabula "embodies the action as a chronological, cause-and-effect chain of events occurring within a given duration and a spatial field" (49); it is something that the reader/viewer reconstructs by using the material given by the actual work of art. The syuzhet "is the actual arrangement and presentation of the fabula in the film" (50); it handles the story events and arranges them according to principles of organization. Another level that helps in the final configuration of the work is the system of style, which uses film techniques to express the syuzhet. Style "simply names the film's systematic use of cinematic devices" (50). Syuzhet and style coexist in narrative films, since they refer to different aspects of the process of production/apprehension of a work of art: "the syuzhet embodies the film as a 'dramaturgical' process; style embodies it as a 'technical' one" (50). Style is not, therefore, at the same level as fabula and syuzhet; style only designates the various ways in which the same information may be presented to the viewer by using the technical array cinema possesses.

Bordwell's model seems to me the best attempt at applying narratological concepts to the study of cinema, because it includes in a single level, the syuzhet, Bal's levels of story and text. This move takes into account the great proximity in cinema between the mechanisms of organization of the fabula and those of the expression of such organization. Celestino Deleyto's "Focalization in Film Narrative" (1991) is a critique of Bal's scheme and an attempt at approximating it to Bordwell's positions. Deleyto's article focuses on focalization, which is placed by Bal at the level of the story; he thinks it belongs to the same level as the activity of narration as understood by Bal, which she places in the text. For Deleyto a film is able to narrate without the existence of an explicit narrator as understood by literary narratology. Narrating is a symbolic activity that does not need to be associated with an identifiable agent. What a viewer does to shape the collection of data given by the film is, mainly, to look, and this "activity requires a textual agent which produces the signs he is looking at" (165). Deleyto calls this activity *focalization* and recalls the direct relationship between the represented and the representation as support for his proposal:

Summing up what has been said so far, we are now in a position to point at two general differences between novel and film from a narrative point of view. In both genres, focalization and narration are key concepts in the analysis of the narrative. In the novel focalization is not explicit in the text, but must be elicited by the critic from the information given by the narrator. We read what the narrator says but only metaphorically do we perceive what the focalizer perceives. In film focalization may be explicit in the text, in general through external or internal "gazes," and works simultaneously and independently from narration. Both activities, focalization and narration are textual (166).

Deleyto, therefore, defends the idea that focalization in film should be placed at the same level as what Bal calls narration. He restricts the meaning of narration as explained by Bal, applying it only to instances of explicit narration (voice-over, onscreen or intertitles) (164). Deleyto perceives another activity at work in cinema that should be placed at the same level as narration and focalization: the activity of representation. Representation includes all the elements of mise-en-scène, the staging of the events in front of the camera, which, according to Deleyto, is textual, too:

> As far as the mise-en-scène is concerned, a film narrative works in a similar way to a play. According to theorists of drama, there is no narration in a play but *representation*. There is a story and, therefore, a fabula; but that story is not narrated but represented by means of actors and a dramatic space, with a certain relationship with the audience (163–164).

Deleyto, therefore, argues that representation, narration, and focalization should be placed at the same level, which he calls the level of the text. He even mentions, although he does not develop this point, the possibility that other aspects, such as character and space, should belong to the same level as the previously mentioned concepts (166). In any case, the interesting notion introduced by Deleyto is that the concepts of narratology devised to account for literary texts must be transformed when applied to cinema, and that this transformation must place concepts that Bal had set on two different levels (story and text) within the same level, whether we call it story, text, or, following Bordwell, syuzhet. The equivalent activity to that of narration in a novel is performed by narration, focalization, and representation in a film (165). Deleyto's scheme is, in the end, similar to Bordwell's: he also accepts the concept of style as the factor that would account for all the possible representations of a certain syuzhet.

Deleyto's analysis of the activity of representation in films coincides, in its general outline, with Edward Branigan's conceptions of narration and what he calls point of view. *Point of View in the Cinema* (1984) expresses his seminal idea, which is taken up by Deleyto, that the process of narration is not personified but constitutes a symbolic activity. Similarly, the camera, traditionally taken to be the origin of cinematic expression, does not exist as a profilmic object that changes place throughout the film; it is, rather, a hypothesis about space constructed by the spectators once they have perceived the filmic material on the screen (39–56). Branigan also coincides with Deleyto when he defines *subjectivity* or *point of view*: for him subjectivity "may be conceived as a specific instance or level of narration where the telling is *attributed* to a character in the narrative and received by us *as if* we were in the situation of a character" (73). The act of representing something in cinema is mainly a creation of space, "a display of the visual through acts of vision" (73). Branigan says that a typical characteristic of classical cinema is its tendency to provide subjectivity by means of spatial variables, justifying its characters spatially and relegating other point-of-view methods to a secondary place (100). This does not mean that the only way to provide points of view is by using spatial variables. The viewer's expectations, color, sound, and dialogue are other ways of expressing subjectivity. This leaves the way open, within Branigan's model, for accounts of subjectivity that place more emphasis on the attitude of the characters, on the position attributed to the characters by the evolving line of emotion and identification, than on the arrangement of space. This is the argument I will use in my discussion of auto-focalization.

In his more recent *Narrative Comprehension and Film* (1992) Branigan remains faithful to his ideas and still links subjectivity to narration. Narration, in this book, consists in controlling the viewer's access to the information contained by the film, which consequently creates abundant differences in knowledge among characters and between the text and the viewer. Subjectivity is a strategy of narration that provides a viewer or speaker with a disparity of knowledge. This helps the narrative control the viewer's access to the knowledge of the fabula (76). Branigan's new account of subjectivity offers support for the conception of attitudinal focalization I will use in my discussion of auto-focalization. Branigan agrees that to create subjectivity a film has to show a character's reaction to the space attributed to him/her. He is consistent about the importance attributed to the presentation of space in his previous book, but here he introduces the attitudinal component as essential for the construction of subjectivity (125–160).

I would now like to outline a brief account of the representing activity of cinema, adopting previously mentioned models and slightly modifying them. I agree with Deleyto's discussion of the activities a film carries out in its communicative process. His model does away with the distinction between story and text that is difficult to handle in cinema, and it accounts for the intimate relationship between the iconic mechanisms of representation and the represented. The only modification I would suggest is briefly suggested by Deleyto himself: space and character should be placed at the same level as the activities of representation, narration, and focalization. The creation of space and character is carried out through these activities (visual presentation, dialogue, performance, etc.) to the extent that, for instance, the appearance of a certain portion of space is usually motivated by a character's gaze, the creation of such a space therefore being inherent to the activity of focalization. In these cases there is no distance between the means of representation (focalization) and the represented (space) that would allow us to define one of them (space) as more abstract, less defined than the other (focalization). I think that we should, therefore, only distinguish a level of the fabula, an abstract level of the cause-effect chronological sequence never shown, and a level of the story, or text, or syuzhet (whatever we wish to call it) that would include all of the more defined, concrete, actualized material.

I also think that we should include the only aspect not dealt with by Deleyto in his article — time — within the syuzhet. The representation of time is also carried out through a visual medium. The creation of time depends on the appearance of actions developing in time on the screen. Time is, therefore, intimately linked to the iconic presentation of events. The short distance between the signifier and the signified is here similar to that in the creation of space or character. Finally, I would include the system of style, technical devices allowing different representations of the same syuzhet, as the third level that would round off the different levels we can distinguish and study in a film narrative.

I hope that the book that follows inspires in its readers the same interest in the subject I felt when I decided to undertake this project. Using Kubrick's words when he was asked about *A Clockwork Orange*, I would like this work to open the door to an art that can make life more enjoyable or more endurable, an art that is always exhilarating and never depressing, whatever its subject matter may be.

Part one of the work will start by introducing an analysis of the ways in which Kubrick's cinema uses formal options. The book's concept of poetics is, therefore, restricted to the description and study of the ways texts employ formal structures, which is a good basis on which to build the edifice of more profound discussion. This abrupt jump into the core of poetics will be gradually clarified as we progress through the intricate array of possibilities opened by the films. Little by little this bare discussion will be clad with further elaborations on the essential stylistic patterns, which will reveal their relevance within a more general system of signification. Let us, therefore, begin with some brief comments on the use of editing.

Scene from The Killing: *Making plans for the robbery.*
Note the elaborate composition of the shot. From left to right:
Elisha Cook Jr., Sterling Hayden, Jay C. Flippen.
© *1956 United Artists Corporation. All rights reserved.*

1: Poetics

Editing

SHOT/REVERSE SHOT SEQUENCES ARE WIDELY employed in Kubrick's cinema. Although many of the cases in which they appear conform with the traditionally accepted use and presentation of the device, they are often altered to produce complex and interesting effects at a formal level. This mixture of adherence to and distortion of classical cinematic strategies hints at Kubrick's special place within contemporary cinema: that of the auteur who approaches classical cinema with both admiration and a desire to react against it. It reveals Kubrick's tendency constantly to parody classicism, in the sense that Linda Hutcheon (1985) understands parody: as an alteration of a code highly admired by the author.[1]

Kubrick's films experiment with the strategy of emphasizing one pole of the sequence over the other. This emphasis on one pole may be explicitly narrational, when it focuses on characters' reactions to what is happening to them or on dialogue to which they listen. It may also be slightly antinarrational, when it stops the narrative flow of information, usually with the effect of demanding the viewer's attention to the beauty or physicality of what is portrayed. But in these cases the strategy is usually integrated into a wider scheme of alterations that are used to qualify the character or to provide the scene with a meaning that is usually coherent with the tone set by the whole film.

In *Killer's Kiss* shot/reverse shot sequences fulfill a particularly important role. These sequences are the basis from which the text evolves into crosscutting, which follows the two main characters, Davy and Gloria, about their respective apartments. The alternation between showing a character's face and showing the reaction of the other character is replaced by the alternation between the two locales, which leads the action on since the film deals with the interaction between the two lonely characters.

---

[1] See Stephen Mamber (1990) on the parodic and intertextual dimension of Kubrick's cinema.

But shot/reverse shot sequences are already altered in this early stage of Kubrick's career. They are transformed into a textual play of foreground/background that is presented in a deep-space composition, without editing and through the peculiar use of lighting. Mise-en-scène sources of light are switched off at certain moments, creating dark foregrounds or backgrounds in which characters conceal themselves and watch the other plane of depth, as the lighted area becomes equivalent to a frame within the frame. This process emphasizes, first, the existence of a deep space that the text decides to explore gradually, and, second, the attitude of the character who is left in the lighted area. This deep-space composition will reappear in several of Kubrick's films, usually without the participation of lighting, turning into one of the marks of his cinematic style.

The Killing also presents several distorted shot/reverse shot sequences. In the breakfast conversation between George and Sherry the sequence starts with two-shots, then focuses on George's reaction exclusively, leaving Sherry offscreen as she carries on the conversation. Here the alteration of the sequence focuses the textual emphasis on George's reaction, which will show him as a weak being in the hands of his ruthless girlfriend. In *Paths of Glory* the device is also altered but in a different manner. In this film the reverse shot is at times withheld much longer than is usual in such sequences. In the initial scene between Mireau and Broulard, the permanence of the first part of the sequence (the shot), and the delay of a reverse shot that would show us Mireau's face as he walks, is used to shock the audience about Mireau's true nature and intentions. After refusing to take the anthill, he immediately changes his mind when he is offered a promotion by Broulard; this comes as a surprise, which is matched by the textual decision finally to show us the longed-for reverse shot that closes the sequence. It seems as if the existence of disinterested human feelings is being linked to the subversion of a classical paradigm. The closure of the sequence means a return to classicism and to the world of ruthless selfishness.[2]

Dr. Strangelove also distorts shot/reverse shot sequences by withholding the reverse shot. Here the alteration of the sequence works in accordance with the general satiric tone of the film. The best example is the confrontation between Mandrake and Ripper in which Mandrake learns about Ripper's decision to order Plan R: the reverse shot of Ripper is withheld for most of the scene, as Mandrake becomes increasingly nervous. The delayed reverse shot comes in the form of a starkly

---

[2] For a study of the potential of focalization to express attitudes in *Paths of Glory*, see Luis Miguel García Mainar (1993a).

lit, extremely low-angle shot that makes Ripper look threatening and dangerously confident. The smoke from his cigar fills the screen, rounding off a vision of madness and authority.

The reverse shot finally showing the woman sniper in *Full Metal Jacket* is also withheld for a long time. We do not learn that the sniper who is killing the members of the platoon is a young girl until the final shoot-out, in which she dies. We get her semi-subjective shot, combined with a zoom shot as she gets ready to fire; but her face is concealed. This hints at the American military's obliviousness to the fact that they were massacring a country that could in no way put up resistance. Here the distortion of the sequence provides a meaning by denying the audience the attitude of the owner of the gaze and by emphasizing the importance of what is being looked at. This shot over the shoulder is similar to the shot in which Barry sees Lady Lyndon for the first time in *Barry Lyndon*. Both are forward zoom shots, and the link established by their formal resemblance may hint at the similar circumstances in which they appear: in both the object of the gaze is, in a way, prey for the person who looks.

Sequences where one pole is held for longer than usual also appear in *Barry Lyndon*. In the scene in which Barry meets the chevalier, the shot showing the back of the chevalier and the door through which Barry enters the room at the far end is held for a long time. The chevalier's reaction to Barry's sudden outburst of feeling does not come until well into the scene and helps maintain the suspense about what his reaction to Barry's confession will be. This formal option links this scene with one of the last scenes in *2001*, where Bowman, as an old man, is seen eating in the present-day room from a similar position to that of the chevalier.

A similar alteration of shot/reverse shot appears in one of the last scenes in *Paths of Glory*, when Colonel Dax informs Broulard of Mireau's order to fire on his own troops during the failed attack. In this case the subversion consists in allowing the characters, mainly the one who is facing us, to distance themselves from the camera. While Dax delivers his information the two characters walk away from the camera toward a door at the far end of the room. Broulard's reaction on learning about the order is given emphasis by a sudden cut to a close-up of his face. Again, this film shows traces of Kubrick's tendency to ascribe importance to one of the poles of the sequence over the other, thereby subverting to some degree the classical paradigm. The negative connotations editing acquires during the film, since it tends to appear accompanying the basest feelings, are finally reversed in the cabaret scene, where the men's sympathy for the young German singer is emphasized through a series of shot/reverse shots.

All of these examples involve concealing information from the viewer, except in the case of shot/reverse shots turning into crosscutting in *Killer's Kiss*. This concealment is invariably accompanied by a textual mark that points out the importance of the scene and of the withheld material for the development of the scene and ultimately of the film. These distortions are also usually accompanied by other stylistic changes that further separate the shot from the reverse shot: from straight angle to low angle (*Dr. Strangelove*), from camera movement to static shot (*Paths of Glory*), from normal motion to slow motion (*Full Metal Jacket*), or change from long shot to close-up (*Paths of Glory*). This extra stylistic effort emphasizes the special relevance of what is suddenly presented to us.

2001 seems to depart from previous films in its use of shot/reverse shot sequences. They are apparently ordinary sequences, where the only exceptional thing is the appearance of computer HAL as a character. Nevertheless, sometimes certain devices act as substitutes for such sequences, adding an element of externality[3] in the process. For instance, the interaction between the computer and one of the men as the crew of the *Discovery* decide to conceal their conversation from HAL is presented through an image of the man on the surface of the machine's eye: it is an internally focalized view of the man through an external effect — the man is shown but without showing him from the position of the machine's eye; the eye is also present in the frame. Here the emphasis is on the externality of the focalization. This externality is gradually being replaced by the growing subjectivity and importance of the computer, HAL, in the narrative, which finally emerges in its most dangerous form in the shot/reverse shot that shows it noticing the conversation being carried out in the insulated pod between Bowman and Poole.

This film presents a wider reflection on subjectivity than the mere consideration of shot/reverse shot sequences. The final segment of the

---

[3] Externality is the result of cinematic processes that privilege textual or syuzhet mechanisms over fabulaic contents. This foregrounding of textual strategies usually produces the effect of distancing the viewer from the film. The processes of exaltation of the iconic, of distortion, and of the setting of distributed information to be linked and processed by the viewer seem to demand a "reading" activity from the reflexive position of an external agent, rather than an activity of identification that a less external conception of cinema would foster.

film is paradigmatic: editing enables the construction of subjective sequences in which Bowman enters what seemed at first to be his own field of vision. The relevance of editing in these sequences is important, as they represent the conclusion of the film: the evolution of humankind is rendered through the cinematic option of editing, which involves the joining together of different spatial and temporal realities; it involves the creation of a distance between shot and shot that the human mind has to join, a process similar to the one at work in the jump in human intelligence represented by the appearance of the Starbaby. Editing and the subjective sequences suggest that in the most essentially cinematic (such as editing) lies the possibility of representing the evolution of a species or of cinema. They suggest that self-consciousness, constructedness, is the way cinema must evolve. This aspect of editing highlights the externality inherent to cinema.

This emphasis on the importance of artificiality is implicitly expressed by the Stargate sequence, since it conveys the progression toward evolution; it is also a composition of shot/reverse shots. Through camera movement, Bowman's point of view is interspersed with reverse shots of his face or of his eye changing color. The progression toward change and evolution is rendered through editing and punctuated by reverse shots. This shot/reverse shot sequence becomes prominent in the conquest of the vanishing point of perspective the Stargate means: the progression toward a distant spatial point placed in the center of the image becomes a metaphor for the relevance of that imaginary unreachable point to the human understanding of space. This, as we will see later, is essential to the understanding of a film that expresses its ideas through spatial variables.

The same externality is also expressed by the partial obliteration of shot/reverse shot sequences. In *Full Metal Jacket* shot/reverse shots are gradually replaced by other means of creating subjectivity. Reverse tracking shots, shots from the ground, and two-shots appear in an attempt to relate focalizer and focalized, hinting at the destruction of the soldiers' humanity during the training period. Nevertheless, some shot/reverse shots appear in the first section of the film in the obscene conversations between the drill instructor and the men. But here the sequences are not conventional, either, since the other character's back is included within the reverse shot. It seems as if the unobtrusive rendering of subjectivity the shot/reverse shot allows was not possible in a film that is precisely trying to discuss the annihilation of personality and independent thought that war carries out in the soldiers.

The distortion of subjectivity devices such as the shot/reverse shot is also employed with the purpose of stylizing the text. Low angles, a combination of long shots and close-ups, and unusually held shot/reverse shots create an atmosphere of detachment. Rhythmical editing, lies introduced through subjectivity, or the excessive formalization of shot/reverse shots also deprive the device of its subjective capacity. In the sports-car scene of *A Clockwork Orange* a close-up of Alex's face is held for most of the scene, showing his wild enjoyment at breaking the law and asserting his free individualism. In his second visit to HOME the text resorts to shot/reverse shots in which Alex's or Mr. Alexander's faces fill the screen and stay for so long that they transform themselves into disturbing elements, hinting at the fear that Alex might be recognized and made to pay for his previous crime in the same locale. When Mr. Alexander finds out that the youngster who is having a bath in his bathroom is the same who raped and killed his wife, the film shows him to us in an extremely low angle in which his face appears as if about to burst and shaking feebly.

Shot/reverse shots of Alex watching the treatment films present another kind of distortion that is not imposed by the form of the sequence but by the compulsion to watch that they present to us. The wide-open eyes, held by cold and strange-looking pincers, offer the viewer an element of content that parallels the distortion of similar sequences with the purpose of shocking the audience; here it is Alex who is shocked at the discovery that something as apparently harmless as watching may become painful, at the realization that what he had created for us in his acts of ultraviolence — views of stylized cruelty — can also affect him as a viewer. The sequences in the scenes where Alex is humiliated before the press are more clearly altered sequences, since they include point of view shots from Alex's position that sometimes become extremely low angles from which the debased youngster submits to the fancies of his masters.

In *Barry Lyndon* a certain stylization occurs in shot/reverse shot sequences, where editing is geared to the rhythm of the extradiegetic music. In a brilliant and beautiful scene Barry seduces Lady Lyndon at the gambling table. The candlelit room holds a play of looks that suggests the interest Barry and Lady Lyndon have in each other. This alternation of looks is edited in such a manner that it seems to follow the rhythm of the extradiegetic piano music that accompanies the scene. The subtle stylization of the scene adds an element of artificiality that results in this case in beauty, creating a warm feeling of love with the aid of formal elements, editing and extradiegetic music, that seem allied to externality and manipulation.

Editing subjectivity also accompanies and suggests lies here, as it does in the textual attempt to conceal Mireau's thirst for power in

Paths of Glory. In Barry's meeting with Lischen, the candlelit scene is filmed in shot/reverse shots as we see Barry lying to the German girl. It seems as if the artificiality, the obtrusive creation of a fiction inherent to the device of editing were being extended to the contents of the scenes. This move lays bare how the artificiality of externality is the source of the main lie: the text.

Editing subjectivity as reinforcing lies also appears in the shot/ reverse shots used in the TV crew scene in *Full Metal Jacket* in the case of Joker. This sequence is linked to deception and irony: the deception television creates about the war and the irony Joker uses in his talk to the TV crew, when he says that he had always wanted to be the first kid on his block to get a "confirmed kill" or that before coming to Vietnam he had always wanted to visit the jewel of Southeast Asia, meet its people "and shoot them." Subjectivity created through shot/reverse shots is here presented as a means of deception that human beings may redirect; in the case of Joker it is redirected through an irony that allows him to show his mixed feelings about what he is doing in the Vietnam War.

Shot/reverse shots are sometimes deprived of their subjective capacity because of the excessive formalization of the sequences. In the interview between Barry and the minister in Berlin in *Barry Lyndon* the shots of the sequence are perfectly balanced, and the characters appear occupying the perfect centre of the composition in an unmoving posture that hints at the rigidity of the system. All of this helps to present the sequences as external, since the Barry we see is not a warm character but a rigid figure mechanically answering the minister's questioning. The subjective capacity of shot/reverse shot sequences is curtailed by the textual tendency to create perfectly balanced or symmetrical shots.

A typical example of formalization in Kubrick's cinema is the appearance of shot/reverse shots with symmetrically placed backs. His sequences of shot/reverse shots are occasionally composed in such a way that the frame shows the object of the subjective gaze "framed" by two backs: sometimes one of these backs belongs to the owner of the gaze, but sometimes the backs have no connection with anybody taking part in the conversation. This device draws attention to the fact that we are watching a text that is creating subjectivity. Its artificiality, its contrived look, does away with the effect of subjectivity: rather than drawing us closer to characters, it detaches us from their concerns and feelings. This strategy is usually accompanied by an attempt on the part of the text to provide a parody or a satire of the character depicted, which is also apparent in the actor's performance.

Lolita offers a clear example during the dance in Ramsdale that represents Quilty's first appearance after the introductory scene. Quilty is surprised by Mrs. Haze's warm and effusive greeting. After he gets rid of her he runs to the woman with whom he came to the dance. As Mrs. Haze follows him he has to carry on the conversation she has started; here Quilty appears framed by the backs of Mrs. Haze and his first partner. The text suggests that Quilty is trapped between two women with whom he has been involved, and that he is afraid his partner might find out about his almost-forgotten quick affair with Mrs. Haze. The interpretation this peculiar sequence of shots suggests is triggered by the externality this device achieves, together with Peter Sellers's obviously comic, almost farcical, performance.

The comic, satiric tone of *Dr. Strangelove* also seems fit for the appearance of this peculiar structure. President Merkin Muffley, also played by Peter Sellers, is at times seen between the backs of two men who are sitting at the huge round table. Apart from the distance this option suggests, critics have pointed out that the shots resemble newspaper photographs. The film constantly describes the president as willing and affable but ineffective, satirizing him as a contributor to the predicament, and this strategy seems to further confirm such a reading of the character.

The Shining marks a step forward in Kubrick's use of shot/reverse shots: here it is not only the form of the shot/reverse shot sequences that is altered but also their contents, their capacity to present us with information that we feel to be truthful. In the bar Jack sees Lloyd after a shot/reverse shot sequence that introduces us to his visions. The ambiguity about the real existence of such visions will be further increased when Danny and Wendy start to share them, and especially when Jack is freed from the storeroom by a voice that we had thought to be part of Jack's hallucinations as part of an aural exchange of information that resembles a shot/reverse shot. This film transforms the reflection on the form of subjectivity as guarantee of truthfulness into a reflection on the capacity of cinema to offer us truth or falsehood independently of its form, a reflection on its intrinsic nature.

Other shot/reverse shot sequences are altered by the powerful presence of Jack Nicholson in the role of Jack. His extreme acting distorts the subjectivity created in many sequences, hinting at something strange behind the mask of his histrionics. He suggests the existence of something that is going to destroy the effect of subjectivity: if subjectivity helps the audience inscribe itself within the text, the eeriness Nicholson provides promises that such an inscription is going to be problematic or that it is going to be more painful than was suggested at first.

This painful inscription is further pointed out by the use of slow dissolves between scenes that link Jack and his family. A special sequence of shot/reverse shots is modified by the presence of a voice-over that belongs to one of the characters but is not part of the dialogue. The voice-over utters the lines of dialogue Halloran uses to communicate to Danny that he, Halloran, can also "shine." Through the subjective sequence the text introduces the phenomenon of the psychic forces that exist in the human mind but that cannot always be mastered, which is the theme of the film. The stylistic subversion is a powerful means of hinting at the theme of the film in an indirect, subtle manner. These strategies gradually create the atmosphere that will make it possible for fantasy to be introduced into the text and finally accepted by the viewer.

The logical conclusion to be drawn about this second use of shot/reverse shot sequences in Kubrick's cinema is that they do not provide identification or subjectivity but lead to externality. They are deprived of their capacity to create and convey subjectivity. Subjectivity is overwhelmed by the textual effort to use its processes to create meaning independently of the signifying force given to it in the fabula.

Editing is obviously one of the main methods cinema possesses in the configuration of meaning. But within editing we may discern a textual attempt to use its workings and to highlight such a use. This is apparent in some cases because of the abandonment of shot/reverse shot sequences, and because sometimes the juxtaposition that editing creates is demanded not so much by the content of the fabula as by a purely textual desire. Therefore, editing in Kubrick may adopt the role of creator of meaning without the intervention of dialogue; it may suggest the independence, the isolation of certain elements within the fabula; or it may create textual patterns with an abstract or content-related significance.

The creation of meaning without the participation of dialogue is evident in *2001* in the scenes in which the monolith and the apes appear together, where the text creates meaning just by editing, by juxtaposing elements — for instance, the scene where the ape discovers the use of the bone as a weapon, which is suggested to be the result of the monolith's influence. Also, the alternation between views of the apes and of the monolith in conjunction with the music suggests the apes' feeling of uncertainty and fear at the presence of such a strange, geometrically "perfect" form in their primitive world of formlessness. The interaction between the two worlds is achieved by the juxtaposition that editing allows.

Juxtaposition as source of meaning may also work by isolating elements. Editing may separate elements within the text and create meaning through this isolation. The basic objective of editing is the joining together of different materials, which, in this way, are made to interact. Kubrick's cinema, however, also shows how editing may separate rather than join. This is apparent in *Dr. Strangelove*, where the suspense and the threat of destruction are born out of the isolation of characters and locales imposed through crosscutting. In the credit-title sequence of *Full Metal Jacket* editing separates men, while the act of shaving their heads joins them together in the community of the Marine Corps, and they are thereby led into the world of Parris Island. The destruction of individuality represented in the sequence uses as its starting point the separation, the distance, the differences among the men as the various kinds of hair give way to the homogeneous buzz cut.

Editing in Kubrick may also create meaning by establishing textual patterns, or by breaking them. This is particularly evident in *Barry Lyndon*, where editing and the zoom shot are combined to create meaning. A cut in the middle of a reverse zoom shot that is introducing a placid view of Lady Lyndon, Barry, and Brian transports us to a brothel, where Barry is enjoying himself in the company of half-naked women. The reverse zoom is continued in this second, edited, shot. The reverse zoom shot, which has become a familiar device introducing every scene, combined with the eruption of the cut, draws attention to the sharp contrast between Lady Lyndon's concept of the family and Barry's. The disruption of a structural pattern that editing produces foregrounds this part of the text.

Such a disruption may adopt a different shape: at a certain point in the film the text departs from its practice of introducing each scene with a reverse zoom shot and suddenly cuts from a close shot of Brian and his father reading a book to a long shot of the two. This disruption marks Barry's solitude after beating up Bullingdon, and such a feeling is more strongly transmitted by means of the emphasis this formal aspect lends it.

Apart from the creation of meaning by juxtaposition or by the breaking of patterns, editing may also acquire the potentiality to shape its own textual patterns. In *Barry Lyndon* the text creates a pattern of recurrence of a long shot of the castle that opens and closes sequences of scenes that represent coherent sections of events and meaning. The narrator's premonition of Brian's death introduces one of these sections after a shot of the castle. The following scenes show the confirmation of the premonition, and they are linked by the presence of the same musical theme in the background throughout the sequence. The sequence ends with a view of the desperation to which the child's death has driven Lady Lyndon and a final long shot of the castle. Editing in this case imposes a formal pattern on the contents of the film and acquires a signifying force that, stemming from the abstract quality of the pattern, extends to the text as a mark of units of meaning.

Strict patterns of editing in the duels are also part of the formalization editing acquires in *Barry Lyndon*. The slow rhythm with which the two duels are edited is accompanied by a perfect balance and symmetry in the compositions and in the order of editing. The idea of the duel as the form that best exemplifies the world of decorum to which Barry finds it so difficult to adapt is emphasized by the strict way in which the duels are shown, following an order imposed by the text on the fabula. The establishment of patterns of recurrence is the first hint of the tendency of Kubrick's films to create stylistic patterns that the text invests with meaning.

Kubrick's well-known tendency to use cuts extensively in his films transforms fades or dissolves into disruptions of a self-imposed rhetoric. These unusual options are not employed for their mere defamiliarizing potential but contain a signifying force that emanates from the rarity of their appearance. One of the only cases in which dissolves are used according to the dictates of classical style is *Killer's Kiss*. Here they are employed to mark the passage into and out of the main character's flashback, which constitutes the text. *Killer's Kiss* also makes extensive use of fades — for instance, after Davy loses the fight, and Gloria is abused by Rapallo; or after Davy meets Gloria at her apartment; or after they fall in love, a scene that is followed by a view of the New York sunset. In this film fades seem to be used according to the dictates and customs of classical cinema. *Spartacus* also makes extensive use of fades and dissolves, as befits a generally more classical film.

Fades, however, may mask ellipses and, at the same time, draw attention to the existence of such ellipses. In *Paths of Glory* fades acquire the capacity to suggest meanings. They appear at particularly important moments in the narrative: when the court martial retires to deliberate, and after Dax informs Broulard of Mireau's order. In these cases the use of the fade suggests the slight hope that the men might be declared innocent or that Broulard might stop the execution. The stern reality that comes up after the fades (the first is followed by a view of the firing squad being instructed, the second by the execution itself) adopts an extra expressive and emotional force in the depiction of blatant in-

justice. A fade in a scene between Sherry and Val in *The Killing* replaces
a sexual encounter and points to a similar use of the fade in a renowned
scene in *Double Indemnity*. This fade does not lead to a different locale
but stays in the same setting, thereby departing from the other uses of
editing in this film. *Lolita* makes consistent use of fades between scenes,
breaking Kubrick's pattern of using straight cuts.

In *2001* fades create a reading practice: they suggest to the viewers
that they are to provide an explanation for the scenes that the fades
link. Fades join most of the scenes that form the "Dawn of Man" section. Here the absence of temporal marks in the scenes makes necessary
the presence of a "grammatical" sign, the fade, that hints at the passage
of time between one scene and the next. Also, the use of fades between
scenes in which there is no dialogue emphasizes the textual effort to
create meaning in independent fragments that develop toward a resolution. The fades warn the viewer that the meaning of the scene will
have to be strictly extracted from the images within the scene, since the
scenes are separated from one another, preventing the creation of a coherent context that would help the viewer shape meaning. The fades
warn us of the unclassical nature of the section.

Fades may create artificiality and draw attention to this artificiality,
marking the device — and, by extension, the text — as part of the old
tradition of storytelling. *Barry Lyndon* uses extradiegetic titles to present the two parts into which the text is divided. These titles do away
with part of the curiosity about what events await Barry and direct our
attention to the way in which they are presented by the text. The titles
are self-conscious marks of textuality that, on the one hand, link the
film with its literary source, claiming the relationship of the film with
the long tradition of storytelling and artificiality, and, on the other, introduce the atmosphere of self-consciousness that permeates the text in
its depiction of images that resemble paintings of the period. Otherwise, the text usually resorts to cuts to link scenes.

The same device of extradiegetic titles is employed by *The Shining*,
in this case with the purpose of contributing to the feeling of urgency
and approaching danger the film provides. The titles refer to the fragments in which the action evolves. They hint at an artificial division of
the time of the fabula by the text, which is guiding us toward the feared
bloody outcome. They suggest that the text knows everything that is
going to happen but is withholding it from us and manipulating our
feelings, threatening us with the approaching presentation of horror. As
the film progresses the titles become more and more specific: they start
with a reference to the interview in which Jack is informed of the par-
ticulars of his job, then change to temporal references that gradually

become more and more precise, as if the text is coming near the point at which it wants to tell us the core of the story, its resolution. This strategy is utterly obtrusive since it points, similarly to the case of *Barry Lyndon,* to the artificiality of the text, as if it wanted to claim for the text, again, a reputed status as example of the old storytelling tradition.

The Shining is also remarkable in its use of dissolves. The text makes use of the slowness inherent to the transition through dissolves to mark the special relationship between the two elements that are joined. Dissolves are strikingly effective in the linking of Jack and his son, Danny. Several shots are joined by slow dissolves from Jack's face to a view of his family, particularly of his son. The unusual slow pace of the device, combined with Nicholson's exaggerated performance, creates an atmosphere of restlessness about the future relationship of the two characters: the possibility that they will become antagonists is clearly suggested.

In the final scene of the film the text uses a dissolve to focus on the photograph on the wall and allows us to see Jack there, in 1921. These dissolves belong to a scene that is shot by an external camera, one that is not motivated by the gaze of any character: it is the text that is using them to probe into the essence of the film, as the scene suggests that everything we thought to be Jack's hallucinations was, in fact, "real" (or else the text has turned into a hallucination). In their externality these dissolves are different from the previous examples: those were linked to Jack's face and seemed to hint that they led to a view of Jack's subjectivity. These final dissolves, however, belong to the text, as if the text were also an accomplice of Jack's — confirming the hypothesis that the text has turned into a hallucination.

Full Metal Jacket also uses dissolves as linking elements between scenes. The slow transition they offer adds a further feeling to the text: not the feeling of action developing but of description being carried out, of characters becoming representatives of ideas and of events becoming metaphors for something that is not there. The slowness of dissolves links fragments of life in an aesthetics of logical thinking on the part of the text. These links introduce the scenes as if they were arguments. They set off this film from the typical war films, where action is sometimes deprived of meaning. Fades acquire a double function: on the one hand, a fade is used as a grammatical mark separating the first part of the film from the second part; and, on the other hand, a fade introduces the scene in which Pyle is beaten up by his mates, achieving a slowness and a contrast between the black of the fade and the strange blue light of the scene. Dissolves are more widely used in the second part of the text, creating the impression that the scenes are fragments of the life of the men at the front that the text joins or leaves as it pleases and thereby achieving an effect of spontaneity and truth that the scenes in the first part could not achieve: they were a reflection of the men's oppression by the rules and rigid structures of the Marine Corps. Particularly interesting is the scene in which Joker watches the lime-covered dead, which is introduced by a dissolve disclosing his face with an expression of disgust at the view. The slowness of the transition, combined with the eerie music, clearly mark Joker's attitude as the relevant element in the scene, as the conversation about the peace button discloses soon afterward.

In conclusion, we may say that fades and dissolves in Kubrick fulfill two functions: first, the traditional classical function of linking and separating fragments of meaning (scenes, sequences), acting as punctuation marks that fit the rules of a grammar; and second, drawing attention to what is elided or linked, in order to make these elements fully significant within the overall scheme of the text's contents. The following discussion deals with Kubrick's cinema as a mixture of classical and nonclassical features.

Editing in Kubrick transforms itself into a force that explores its own possibilities within the cinematic code. The films exploit the capacity of crosscutting to suggest both interaction and isolation among elements; they exploit the classical as well as the nonclassical uses of montage, the capacity of match-cuts to mix subjectivity and externality, and the mixture of spatial continuity (with the resulting absence of self-consciousness) and exaltation of space as beauty, artifact, provided by long takes.

So far, we have studied editing's capacity to join elements in the text, elements that are made to interact as they are shown to share a common space within the film. Editing may also, however, draw attention to its capacity to separate elements, as we have seen in the previous comments on fades and dissolves, or to relate elements that are not spatially contiguous. The double nature of crosscutting is intrinsic to its stylistic nature: the joining of two elements may also be exploited to distance these elements. *Killer's Kiss* begins with shot/reverse shots that show the two main characters' isolation in their respective apartments: the characters can see each other through their windows. This distance begins to be bridged when the text continues to focus on the lives of the two characters when they are not in their apartments. Shot/reverse shots are, therefore, transformed into crosscutting, which follows Davy and Gloria in their respective occupations: Davy boxing, Gloria dancing. These crosscut scenes are an anticipation of the meeting of the couple, who will see a way out of their problems in their relationship and in their escape to the country. The separation imposed by shot/reverse shots and crosscutting is the formal expression of the oppressive worlds in which the two characters live. Their meeting will mean both a resolution of their predicaments at a fabulaic level and a transformation of editing into other formal strategies that can better express such a meeting.

The Killing and *Dr. Strangelove* are paradigmatic films with respect to crosscutting in Kubrick's work. *The Killing* builds its dramatic force on the alternation of scenes that the narrator announces as having happened at the same time; the feeling of omniscience and the constant change of point of view enable the text to suggest that it can offer us the whole truth of what happened. Crosscutting serves the purpose of striving toward psychological realism, as well as of creating suspense about the outcome of something that we know is going to take place. *Dr. Strangelove* is also based on the strategy of crosscutting, which allows the audience to follow the development of the action in the three locales. This linking function, contributing to suspense, emphasizes at the same time the separation, the distance between the different locales, which is a metaphor for the distance that separates the characters, for their incapacity to understand each other, and especially for Ripper's isolation in his perturbed mental world of communist threat.

Montage sequences exemplify Kubrick's fondness for mixing classical and modernist uses of stylistic strategies. An example of a classical use of montage sequences appears in *Killer's Kiss* at the start of the film: views of posters announcing the forthcoming fight are edited together to let the audience know that Davy is a boxer. In *Spartacus* montage sequences are used in the depiction of the training the slaves undergo both in the gladiators' school and afterward when they are free. *Full Metal Jacket* uses montage sequences to portray the training of the soldiers on the island. The quick combination of shots showing similar activities by means of dissolves is a typically classical way of presenting the improvement of characters in such an activity. Montage sequences of this kind attempt to condense time, in which — it is suggested — no important event, apart from the training itself, has happened. *A Clockwork Orange* introduces a similarly classical use of these sequences: near the end the film tells us how Alex's rehabilitation and conformity to the government means the success of the treatment. This is presented by means of newspaper headlines, as in so many classical films. In this case, however, the use of eerie extradiegetic music in the background helps to set off the device from straight uses of classicism. Within this same film we find an extremely unclassical montage sequence: the fast editing to the rhythm of different shots from different angles of the Christ figures Alex has in his room makes the sequence resemble the films of Eisenstein. The sequence shows different parts of the figures, which are put together in such a manner that they seem to be dancing to the music in the background The fragmenting of an element of mise-en-scène and its posterior elaboration is completely alien to classical models of filmmaking, since it reveals a powerful tool of manipulation and creation of meaning in the process of montage, which in classical cinema is supposed to be subservient to the unobtrusive depiction of the fabula. This kind of montage attempts to suggest an idea by creating it before our eyes rather than by showing us how it emerges from the flow of the fabula. This montage does not create temporal or spatial ellipses; it does not advance the fabula in these respects but attempts to defamiliarize the option of montage, to create an antireligious parody and mix it with a hint of Alex's fondness for blood and suffering.

Graphic matches enact a shift from subjectivity to externality. For instance the match-cut from bone to spaceship in *2001* offers perhaps the longest temporal ellipsis in the history of cinema (combined with a spatial ellipsis). It involves a passage from a shot that has a certain subjective force, since the bone has been thrown by the ape and there is a relationship of contiguity between them, to a shot that is utterly external in its presentation. The view of the spaceship does not belong to any character and cannot be attributed to any contiguous person; and the following dance to "The Blue Danube Waltz" is meant to be enjoyed as a spectacle, not as the representation of anybody's perception or subjectivity. This passage reveals the metaphorical meaning of the cut: human beings have developed into intelligent beings capable of building spaceships, but this development has stemmed from their desire to dominate and kill, which made them create tools, machines, and so on. The spaceship represents a more developed stage of humankind; but it still threatens to become a destructive weapon, since such a possibility lies at the core of its existence.

The graphic dissolve from the maze inside the hotel to the maze outside in *The Shining* also presents a passage from a subjective view to an external one through a spatial ellipsis. This move forebodes Jack's disturbed mind and its effect on his family, which is inside the real maze. The metaphor created seems to resort to a verbal game: Jack is in a maze (confused), and his family is, too (trapped with Jack inside). The dissolve is a mixture of subjectivity and externality: the external view gives us information about Jack's subjectivity.

Long takes are widely used by Kubrick to maintain a spatio-temporal continuity closely related to realism but certain films are more consistent in the use of this stylistic option. *Lolita* extensively uses long takes to create signifying units of a closed nature, which conjure up the impression that each scene is going to include a development and a conclusion. *Barry Lyndon* uses long takes in conjunction with reverse zoom shots and depth of field. The film turns space into a signifying variable: the characters have enough time to explore the different planes of depth, using this space as an aid in the expression of the idea of the scene. In a sequence shot Barry and Nora approach the foreground from the distance. The long take allows the text to use the space of the shot to express the growing jealousy Barry feels because his cousin has danced with another man. The dialogue ends when Barry can no longer bear Nora's indifference and says that if she is so fond of that man she'd better ask him to accompany her. This last part of the dialogue is uttered once the two characters have reached the foreground of the shot, almost achieving a close-up. The development of the dialogue is accompanied and emphasized by the movement of the characters and by the change in the dimensions of the characters that are allowed by the long take. On the other hand, long takes in this film also create beautiful views resembling paintings of the period, which helps the formalization of the film as a textual artifact.

Cinematographic Properties

Tracking shots in Kubrick fulfill a specific task: they establish a relationship between at least two elements within the shot. These elements are usually the space of the setting and the character. We must distinguish between two types of tracking shots: those that are accompanied by character movement and those that are not. Among the first, lateral tracking shots are one of Kubrick's constant stylistic marks. These lateral shots may only link characters, as is the case in *The Killing*, where the shot moves with a character until he meets other characters and thereby provides the spatial proximity necessary for the action to start. The scenes in Johnny's apartment constantly present this camera movement, which explores the apartment as it links Johnny and his friends. These shots may also have the effect of relating character and space. In *Paths of Glory* the attack on the Anthill led by Dax is presented by means of a lateral tracking shot that follows the progression of the soldiers across no man's land; the setting they traverse is, in its barren look, an expression of the rotten logic that has led them to that suicidal action. Later Dax visits Broulard during an elegant ball, and the scene employs the same kind of shot with the same screen direction: from right to left. In this case Broulard's high position within the military organization is emphasized by the milieu he inhabits, to which the text relates him by means of the tracking shot.

A similar effect is produced by this kind of shot in *Spartacus*, where Spartacus watches his men train for the battle as the text emphasizes that the strength of this leader stems from his similarity with his men, not from his patronizing difference. *Lolita* introduces a variation in the use of the device: it becomes much more self-conscious than it was before. Tracking shots laterally following the characters as they cross from one room of the house to another are clearly reminiscent of the use of the same stylistic option by Max Ophuls, a director for whom Kubrick has confessed his admiration.

This self-consciousness constitutes the first hint at the questions the device will suggest in later films. In *2001* one of the first sequences set in the modern era shows several spaceships dancing to the rhythm of the extradiegetic classical music. Here the lateral tracking shots are transformed into camera movements in almost every direction. The relationship between the spaceships and the background of black space questions the concept of camera movement, since it is difficult to distinguish whether it is the spaceship that moves or the camera. The meaning of the sequence is produced by the rhythmical way in which the spaceships appear and disappear from the screen, not from the perfect and constant accommodation within the frame that previous cases of tracking shots presented. It seems as if the sequence is trying to prove the relativity of space and movement, with narrative effects within the film and with formal implications as to the artificiality and the manipulations of cinema. *Full Metal Jacket* takes this idea further. One scene shows a TV or movie camera shooting the men during an enemy attack: the lateral tracking shot follows the camera as it moves laterally, recording the sentences the men direct at it. The background is filled by the sound of combat, the middle ground by the soldiers, and the foreground by the recording camera. The scene introduces a third element within the relationship character/space: the movie camera for which turns in the uttering of dialogue are established. The appearance of a real camera that governs this process highlights the fact that the film itself is nothing but this: a constant staging, an arrangement of the action so that the camera can record it. The movement of the camera is revealed as allied to such artificiality, thereby revealing that the essence of movement in cinema is also part of a previous artificial staging of the action. The film nevertheless offers a final scene that seems to return the "lost prestige" to the device: the soldiers feel safe in the communal act of singing as they walk, laterally followed by the camera.

Tracking shots in Kubrick's films also offer us views of characters from the front as they walk or run toward us. These shots foreground the importance of the characters over the setting they inhabit. In *Paths of Glory* Mireau's visit to his men is presented in a tracking shot from the front as he walks along the trenches, suggesting that for Mireau his own interests are more important than his men, whom he is ready to massacre to satisfy his thirst for military success. In *A Clockwork Orange* Alex walks into the record shop dressed in a way that reminds us of earlier periods; the shot from the front foregrounds his costume and his confident smile, which matches the powerful tone of voice he uses when addressing the shop assistant. *Barry Lyndon* contains a similar scene: Lord Bullingdon enters a club looking for Barry, determined to demand satisfaction from him; the tracking shot from the front draws the viewer's attention to the gentle manner in which Bullingdon is dressed and to the expression on his face, a mixture of fear and despising hatred. The use of the device in *The Shining* also stresses the physicality of a character's features: in Jack's mad chase after Danny in the snow-covered maze the shot helps make clear that Jack's madness has made him unaware of the space he is traversing; his getting lost is, therefore, a natural consequence. The capacity of the device to portray human beings' lack of relation to space is increasingly employed by the later films. *Full Metal Jacket* offers shots of men running in formation guided by the drill instructor; these shots foreground the situation of men of diverse natures who are made to march in a square pattern, forced to reject their individuality and accept the instructor's code of behavior as a norm. This emphasis on the process of homogenization they undergo is more evident than the inscription within the space of Parris Island, which appears in the background of the shots.

Other types of tracking shots, however, relate characters to the spaces they inhabit. Tracking shots that follow characters establish a clear relationship between the character and the setting, sometimes creating a meaning that is coherent with the rest of the film. In *Paths of Glory* the initial Mireau-Broulard conversation is presented by a camera movement that follows the characters around the richly decorated room of the chateau. The characters are clearly linked to this world of sophistication, of delicate art and exquisite manners, therefore setting a strong contrast with the way of life and values of the men in the trenches, who are always shown by means of camera movements which follow a straight line. *The Shining* starts with similar camera movements following Jack's car as he approaches the hotel along the mountain road; in the hotel, Jack's movements in the hall and into the manager's office are also offered by a tracking shot that follows him around. These camera movements inscribe the character in his space, suggesting that he belongs, in the world of mystery and threat that these movements will later link with the maze and the maze-like ramblings of Danny through the corridors of the hotel.

Tracking shots that offer us the point of view of a certain character emphasize the centrality of the space the character inhabits. In *Paths of Glory* Dax walks through the trenches just before leading his men in the attack. The text shows us his point of view, revealing frightened men who seem to be encouraged by Dax's presence and proximity to them. The danger together with sympathy that the scene elicits is mainly suggested by these point-of-view tracking shots, which pierce the semi-darkness of the trenches to unveil staring eyes and dirty faces. In this case character allows space and setting to provide the meaning of sympathy which in other parts of the text is reserved exclusively to character. This type of shot acquires a central role in certain Kubrick films. In *2001* the Stargate sequence presents us with Bowman's point of view as he rapidly progresses through the fantastic space that appears before him. Humankind's development is here described through a metaphor as progression through space within a character's point of view. This metaphorical purpose of the text is consistent with the importance attributed to space throughout the narrative. In *The Shining* Danny's journeys through the corridors of the hotel are used by the text to offer us, by means of his low-angle point of view, the threatening aspect the hotel has for the boy. The shots emphasize the appearance of the setting, together with its capacity to elicit an emotional response from the audience.

Tracking shots may also appear without character movement. In Kubrick's films reverse and forward tracking shots suggest some kind of interaction between character and space. Reverse tracking shots set space as a reflection of the character's interiority or situation within the fabula. The reverse shot starts with a view of the character, which is broadened to accommodate the space surrounding the character; this space thereby becomes qualified with the meanings the character carries. The initial shot of *A Clockwork Orange* is of this type: it includes only Alex at first, but the frame gradually includes his mates and then the Korova Milk Bar, decorated in such a way that it introduces several topics of the film associated with Alex's personality. Aesthetic estrangement and the consideration of women as mere objects of sexual desire will be revealed as part of Alex's ideology. In *Full Metal Jacket* Joker and Rafterman bump into the effects of a recent raid: a ditch is full of dead bodies that have been covered with lime and are ready to be communally buried. The scene starts with a close-up of Joker that quickly tracks back to include the ditch at which he is looking; the scene is relevant in the depiction of the development of Joker in his contact with the war. At the point at which it appears it represents a stage between Joker's period of training, characterized by his constant rebellious behavior, and his surrender to the realities of war, which will finally lead him to accept the massacre and feel happy just to remain alive. In this scene the space (setting) represents Joker's moment of entering into contact with such cruelty and injustice; it is an expression of the inner struggle that is taking place in Joker at the moment.

Forward tracking shots suggest that the characters are reflections of the space they inhabit. *The Shining* ends with a tracking shot that shows a photograph of a 1921 ball at the Overlook Hotel — only to disclose Jack in the photograph, dressed in the fashion of the time. The text focuses on him to add the final hint that the hotel is a place where time does not pass, that its inhabitants have always lived there. The view of Jack in 1921 finally suggests that what we saw before was a fantasy and that we are forced to believe it. If Jack has lived in the hotel all this time, then the claims made by those fantastic characters are true, and the whole text is a fantasy. The text's emphasis on the character is an expression of the idea that this character is essential for the understanding of the setting in which the fabula takes place.

Kubrick's use of tracking shots exploits their capacity to relate characters and setting (space) in many ways. But a common characteristic of all of these ways is their high degree of self-consciousness. Self-consciousness of the workings of the camera is inherent to camera movements that are not accompanied by character movement, but in Kubrick the special nature of the tracking shots that do show character movement renders them also highly self-conscious. This means that the films turn an element of style into a fully signifying force, independently of the contents the tracking shots convey. The nature of the camera movement prefigures what the interaction among the elements in the shot will be.

Panning shots show an attempt to preserve spatial continuity, although from this basic notion Kubrick's cinema extends the function of this stylistic strategy to that of point-of-view shots. In Kubrick, panning shots fulfill the task of linking characters while preserving spatial continuity, as in *Killer's Kiss,* where a panning shot joins Davy in his apartment with Gloria in hers. The future relationship is here foreshadowed by the textual desire to link them and to express the curiosity they feel about one another. Panning shots may go a step further and expressively present the relationships among several characters; in *Barry Lyndon,* a panning shot shows Bullingdon pacing the room from side to side, while Runt and the family's accountant are seated at a table in the middle of the room. Bullingdon's walk is followed by the camera, which only shows the other two characters when he walks past them. The standing position of Bullingdon, together with his impatient walk, suggest his impetuous nature and his decision to react against Barry, while the other two characters are presented as second in rank, since they do not seem to be able to act (which is expressed by their static position on the chairs).

Panning shots in Kubrick may also become part of a subjective shot. The movement of the camera scanning the space surrounding it from what seems a static position is a suitable form for the attribution of such a view to a character in the text. A clear example can be found in *Barry Lyndon* when Lady Lyndon appears for the first time. The voice-over informs us of Barry's intention to marry a woman of a genteel family and starts to describe Lady Lyndon; meanwhile, the camera leaves Barry and the chevalier offscreen and moves to focus on a figure in the background garden; then pans to accommodate her and her family (husband, son, and Reverend Runt) as they walk along a garden path. The connection between voice-over dialogue and camera movement, which starts from a position close to where Barry is sitting, transforms camera movement into part of a subjective shot.

The Shining offers a similar example. When Wendy finds Jack's notes and notices he keeps writing the same sentence for pages and pages, she stands dumbfounded by her husband's typewriter. The text suddenly changes from a close view of her to a long shot that includes part of a wall on one side; the camera pans to perfectly frame Wendy, and we realize that this shot might be a character's point of view. Our hypothesis is quickly confirmed as Jack appears in the frame and the shot is interpreted as part of his view.

Reframing is another attempt at spatial continuity that the films transform into an expression of the text's constriction on the fabula and, by extension, on the characters. Kubrick uses the slight follow focus to include a moving character in order to maintain spatial continuity, as well as textually shape the laws that govern the characters at a fabulaic level (their being trapped in a cage, etc.). In *Killer's Kiss* Davy, in his escape from Rapallo, climbs up to a building's roof, walks all over the roof, and tries every door leading to the stairs. All of them seem to be locked, and he has to return to the place where he reached the roof. He finally finds an open door and continues his escape. Davy's run on the roof starts in the bottom left corner of the frame; he continues to the top left corner, then to the top right, and finally to the bottom right. The camera is forced to reframe Davy while he remains on the roof to keep the spatial continuity to render the scene properly. At the same time, it suggests that Davy is trapped within the laws of the text and is going to have to face Rapallo.

Kubrick's films also question the issue of the nature of reframing and show how it is, in fact, a textual manipulation. *2001* is a paradigmatic example. In this film the camera has to reframe a character in an unusual way: the flight attendant in the spaceship places herself upside down in the weightless space as she carries food trays to the crew. Once she is completely upside down, the camera revolves and presents the flight attendant right side up. This movement shows the relativity of spatial directions in the creation of spatial coherence: the movement fools the viewer, modifying the conditions of viewing in a fairly obtrusive way. The movement shows that coherence in the cinema is always the product of a construction. In the same film we find another case of reframing that is relevant: one of the two members of the crew aboard the *Discovery* is running and shadow-boxing along a circular walk. The camera is placed in such a way that the character can remain onscreen for the whole length of his run with only a slight camera movement. Continuous space is, therefore, rendered by a simple camera movement as long as it is a deceptively continuous space, produced by means of an artificial nonstop circular "runway." Here the deception is not so much exclusive of camera movement but previous to it and performed by mise-en-scène (setting). In this film reframing lays bare the existence of a tacit code of spatial variables that allows the configuration of coherent space easily graspable by the audience.

With respect to angle, the most remarkable cases are low-angle shots in *Killer's Kiss, The Shining,* and *Dr. Strangelove,* and *A Clockwork Orange.* Most of the low angles are part of a strategy of distortion of subjective structures, which inevitably lead to externality, the destruction of identification with the character, detachment from the text. They are also linked to a high degree of self-consciousness, which usually fits the tone and the generic features of the text. Films noirs, modern-age satires, and modern horror stories employ this strategy as part of their generic stock of stylistic options or as an aid to the overall distortion of the reality of the text they attempt to portray.

Among the most remarkable aspects concerning distance are long shots in battle sequences in *Spartacus* and *Barry Lyndon* that express the nature of the different armies through their arrangement and their movement. Long shots also emphasize, and allow the expressive nature of mise-en-scène. In *Spartacus* the slaves' army stands for freedom, and this is shown in their free arrangement during the attacks; the Romans are the rule and the power, and they are arranged in perfect squares. In

Barry Lyndon the perfect symmetry the army displays during the attacks reveals its expertise in killing, whereas the dissolute and oppressive nature of the army is shown in scenes of the soldiers' daily life.

Kubrick's films use the strategy of suddenly cutting from a long shot to a close-up, causing surprise in the audience and achieving the aesthetic effect of the eruption of a highly expressive close-up in a scene that had promised to keep us at a distance from the action. This happens in the ball scene between Dax and Broulard in *Paths of Glory*, as we have already seen, and constitutes an alteration of a subjective sequence. In *A Clockwork Orange* we find the structure in the scene in which Alex and his droogs beat the old drunkard. The long shadows cast by the gang are shown in a long shot as they approach the old man. As Alex begins to talk to him the text cuts to a close-up of Alex's ruthless face. In both cases the scenes play with the audience's expectations: they promise no emotional involvement through the long shot, only to suddenly introduce a vision of ruthlessness that shocks the viewer into sharing the feelings of the characters in the scene.

Close-ups are used to reveal the true natures of characters; they use the emphasis on the physicality of the image to approximate the character's nature to the viewer and to make it significant for the development of the plot. Most of the time this importance is marked not through what characters convey but through the mere emphasis on their physicality: therefore, it is a purely textual emphasis, a textual strategy, a stylistic product. In *Killer's Kiss* close-ups are invariably accompanied by distortion: Davy's face is seen in close-up through the fishbowl suggesting his being trapped; Rapallo's evil nature is conveyed by starkly lit close-ups.

In *Dr. Strangelove* almost every character is the object of close-ups, which, together with lighting, create the atmosphere of nightmare the theme demands. In *Paths of Glory* Dax reveals his true feelings to Broulard in one of the last scenes, and the text resorts to a close-up. *Spartacus* uses close-ups in the tender love scene between Varinia and the main character after the freed slaves have learned, and dare, to express their feelings — the main idea in the first part of the film. *Barry Lyndon* shows Barry's inexpressive face in medium shots to emphasize his incapacity to survive in the society he has joined through his marriage. Barry's innocence and unsophistication are constantly suggested by shots that present an attractive face, a good person, but no spirit to pretend convincingly to be what he is not. In conclusion, we may say that both the strategies of angle and of distance of framing are used by the texts to emphasize the physicality of the image, which is revealed as a strong contributor to the expression of meaning.

Color in Kubrick's cinema suggests meaning by establishing links with external elements, with elements within the same text, or with other elements of conventional genres. Color, in short, helps in the creation of symbols and metaphors. Color provides one element of the metaphor; the other is helped out by color and rounded off by the context formed by the whole film. Context helps in the elaboration of a coherent meaning that perfectly fits the rest of the text.

2001 is a particularly relevant film in this respect. The gradual humanization of the computer HAL is the cause of the death of most of the crew. The machine's capacity to have feelings becomes apparent in the scene in which Bowman disconnects HAL. The computer's desperate attempt to stop Bowman reveals that the machine is afraid to die and is sad at the moment of its death. The connection computer-human being is further suggested by the red color of the chamber Bowman opens to disconnect HAL. The metaphor of this chamber as the vital organs of the machine drives home the idea that the computer has human feelings.

Also in *2001,* color is significant in the Stargate sequence. During the journey the tonalities surrounding Bowman, which are reflected in his eye, change from the warm colors of humanity to the cool colors of further intelligence. He reaches a white room — white meaning the conjunction of all colors, the stage of the journey where a totalizing answer is going to be given to the process. The same white color appeared in the *Discovery* and the other spaceships in the film, representing the pinnacle of intelligence humankind was capable of reaching at that stage, which encompassed all the previous stages of humankind. The color brought in by the monolith is precisely the opposite: black. This new step ahead of humankind will again spring from the reconciliation of opposites: the baby represents a new human being capable of understanding and mastering all the contradictions and mysteries of the universe, a human being with a developed intelligence fit to match the wonders of space.

Kubrick's films also dismantle conventions about the use of color in genres and narrative modes. In *A Clockwork Orange* color is relevant in the presentation of the claustrophobia pervading Alex's parents' house, but the excessively bright, jarring colors do not provide the same connotations they bring to other genres. Musicals and melodramas use bright colors in mise-en-scène to shape an atmosphere of gentle theatricality or fantasy, or to accompany the expression of the characters' feelings in texts that usually present an intense exploration of feeling. Here bright colors express precisely the opposite: the dismemberment of a family where no love bonds exist, a world where Alex is not a son but a stranger. *A Clockwork Orange* also uses white as an expression of threat. The initial scene in threatening white and the HOME scene also dismantle conventions about color in cinema: the white of perfection leads to destruction.

The Shining subverts horror-film codes since the cleanliness associated with the bright colors shows a text speeding toward madness. Films in the horror genre seem to demand dark colors and scarce lighting where the mysterious hides, waiting for the characters. In *The Shining* the idea that the hotel is haunted is expressed through the "shining" walls and floors, where "shining" suggests the supernatural as exemplified by Danny. In contrast, Jack finds refuge in the ballroom and the bar where the past survives, which exhibit dark colors — friendlier colors, according to the system of codes set by the film. The bar, however, contains a rest room decorated in a jarring red, where Grady informs Jack that he, Jack, has always lived there and persuades him to kill his family in order to "correct" them. The friendly atmosphere is concealing the reality of the return to the past: Jack's mental breakdown, which begins to pervade the whole of the film. The same red color appears in the carpet on which Danny plays, and it is also the color of the blood coming out of the elevators in his recurring vision.

Full Metal Jacket also uses this code concerning color. The first part presents shining floors and ceilings in the barracks. Pyle's death takes place in the latrines Joker and Cowboy had been cleaning, suggesting that his friends and their submission to the inhuman rules of the Marines have caused his death. Furthermore, they have actively taken part in the death, since they helped to "clean" the "head" (the Marine term for latrine) of the platoon and to conceal the brutality of the military discipline. In fact, Cowboy and Joker had led the attack on Pyle that led to his mental degradation and death. Color thus points to Cowboy and Joker as the cause of Pyle's death. The cleanliness that is usually associated with warm familiarity in cinema here designates madness, and, therefore, also suggests the partial invisibility of the codes that govern the Marines, the concealed ideology behind the Corps. The initial scene in the second part employs bright colors that make the Vietnamese city look like an American one, suggesting the process of transformation into an American issue that the war had undergone — to the point of disregarding the interests of the inhabitants the Americans were said to be helping. In this case color is used more traditionally, linking brightness with the American way of life and urban civilization as many mainstream films do. This use of color matches the use of popular American music in the soundtrack: "These Boots Were Made for Walking" sounds in the background.

Depth of field in Kubrick is usually the expression of a textual attempt to portray the ways in which the characters relate to one another or to their milieu, which tends to be a source of meaning. Depth of field emphasizes the capacity of mise-en-scène to carry meaning. In most cases this interaction is presented unobtrusively, but at other times the text engages in a process of distortion (usually with a satiric or parodic purpose) that is carried out in an explicit fashion. In short, Kubrick's cinema exhaustively explores the possibilities of depth of field, using it and questioning it. This seems to be a characteristic of Kubrick's films: they use stylistic devices in traditional as well as in untraditional ways and question their use.

Depth of field links characters and elements on the screen in both realistic and obtrusive ways. *Killer's Kiss* offers examples of both tendencies. Shots in which Davy is in the foreground while Gloria remains in the background, both in their apartments, establish the first links between them in a relatively unobtrusive manner. A particularly interesting one has Davy watching Gloria undress. This is shown in a view of Davy next to a mirror that reveals the object of his gaze; the shot achieves subjectivity without the use of editing. The title[4] "Mind your step!," warning the character and the audience of the danger that looms over the couple in their visit to Rapallo, is an example of the explicit use of depth of field as an element of relation, since depth of field allows the interaction of title and character.

Dr. Strangelove presents depth of field as an instrument of obtrusive commentary aiding satire. In the meeting of Ripper and Mandrake the distorted shot/reverse shot is possible because the text resorts to depth of field to fit both characters in the frame: while Mandrake walks to the end of the room, the text holds the shot from a position behind Ripper's back. Also part of a distorted shot/reverse shot is the low-angle view of Turgidson, the title of his book, and the world map in the background. Here the obtrusiveness of the title is apparent, since it qualifies Turgidson as a mass murderer. Apart from this explicit use of titles, the film resorts to depth of field in compositions that show characters holding different views about the events. Depth of field allows the text to include opposing views in a single shot, which permits us to see the reaction of a character to what another character is saying. A paradigmatic scene introduces the Russian ambassador informing the

---

[4] By title I mean any element of mise-en-scène that includes verbal language and which, in the case of Kubrick, usually comment on the contents of the shot. Titles appear in notices, notebooks, etc., belonging to the mise-en-scène.

Americans of the Doomsday Device. The ambassador and the president are in the foreground, while the round table with the other members of the War Room remains in the foreground. Here not only the president's reaction but also the reaction of the rest of the War Room is offered as relevant.

Within the obtrusive uses of depth of field we find examples in which it is used to exalt the physicality, the iconicity, and the beauty of the image. In *Barry Lyndon* depth of field in long takes discloses subjectivity, although the inexpressiveness of the characters creates a certain detachment from the fabula. A contrast is created between the use of depth of field after introductory reverse zooms and the use of handheld camera shots: Barry's only outburst of spontaneity and anger is shown in a handheld shot that breaks a pattern of depth-of-field scenes. Depth of field is allied to decorum, to the worship of exteriority, of politeness, while handheld shots are allied to genuineness and sincerity. The prevalence of depth of field throughout the film points to the privileging of the iconicity of the image over other considerations. The deep space created by reverse zoom shots is not usually employed narratively in its fullness. The use of deep space for non-narrative purposes marks the text's tendency to privilege description and textuality over fabula.

Depth of field in *Barry Lyndon* is also used as a realistic device that contributes to the expression of how characters relate to one another: characters separate and leave at both ends of compositions in depth, or they progress from one plane of depth to the other and stay there together, hinting at their closeness. Typical examples are Redmond seeing his cousin Nora home and Captain Grogan seeing Barry home. The encounter between Barry and the chevalier in the latter's room also uses depth of field. This scene's similarity with the last scenes of *2001* suggests that it is relevant to the consideration of the stylistic strategy. In this case the distance created by the two planes of depth is not obliterated by the disappearance of one of the poles but is bridged by one of the characters (Barry) who walks toward the other. The space between the two characters is shown as relevant, if only to state that the union of the two has started from their distance. Depth of field is thus reinforced in its capacity to relate elements of the fabula. This is one of the differences between *2001* and *Barry Lyndon:* their differing conceptions of space as ambiguity in the one case and as an element that fixes meaning in the other.

Within the realistic use of depth of field we also find cases in which the device shows the interaction between opposing characters and marks their opposing natures. In *Paths of Glory* depth of field is used to accommodate within the same shot characters who represent differing worlds and ideas. These scenes are invariably examples of confrontation between the world of the chateau and the world of the trenches, and the stylistic strategy of depth of field is essential in the depiction of the central theme of the film. The initial scene between Mireau and Brou-lard in the chateau room presents two characters with apparently differ-ent views on the cost in human lives a victory is worth; although the scene finally discloses that the views of the two men are not different in the end, the scene is performed in an atmosphere of confrontation that is aided by the use of depth of field. After the interview Broulard and Mireau hold with Dax, where they discuss the course of action to fol-low to punish the soldiers for their "cowardice," the conflicting posi-tions of Mireau and Dax are made clear. When they are outside the room where the interview was held, a deep-focus shot includes Mireau in the foreground talking to Broulard and Dax in the background on his way up a flight of stairs talking to one of his men. The relationship of antagonism is stressed by the textual decision to include them both in the same shot, with the added significance that Dax is physically placed in a higher position than Mireau, hinting at his higher moral standard: he has been forced to accept the trial of three of his men, and he has openly expressed his disagreement with the decision. This same use of depth of field reappears during the court martial, where the text organizes most of the shots in two planes of depth that include, al-though separated, the three men and the jury. Finally, the interview in which Dax informs Broulard of Mireau's order during the attack also employs depth of field.

In *Lolita* depth of field is clearly allied with the creation of irony, showing the different degrees of knowledge possessed by the characters in a realistic move to convey to the audience as much information about the fabula as possible. Shot/reverse shot sequences seem to evolve into depth of field, through which subjectivity is achieved. Depth of field allows the presence of focalizer and focalized in the same frame, a complete change from previous films. Both focalizer and fo-calized are the object of our gaze, making it unnecessary for the text to resort to editing to clarify the status and meaning of the presented ma-terial. Nevertheless, the film still privileges one element over the other. In the scene in which Humbert sees Lolita for the first time (when Charlotte leads him to the garden in her attempt to persuade him to stay at her house), the text sticks to editing and emphasis on one of the poles — Humbert, in this case. Later, a similar scene marks the change toward depth of field: a camera movement discloses Humbert atten-tively watching offscreen; as the camera tracks back we are shown the object of his gaze: Lolita playing in the garden. The evolution to depth of field exists, but the text still strives to focus our attention on Humbert, the most important character in the scene and the center of consciousness in the text. Therefore, there is still a certain emphasis on one of the poles that the film privileges.

The text further develops this strategy in several scenes that employ depth of field. One of these is the scene in which Humbert and Lolita check into the hotel: while the couple are talking to the clerk Quilty and a woman appear in the background, but Humbert and Lolita do not see them. At a certain moment Quilty appears in the foreground, observing Humbert and Lolita, who are still unaware of his presence. Later, Quilty pretends to be a policeman while chatting with Humbert on the porch. Quilty is in the foreground looking at us, and Humbert cannot see his face. These two scenes are examples of the film's constant game with knowledge: the audience knows that Quilty is following the main characters, while they remain oblivious to the fact. These scenes emphasize the interaction between two poles (in this case, planes of depth) which are isolated from one another because of the lack of knowledge of one of them. This evolution of the textual strategy means a change from the distortion of a textual device in order to emphasize one element over the other to the use of a similar binary device in order to make clear the interaction between the two elements and their capacity to create meaning. A similar use of depth of field occurs when Humbert knows that Charlotte is planning to send Lolita away from the summer camp to a boarding school; Humbert's annoyance at the possibility of not being able to see Lolita leads him to consider killing Charlotte. This is suggested in a deep-focus composition in which a revolver appears in the foreground, Humbert in the middle ground in bed, and Charlotte in the background. Humbert is looking at the gun while he listens to Charlotte, his back turned to her. The effect of Charlotte's words and Humbert's concealed desire for the girl are presented to the audience but never to Charlotte, who remains oblivious to Humbert's real feelings.

Analysis of depth of field also suggests complex theoretical responses to the contents of the fabula, responses which at the same time place the workings of depth of field in a new light. In *2001* the final scene that denies the reliability of depth of field in the new world of supraintelligence is a good example of this less traditional use of the device. *2001* introduces uses of depth of field that allow the inclusion and interaction of several elements, but the meaning that is to be extracted from such juxtapositions demands a great imaginative effort, a great capacity to make hypotheses, from the audience. The alignment of the three planets and the sequences of spaceships and planets dancing to music use several planes of depth and shape scenes that require the audience to abstract a meaning from them. The device seems to produce greater complexity and ambiguity rather than a more accurate depiction of reality, as the examples in the discussion of editing did. Depth of field is also relevant in the scene in which HAL sees Dave and Poole inside the pod discussing the situation of the computer. Here the machine is introduced into the group of men in command — and not only that, but the text reveals that the machine is in a stronger position than the men, since HAL has understood what the men are talking about, whereas they do not suspect anything. Depth of field in this case expresses the evolution of the machine, which is now able to become part of the commanding crew. The idea of improvement from such a state of affairs is also suggested by depth of field: in the last scene in the eighteenth-century room the two planes of depth that the point-of-view shots create are disassembled by the fact that the character that the text presents as the origin of space does not appear in subsequent shots, therefore rendering the use of depth of field ineffective. The progression of humankind which Bowman's transformations point to is carried out at the expense of the strategy of depth of field, therefore demanding reasons, meanings, why this has been done in such a way. One suggestion might be that the relationships between elements which depth of field is capable of expressing in cinema are now considered traditional, and therefore ineffective in expressing the step ahead in the development of intelligence that this final part means.

Questions of perspective also contribute to the eliciting of complex responses from the audience. Kubrick's cinema reflects on questions of space and presents space as constructed, as artifice. This is, again, especially evident in *2001*. As we have already noted, the endless track on which Poole runs creates a distorted perspective. Also, in the *Discovery* section, during the repair of the failure reported by HAL the shots of the man out in space are edited together without showing us any unmoving points of reference, making it impossible to discern the proper position of verticality for the man or the exact position of the spaceship, which is moving at the same time. This uncertainty about the real nature of the space created by the text and about the spatial relationships present in the shots is a similar effect to that sought by experimental films. The aim of experimental cinema is to explore the possibilities textual strategies offer the artist to construct stories in time and space. This exploration tends to work by questioning codes established by classical cinema. *2001* is, therefore, close to experimentalism in its handling of space.

The use of process work also contributes to the creation of deceptive space. Since the conjunction of foreground and background is artificial — it does not really exist but is a product of the workings of the text — the depth is nonexistent, and, therefore, perspective does not in fact exist. This is so in the rear projections in "The Dawn of Man" and in the matte work in those scenes where one spaceship lands on another and is lowered as if on an elevator.

These scenes present the viewer with elements of mise-en-scène or editing that question the notion of perspective, traditionally understood as linear perspective. Perspective is supposed to arrange lines within a picture to order the different planes of depth and make the image coherently readable. Readability also demands that the viewer be able to distinguish the bottom from the top of the image. These two aspects of space, which perspective helps to discern, are questioned by *2001*. The conclusion should, therefore, be that the text extends to its style the discussion of the nature and evolution of intelligence that the film is carrying out, and that the configuration of space as part of style is brought into this discussion. The cases of depth of field that we saw in the first section were capable of relating elements in the text and, therefore, of creating meaning. This second section has, nevertheless, suggested that depth of field is not so capable of fulfilling a narrative role, in what seems a direct attack on the idea that space (and, by extension, the visible, cinema) can express a truthful relationship with reality.

Mise-en-scène

Mise-en-scène is formalized to an extent that reveals the texts' attempt to elicit meaning by means of textual options of style rather than by the spontaneous development of characters who would develop the theme of the film. Setting shares this tendency, working toward an apparent formalization of the locales, ascribing them clear-cut meanings. In some films different settings accompany changes in the development of the plot; in other films the settings accompany opposing points of view, becoming representations of the struggling forces in the fabula. And in a few cases the settings remain unchanged throughout the text, representing both the external and the mental milieux the characters inhabit.

Killer's Kiss belongs to the group of films whose settings accompany the development of the narrative. The dancing club becomes a representation of Gloria, the boxing palace stands for Davy, and the apartment building is the place where these two settings are left behind, where the exploitation the two characters suffer is transformed into gentle interchange between the two and into the final romance. Davy's nightmare scene anticipates the setting of the Rapallo-Davy chase that takes place later in the film. The setting in the nightmare as a foreshadowing of Davy's later predicament suggests that Davy is trapped in his own interiority. The state of isolation suggested by the settings associated with each of the two characters will be solved by the appearance of a third one, their apartments, which allows the interaction between Davy and Gloria and their decision to escape the bonds of oppression that tie them.

In *Spartacus* the gladiator school is a site of oppression that is gradually transformed, because of the growing consciousness of the slaves, into a place of redemption. This transformation hints that the slaves can change and shape their future, that they can control their own destiny. Against this conviction the film offers Rome, the origin of slavery, which attempts to counteract the slaves' awareness about their own situation. The outdoor fields initially represent the first possibility and experience of freedom: community among the slaves, friendship, the love of Spartacus and Varinia. But they are gradually transformed into the site of the end of the dream, where the slaves are defeated by the Romans. The settings become representations of ideas as the text evolves from one to another; but at the same time the settings themselves evolve, coinciding with the development of the plot.

In *2001* the plot starts in the apes' desolate world, standing for pre-civilization, for primitive mental work that is evolving toward intelligence, the desire to kill being the first hint of the development of the apes' intellect. Dr. Floyd's setting reveals a world where everything has been devised so that intelligence is employed to master nature and the immediate surroundings. The *Discovery* means a step ahead: intelligence is being handed over to pure intelligence, to the machine. In "Beyond the Infinite" intelligence is surpassed as a new human being is born. The evolution of settings paralleling the development of the plot is clear.

In *Full Metal Jacket* the settings are also given the capacity to signify. Parris Island is the setting of rule, order, and dehumanization in the attempt to turn the men into machines — killing machines. Vietnam is the setting where such a rule is disrupted, where human freedom is used to oppress the weak; it is the setting where the process undergone in the first part is seen to lead the soldiers not to the achievement of logic or order but to degradation into horror. This setting means, on the other hand, the confirmation of that at which the first part hinted: here the soldiers become isolated individuals who do not want to think about their deeds; they just want to go on killing in an attempt to survive.

Paths of Glory exemplifies how different settings may become representations of opposing forces that are never reconciled. The clear-cut division sets off the men living in the trenches, the soldiers, with the connotations of honesty and simplicity they carry, from those living in the chateau, the generals, who exhibit a sophistication that masks their cruelty. The confrontation between the two sets of ideas represented by the two settings is the theme of the film. These ideas are shown to be irreconcilable; the film says so explicitly when, in the last section, the generals are in the chateau having breakfast, and the men are listening to a German prisoner sing before they return to the trenches. *Dr. Strangelove* also employs settings as meaningful pieces of the text. The isolation of the various locales is essential to the understanding of the mad chase toward death. Human isolation is proposed as its cause, and setting is the expression of such isolation.

A Clockwork Orange is an example of the use of settings as consistent representations of a single idea that remains uncontested throughout the text. All settings are of the same kind, and all express the same meanings: alienation; threat; the dehumanization of a world that degrades the individual, only to blame him/her for such a degradation. *The Shining* also exemplifies this tendency. All settings are of the same kind since they are all within the same building, the Overlook Hotel. All of them express isolation and maze-like structures that resemble the complex movements of Jack's brain in his journey toward madness.

The arrangement of characters, or characters and props, within the space of the frame is significant in several of Kubrick's films. In *Lolita* a composition of the gun plus Humbert plus Charlotte hints at Humbert's thought of killing Charlotte when he learns that she has decided to send Lolita from the summer camp straight to a boarding school. In *Killer's Kiss* the final scene repeats the composition of the first; the only difference is the presence of Gloria, who meets Davy at the station. The girl is the cause of the sudden turn Davy's life has taken.

The composition of the shots usually produces an effect of externality. Kubrick's cinema tends to search for perfect, sometimes symmetrical compositions. This searching is especially apparent in the initial and final scenes of certain films. *The Killing* ends with a composition in which the "The End" title is framed by the two policemen who are approaching Johnny to arrest him. The perfection of the shot emphasizes Johnny's predicament and the feeling of entrapment into which the text moves after the well-prepared plan goes wrong. In *Paths of Glory* the initial and final scenes present straight lines that form corridors through which the characters walk: the generals inside the chateau at the beginning, the three soldiers toward the stakes where they are to be executed at the end. These lines seem to hint at the constant manipulation of human life that human constructs (in this case, the army and its generals) effect.

This same purpose illuminates the use of perfectly balanced compositions in *Barry Lyndon*. In this film framing is only one of the strategies that emphasize the idea of society constricting the life of a free individual. *Lolita* plays with this idea of society, or certain people, manipulating others, and it also employs symmetrical compositions to suggest it. At the ball Quilty and Charlotte interchange some talk in which Quilty reveals that he knows more about Charlotte's daughter than the mother does, while Charlotte is trying to make Quilty remember the good time they had together. The compositions that render this portion of the fabula present three characters inside the frame, two of them with their backs turned to us and framing the other character, who faces us. The text seems to be playing with the idea of who is "framing," who is trying to deceive, whom in this conversation.

This capacity of perfect compositions to suggest meaning appears in a more refined manner in *2001* and *Full Metal Jacket*, where traditional perspective is used as a symbol of tradition — one that must be transcended, in the case of *2001*. In Kubrick's science-fiction film a distorted/impossible perspective in the *Discovery* scenes gives way to the search for the unknown and regeneration in the origin of perspective, of space.

Kubrick tends to include similar compositions in different films, providing support for the hypothesis that stylistic devices have a constant, pervading meaning in his oeuvre, a meaning that may be cited in a film by the appearance of a similar composition to one in a previous film. The shot of the men behind bars in Johnny's apartment in *The Killing,* suggesting that they are already in jail, also appears in *Killer's Kiss* and in *Spartacus,* to mention only the most obvious examples. The shot in *2001* of the apes framed in their entirety, plus the ground and the sky that "frame" them, reappears in *Full Metal Jacket* when Cowboy is shot dead, as if to hint that Cowboy represents the modern ape and that humankind has not evolved as much as *2001* might have wished but keeps on destroying itself. Also, the shot of Bowman in the old room in *2001,* in which he is framed from the back as he eats, finds a similar composition in *Barry Lyndon* when the chevalier meets Barry for the first time: here the chevalier is eating and is shown from the back. The composition hints that the step forward of intelligence was a challenge to the rules of the time, since it is now enacted by a gambler, someone who has learned to use society for his own ends, mastering the structures that make up knowledge and human relationships.

Elements of mise-en-scène are used as conveyors of meaning that are sometimes related to the creation of metaphors. A criterion that might help us distinguish different groups within Kubrick's films is the degree of obtrusiveness of the device: some of them clearly cue their reading as metaphors, while others are more subtly concealed.

Overt cases of the functioning of props can be found in *Killer's Kiss*. The pictures on the mirror tell us about the rural, pastoral way of life Davy's family lead in Oregon, as opposed to his own life of solitude and prize fights. The sign "Mind Your Step" over the stairs leading Gloria to Rapallo's office constitutes an intrusion of the text into the fabula. Props in the form of self-conscious titles also appear in *Dr. Strangelove*, qualifying Turgidson and Ripper, and in *Full Metal Jacket*, describing the manipulation of information that is carried out in the newspaper office. Lolita's props in *Lolita* — her lollipops, hoop, Coke and potato chips — suggest her vulgarity and childishness and reinforce Humbert's unawareness of Lolita's defects. For him she is just an adorable, attractive nymphet. In *A Clockwork Orange* the Beethoven bust, the penis-like sculpture, the furniture in HOME and the Christ figures in Alex's room become meaningful through an obvious textual effort to make them so. They tell us about Alex's fondness of music, the contrast between the art Alex enjoys and the modern art he despises because he does not understand it. This metaphor suggests that he is a modern-age criminal only in appearance. He identifies with traditional art and rejects what does not fit his pre-established codes, hinting that he is a product of society as it has evolved until then, not an inexplicable degradation of humankind. Alex is the result of traditional conceptions of social relation, if we follow the interpretive line opened by props in the film.

More covert uses of props appear in *Killer's Kiss* in the use of mannequins in the final fight, which hints at the manipulation of people Rapallo exercises throughout the film and is suggested here when Rapallo uses the mannequins as weapons. In *Paths of Glory* the three stakes to which the condemned soldiers are tied reenact the death of Jesus Christ and the two thieves, hinting that the soldiers are always innocent victims in the game of war. *2001* uses food as a symbol of humanity, and the film evolves from the raw meat of "The Dawn of Man" section to the synthetic food Bowman and Poole eat and finally to the traditional dish the aged Bowman eats in the white room. It seems as if the film has returned to an age where human beings are properly human and eat proper food. The bone transforming into a spaceship marks not only a change in time but also the evolution of intelligence, although intelligence is, in a way, still the same, since it still needs to kill to survive. HAL represents the development of intelligence together with the loss of humanity on the part of the human crew, the machine becoming more human than Bowman or Poole. The monolith is the symbol of intelligence, of the developing capacities of individuals, which are only a potentiality in the first stages of the film but are quickly shown to bloom. The Starchild is the new specimen of humankind, a new being capable of transcending the traditional boundaries of intelligence.

Some props, and sometimes also similar events, recur in several films. This repetition allows the intertextual interaction of some films on others and the commentary of new texts on old ones and vice-versa. The mask Johnny uses in *The Killing* is similar to the one Alex puts on during the rape scene in HOME in *A Clockwork Orange,* perhaps hinting at the different nature of outlaws (in the past they had an aim in mind; nowadays their only concern is destruction) and also at their similarities: both elicit sympathy from the audience by presenting themselves as playing a role that is different from their real nature, by calling attention to their self-consciousness as actors.

The crosses in *Paths of Glory* and *Spartacus* link innocent victims to the religious tradition started by the figure of Jesus Christ. In both films the men die in the company of other men who have suffered a similar injustice, and the scenes suggest that human beings are never free to choose their own destiny or express their own ideas, that the power relations at work in every society are always stronger than the will of the individual, and that the individual will always be defeated. The killing of the ape in *2001* is similar to the fight to the death Spartacus and Draba are forced to perform for the Roman nobles. It seems as if this fight in *Spartacus* is linking the apes' fight with the modern era, suggesting that the criminal instincts in the human being have existed in all the stages of history.

Costume and make-up as means of expression are found everywhere in the cinema of Stanley Kubrick. Charlotte's leopard skin in *Lolita* suggests her aroused sexuality, which Humbert cannot control. Alex's suit and make-up in *A Clockwork Orange* suggest the eeriness of an artistic option expressed by costume and matched by the dehumanized world in which Alex and his droogs survive. Dax's unbuttoned jacket in *Paths of Glory* hints at his contempt for military formalities. Spartacus's loose, simple costume befits a former slave experiencing freedom. The use of make-up in *Dr. Strangelove* to create three characters out of one actor is a self-conscious move that matches the overall distortion of the text. The plain, all-alike suits in Floyd's world in *2001* hint at the uniformity of the people living in such a dehumanized environment. The sophisticated costumes and heavy make-up in *Barry Lyndon* emphasize the world of external appearance and decorum with which Barry tries to cope. The ordinary clothes in *The Shining* hide the extraordinary, matching the development of the film from a family picture into a horror movie where fantasy is revealed to have existed from the beginning. In *Full Metal Jacket* Joker's helmet with the inscription "Born to Kill" and the peace button on his uniform suggest the ambiguous status of the main character, who is undergoing the extreme experience of having to adapt himself to the reality of war.

The inexpressive nature of characters is used as a tool by the narrative, revealing Kubrick's ever-present tendency to treat characters as mere accessories of the textual manipulations he effects to create meaning. He disregards characters as flesh-and-blood beings capable of complex reactions and refuses to give the presentation of the characters' psychology a relevant place in his films. Therefore, in *Killer's Kiss* and *The Killing* expression is assigned to voice-over or to elements of mise-en-scène other than acting. In *2001* the narrative force is handed over to plot and space, since characters are deprived of their capacity to show their feelings. *Barry Lyndon*, where the main character is particularly bland, is greatly aided by the choice of an actor such as Ryan O'Neal; the actor's inexpressive face is perfect for a character who, unable to adapt to the new social position he has acquired, remains impassive because he does not know how to behave in a world to which he does not belong. The first part of *Full Metal Jacket* employs this same lack of expression as a hint of the dehumanization that military training confers on the soldiers. Inexpressive natures are forced to burst out in violent rages through which the soldiers show their growing disposition to be aggressive and kill; an example is the violent conversation in which Hartman forces Joker to show him his "war face." In the second part the soldiers adopt clichéd poses toward the events. Joker's expression reveals an ironic, detached attitude to the war, although in the end he will become one more "empty head."

Obviousness, almost self-indulgence, of acting is present in some cases, with the purpose of creating a satiric or farcical text, emphasizing the physical quality of the actor, or depicting a landscape of madness. In *Lolita* Quilty is played by the same actor who also impersonates other characters, by using disguises, throughout the film. Several characters are also played by the same actor in *Dr. Strangelove* (Peter Sellers, as in *Lolita*) with the degree of self-consciousness this involves. All these characters in the two films present us with more or less exaggerated examples of acting, where the actor's histrionics can be interpreted as an extra signifying force that is added to the dialogue and the plot. In *Spartacus* acting attempts to exploit the star status of Kirk Douglas and Jean Simmons, and also their physical appearance in prolonged close-ups. In *The Shining* Jack Nicholson uses self-indulgent acting, which reminds us of so many of his previous films, to express the character's madness, his incapacity to escape from his fantasies, to stop being ruled by his decaying mind.

Character movement is rendered relevant as it turns space into another protagonist of the text. In the journey through the Stargate toward the development of intelligence in a new human being in *2001*, the movement of the character is essential to describe the progression through space that the film chooses as its metaphorical conclusion. Movement reveals the constructed nature of space in the scenes where the flight attendant appears walking upside down, or in the deceptive continuity of space that the track seems to create while Poole runs, all of which points to the deceptive nature of space in cinema. In *Full Metal Jacket* character movement reinforces the contrasts between the two parts of the film. Soldiers move in fixed patterns (in military formation) on the island, according to the dictates of military order. In Vietnam movement is freer; the men are not forced to follow any pattern, and in a way they feel at a loss without such an obligation to follow a predetermined movement. In the Mickey Mouse song of the final scene the characters return to the formation-like movement, expressing Joker's acceptance of the survival code imposed by the war.

The stylization of the characters' movement usually serves the purpose, by mixing the originality or beauty of the form with outrageously indecent or immoral contents, of laying bare the falsifying capacity of cinema and of texts in general. In *A Clockwork Orange* the "Singin' in the Rain" dance number mixes the gay lyrics, lively music, and dance with the rape scene at HOME, thereby pointing to the mixture of cruelty and sophistication in Alex. *Barry Lyndon* provides one of the most beautiful moments in the cinema of Stanley Kubrick in the candlelit scene in which Barry and Lady Lyndon meet at the gambling table. The movements of their eyes and faces are geared to the music through acting and editing. Music and visual spectacle, which shape a warm, romantic scene, are mixed with the coldness of the wooing and the contrived nature of their "love": Barry is deceiving Lady Lyndon, since he is only interested in improving his social status. The scene is followed by a cold kiss in the blue light and the narrator's blunt remark that Lady Lyndon quickly fell into Barry's trap.

"Noir" lighting is typical of certain films by Kubrick. Stark lighting and a single source of light onscreen are apparent in *Killer's Kiss, The Killing,* and *Dr. Strangelove.* The use of a light onscreen is far from being an element of realism in Kubrick's cinema; rather, the links with film noir that this lighting suggest hint at the distortion at work in the text, at the dangerous moral ambiguity and threatening atmosphere that pervades these texts.

Light is also employed as a means of separating two milieux, plots, or settings. In *Paths of Glory* the chateau is flooded in three-point lighting, while the trenches are starkly lit. *Lolita* creates scenes of threat or mental breakdown with the help of "noir" lighting: for instance, in the introductory sequence at Quilty's mansion and the final scenes at the hospital, in which Humbert almost goes mad when he realizes that Lolita has left him.

Spectacle as the result of big production values uses standard three-point lighting. *2001, Spartacus, A Clockwork Orange* (even though it is not a big production, the atmosphere of clarity and well-defined spaces approximates it to such a production), *The Shining,* and *Full Metal Jacket* all use standard lighting, which usually makes the symbolism of color and cleanliness at work in the films more evident.

Lighting is transformed into a source of beauty, tending to emphasize the beauty of the visuals: in *Barry Lyndon* candlelit scenes, softly lit scenes, and scenes shot with natural light are so carefully planned with respect to lighting, color, costumes, etc. that the impression of beauty is achieved. This effect suggests the coldness and rigidity that such beautiful appearance conceals and, consequently, the deceptive nature of cinema, here represented by beauty. Blue lighting in *The Shining, Full Metal Jacket,* and *Barry Lyndon* seems to be used to create beautiful scenes that usually accompany cruel contents, such as killings, beatings, and false demonstrations of love. The use of blue lighting is the conjunction of a strategy of beauty with the inherent criticism of the search for beauty that the contents imposes.

Sound

Music is a particularly relevant aspect of Kubrick's style, since he consistently confers on it a great signifying potential. The texts exploit this nature of music (both diegetic and extradiegetic).

Extradiegetic music is often given the role of suggesting meaning. In the credit-title sequence of *Dr. Strangelove* the confrontation, and also the common origin, of war (death) and maternity (life) is suggested by the music on the soundtrack, which quickly introduces one of the main ideas in the film: the connection between desire and destruction. In *2001* all of the musical themes acquire meaning as they consistently accompany the same visual portions. The credit-title theme appears whenever the conjunction of the planets is shown, hinting at a turning point for the text and for humankind. The monolith's theme is coherent, in its absence of melody, with the noise heard during the Stargate sequence: both foreshadow the jump in the development of human intelligence. The monolith warns us about such a jump, and in the Stargate sequence we experience it. Strauss's "Blue Danube Waltz" theme, in its melodic richness, seems to present a contrast with the previous examples of music in *2001*. It seems as if the waltz music perfectly matches the movements of the spaceships in outer space, suggesting the self-satisfaction that this stage of technological development has produced in humankind; nobody seems to question whether such a development has, in fact, meant an improvement in the lives of people, or whether, as the film points out, such a development may not be so satisfactory after all, since it involves the loss of one of the qualities that define the human being: the capacity to communicate with one another.

Full Metal Jacket employs quite a different kind of music. Here we find popular music, which can produce meaning in two ways: through its musical features (rhythm, melody, lyrics, etc.) and through the connotations such songs may suggest to the viewer, who is supposed to share the culture that has produced them. The credit-title music emphasizes the popular nature of the Vietnam War, singing about the common experience for every American boy in those days of being called up, while the visuals show that the multiplicity of the people is being obliterated as they are shaved into exact replicas of the other soldiers. The song points out the contrast between what popular culture suggested the war was and the real thing, and the difficulty in offering an unbiased text about it. The initial scene of the second part presents a song, "These Boots Were Made for Walkin'," which encapsulates clichéd American attitudes toward the war. It matches the visual, a Vietnamese city that looks completely American, and shows how partial any view of the war is bound to be, since all accounts are born out of clichéd, biased approaches. The words of the song say: "one of these days these boots are gonna walk all over you," mixing a reference to the typical American tendency to spread its clichéd culture and to act according to it, and the result of such conduct in Vietnam, where the Americans are actually walking over the inhabitants of the country. The final Mickey Mouse song contrasts with the formation songs, while the similar physical organization and movement of the characters suggests a comparison. The American soldiers are more like children, frightened and happy to be alive, than like killing machines.

Extradiegetic music can also be used to mark the relevance of a character: in *Killer's Kiss* specific musical themes are ascribed to each of the two main characters, Davy and Gloria. These themes suggest the nature of their personalities, with Davy appearing accompanied by a tense score while Gloria's music is more relaxed and friendly.

Extradiegetic music can be opposed to diegetic music to emphasize the theme of the film. In *Paths of Glory* the sound of the drums during the attack and execution scenes is clearly set against the final song in the cabaret scene. The world of military discipline and rule is shown to be inadequate, since it evolves into injustice. The final song by the German girl means the return to human values, which is further stressed by the change to a form of music that contains lyrics and is performed by a human voice, not just by an instrument. In *Dr. Strangelove* the music from the transistor radio Mandrake finds is lively and contains no reference to the theme of the film, representing how civilian life is completely obliterated by the ideology at work in the fabula of the film. This music contrasts with the music in the credit-sequence and that in the final explosion scene, which is clearly related, although ironically, to the theme developed by the film: the links between desire and death. In *The Shining* extradiegetic music is ominous and lacks melody, matching the horror story, whereas the diegetic music heard at the ball is melodic, soft, and friendly. Music helps to contrast the two worlds, to indicate the passage from one to the other, and to suggest the ambiguous attraction the world of the past (of mental disturbance) has not only for Jack but also for the audience.

Extradiegetic and diegetic music may join forces in the depiction of the film's themes. The formal coincidence between the features of extradiegetic and diegetic music creates a coherence that contributes to the unambiguous establishment of the texts' sets of ideas. In *Lolita* both the credit-title music and the diegetic music at the ball emphasize the artificiality of acting, the aesthetic move acting implies, something Humbert does not realize. The credit sequence shows Humbert painting Lolita's toes, transforming her into what he expects her to be: an adorable young nymphet. He is changing Lolita into something she is not, just as the actress playing Lolita has created the artifice of her character. In the ball sequence Quilty proves his ability to see reality behind the curtains of appearance; he can discern where pretense is because he is an artist: he knows that Lolita is in his hands, something Charlotte ignores. In *A Clockwork Orange* diegetic and extradiegetic music are allied in the depiction of the ideas of art alienating Alex and of the existence of a common origin for art and violence. *Barry Lyndon* presents extradiegetic music that accompanies the depiction of the world of decorum in the society of the time. Diegetic music appears in Bullingdon's scene and fulfills the same task. It is this music, and the formal gathering to enjoy it, that emphasize the turning point of the text and Barry's abandonment of decorum in beating Bullingdon.

A characteristic feature of Kubrick's cinema is the use of a theme of extradiegetic music that extends over several scenes, which are joined together thematically with the help of the musical theme, turning music into a textual mark of significant fragments, a creator of textual patterns. This is particularly evident in *Barry Lyndon,* which sets textual patterns through music. Music marks the beginning and end of fragments which contain a coherent meaning independent from the preceding and the following material. This is only part of this film's tendency to organize its material in the most "beautiful" possible way, with the purpose of emphasizing the physicality of the text — here with the obvious help of extradiegetic music. In *Lolita* this technique seems to help the quick succession of events. This happens in the drive-in movie scene, which is joined with a view of Lolita playing with her hoop in the garden; both scenes suggest the growing friendship between Humbert and Lolita. Such a link also appears when the music in the bath scene that follows Charlotte's death extends over to the scene of Humbert picking up Lolita at the camp. In *Full Metal Jacket* this technique links scenes that criticize the biased nature of all accounts of the war, especially by TV, and also by the film itself. The artificiality of the linking is accompanied by the reference to the constructed nature of cinema (its bias). This happens in the scene in which the soldiers are being filmed by a TV camera in the middle of an enemy attack, a scene that is introduced by the music that had started in a previous scene where an officer had killed several Viet Cong soldiers.

Music in Kubrick reveals a general tendency that can be observed in almost every component of style he uses in his films: the self-conscious exploitation of stylistic options. Kubrick's films exploit the signifying potential of extradiegetic music and, consequently, its inherent self-consciousness. This self-consciousness is further employed to join scenes by means of extradiegetic music, creating sections with coherent, independent meaning within the texts.

Voice-over narration in Kubrick usually works as a creator of what we see, as a controller of the information we are given and the way in which this is done. This is so in *Killer's Kiss,* where the main character's voice introduces the flashback that will tell us what has happened to him in the previous days. The voice-over narration in *The Killing* also shows the reliability of the creator of what we see. It invests what we see with meaning by exhibiting an extreme control over the development and chronological arrangement of the steps in the plan. The narrator in *Lolita* acts as if controlling the text ("we are now six months later in . . . "), and he uses a careful diction to warn us about his calculating mind, one that is going to conceal his feelings to satisfy his desire. The narrator seems oblivious to the superior knowledge of the situation Lolita has; this voice is used as a means of indicating the different levels of knowledge at work in the film.

2001 has no voice-over narration, only silence. Silence prevails in the apes' scenes, showing nature at its most essential, uncorrupted by the sound of human language. Language is here equated with development. In *A Clockwork Orange* the narration is alienating, drawing attention to itself as internal. It is also ironic toward the events in the narrative: "a night of considerable energy expenditure . . . ," says the voice after beating up the old man, stealing a car, ravaging a house, and raping the owner. The voice alternately distances us from and draws us to the text, to the possible sympathy we may feel for the protagonist. In *Barry Lyndon* the voice is ironic, compressing information, playing with the audience (moving Barry toward and detaching him from the audience), doing away with the beauty the text creates by introducing into each scene the human factor, which is usually gross and base. It tells us that Lischen had had many short affairs like the one she had with Barry, destroying the apparent sincerity and true affection the film had suggested; it also remarks that Lady Lyndon was quickly won over to Barry, doing away with the potential tenderness we had guessed in their first meeting.

Voice-over narration in Kubrick evolves from an element that shows the mastery of the text by itself, an element of coherence that assures the perfect fitting of each element in the first films, to a more detached, ironic relationship of narrator to text that hints at the growing feeling in the later films that reality cannot be controlled and that the text is unable to present it to us in a clear, reassuring way. This passage seems to be marked by the absence of voice-over narration in *2001*, a reference to the organizing, clarifying function it had fulfilled in Kubrick's films up to then, which would not have been coherent with the spirit of this revolutionary film.

The effect of the form of dialogue, rather than of the contents, is characteristically exploited. Meaning stems from the physical quality of the dialogue rather than from the things that are said. In *Lolita* all characters are qualified by their speech. Humbert's soft tone and chosen diction fits his image as a cultured person. Quilty's tone, with sudden changes in intonation and diction in the first scene, qualify him as capable of playing with language (of fooling people, of sophistication). *A Clockwork Orange* uses the stylized talk of most characters as part of the general strategy of distancing the characters from the audience. This stylization is reflected in their use of incomprehensible words that strike us with their sonority, their quality as sound, since we can only guess what they mean.[5] The pace and tone of delivery are also carefully stylized to draw attention to the physical dimension of sound. In *Full Metal Jacket* the content of dialogue is relevant, but so is its tone. Hartman's high tone contrasts with the soft tone employed by Joker when he is finally allowed to speak to Pyle. The second character is, therefore, the embodiment of the human qualities of sympathy and gentleness Hartman lacks. In the *Stars and Stripes* scenes we see how the newspaper manipulates the war through language: form is privileged over content as a method of manipulation; discourse is reduced to a collection of news that sticks to the stylistic rules imposed by the military command.

In *Paths of Glory* Mireau's booming voice contrasts with Dax's calmer way of delivering his lines. In *Spartacus* the difference between the American accent of slaves and the British accent of masters further stresses the distance between them. Also, the masters are more sophisticated with regard to diction, tone and pace of delivery. When the slaves become more conscious of their human qualities they use a soft tone and slow delivery (Antoninus when he recites the poem in front of the men; Spartacus and Varinia in the scene in which they confess their love). The scarcity of dialogue in *2001* confers more importance on it when it appears. We usually find a formal, calm and soft tone of voice that hides the real thoughts of the person or machine. During the voice-print identification language is reduced to a mere vehicle of formal communication, not human communication, as opposed to the apes' grunts, which were at least sincere in their threat. In *Barry Lyndon* characters convey their status through the formal features of their speech. Barry seems to fall outside the world of decorum because of his feigned polite accent and speech. *The Shining* uses Jack's diction and delivery to show his sophisticated nature, which seems capable of anything. The Jack-Grady dialogue in the rest room is really civilized on the part of Grady, with a careful, stylized delivery that becomes threatening and fits Jack's apparent capacity to master his reality in a violent way.

---

[5] For a discussion of the defamiliarizing strategies and the different textual contexts at work in *A Clockwork Orange*, see García Mainar (1992b).

The contents of dialogue also separate the characters, ascribing specific features to each. In all films the contents help to distinguish the characters from one another, but in some films the importance of language is more consistently suggested than in others, to the point that language becomes one of the main themes of the film. This happens in *Dr. Strangelove, A Clockwork Orange,* and *Full Metal Jacket,* but it is not as apparent in the rest of Kubrick's films. In *Dr. Strangelove* the contents of dialogues are essential to express Turgidson's and Ripper's detachment from reality, the twisted logic that leads them to propose total destruction to solve the Russian threat. The stylized dialogue of *A Clockwork Orange* conveys Alex's degraded ideology of violence and brutality, which is set against the minister's apparent discourse of friendship. In *Full Metal Jacket* the abusive talk by Hartman reveals his bigotry and hatred of anything or anybody that does not fit his narrow American ideology. This has an extension in the clichéd ideas expressed by the soldiers and in Joker's quotations from John Wayne, who has become the representative of American violence through his characteristic roles in Westerns and war movies.

Dialogue is also a powerful source of intertextual meaning. Elements of dialogue may easily be made to refer to other texts (filmic or not) and even to previous films by Kubrick. Humbert's reading of a poem by Poe to Lolita hints at Humbert's cultured nature and Lolita's unsophisticated personality; the poem suggests a world of aesthetic refinement to which the reader can easily link Humbert. Joker's references to John Wayne suggest that the events and types in *Full Metal Jacket* are similar to those of Westerns, and that Kubrick's film is, as these were, a reflection of the American myth of the frontier and the preservation of freedom that the soldiers say they are fighting for. Kubrick's films occasionally make slight and quick references to his own work. The clearest example appears at the beginning of *Lolita:* in the scene at the ranch Quilty makes his entrance by taking aside the sheet that has been covering him on a chair and saying "I'm Spartacus," in a clear reference to Kubrick's previous film. This starts the game of irony that the text carries on at the expense of Humbert: the text presents clues to the plot Quilty has set, but these are only recognizable for the audience; Humbert remains oblivious to them.

Sound effects are elements that in some cases perform the function of dialogue. They can be considered examples of the stylization of form that also affects dialogue; they are all form and no content. They are mainly relevant in the setting of contrasts between scenes. Further realism is achieved by the juxtaposition of scenes with music and outdoor scenes filled by noise — for instance, in *Killer's Kiss.* Also, the noise of ape grunts is followed by the waltz music after the match-cut in *2001,* emphasizing the jump in time by linking two types of dances: the primitive one of the apes gives way to the sophistication of that of the spaceships. In the same film the use of silence during the outings of the astronauts in the space surrounding the *Discovery* is significant, since it intensifies the men's breathing that can be heard on the soundtrack, setting the contrast between the fragility of human life and the immensity of outer space.

Sound effects may suggest the performance of an action and replace verbal language. Language is usually associated with human qualities and actions. When the machines take over in *2001* during the death of the hibernating people and during Bowman's trip outside the *Discovery,* sound becomes the tool through which the text expresses the evolution of the action. The intermittent sounds that mean that the crew are alive are replaced by the constant sound of death. Bowman's breathing marks his growing concern when HAL does not allow him back in the ship and his anger while disconnecting the computer. Human beings become mad in *The Shining,* and this is expressed through Jack's banging of the ball in the lounge.

Dialogue shows again the overall process of formalization of elements that usually takes place independently of the meaning explicitly expressed by the text. Here dialogue is used in the traditional way, as conveyor of meaning through the lines it contains, but, following the general tendency of Kubrick's cinema, it is also made to signify by turning its form (its physical qualities) into an element fraught with meaning. So dialogue also confirms the attempt of Kubrick's films to exploit any single element of signification to add complexity to the text. This is even stressed by the appearance of intertextual references in lines of dialogue, which suggest the status of films as products of a web of signification that is more complex than it seems at first sight and that hints at the idea that the text cannot be controlled by itself but is in the middle of a whirlpool of meanings, some of which are external to it.

Narrative Organization:
Symmetry and Parallelisms

This section will undertake the description of structures that affect and construct larger portions of material than the previously studied stylistic strategies did. It will attempt to reveal the existence of systems of signification devised by the interaction of stylistic structures.

In Kubrick's films we find many examples of elements that are organized in such a way that they create symmetrical textual patterns. *Killer's Kiss* and *Lolita* end in the same settings in which they started, as if the circular move performed by the film means the culmination of a process that had led us to the present state — as if such a present state had been the focus of the whole text, which now returns to its origin and raison d'être. Apart from this, most of Kubrick's films show a division into two parts. *Paths of Glory* has a first section devoted to the men at war and a second devoted to the soldiers in court. *Spartacus* is divided into scenes of the slaves becoming conscious of their humanity and scenes of the fight against the oppressor. The first part of *Lolita* deals with Humbert's game of seduction of Lolita, the second with Lolita's revenge on Humbert. The process of development toward intelligence in *2001* features a first part devoted to the apes and the climax of the bone-throwing scene, and a second part devoted to the same process undergone by the spacemen. *A Clockwork Orange* shows first how Alex bullies society in order to contrast it later with society bullying Alex. Barry Lyndon's rise in the first part is followed by his decline in the second part. The somewhat realistic depiction of Jack's degradation in the first part of *The Shining* is followed by the text's swerving toward fantasy. The first section of *Full Metal Jacket* shows the military training that takes place on Parris Island, the second shows the actual war in Vietnam.

This symmetrical layout is an obvious source of meaning, since the second part is usually understood in its relationship with the first, and vice-versa; and the contrasts and oppositions between them, as much as the similarities, become interpretable signs. The two parts usually follow similar patterns of development, creating parallelisms that emphasize similarities and differences between them. These parallelisms may be set in many ways, thereby shaping many types, from stylistic to fabulaic.

The ordering of the fabula carried out by the text may be used with the purpose of linking scenes taking place at different times. These links usually provide contrasts or oppositions, a frequent strategy in Kubrick's work. The last scene of the first part of *Paths of Glory* is the French attack on the Germans; the last scene of the second part is the cabaret scene in which the French soldiers listen to a German girl sing and finally join in, feeling sympathy — the sympathy the French officers did not show toward their men. The link established by the text suggests that the real differences that make war possible are not the ones the army presents to us but the differences in rank and power, as well as in social class, which have nothing to do with nationality. Similar cases in which the placement of a scene establishes links with other scenes in the same text are found in *Spartacus:* the fight between Spartacus and Draba is followed by the slaves-Romans fight, which shows the progress of the slaves' awareness of their own status and rights and is also linked with the final fight between Spartacus and his friend Antoninus, which marks the slaves' defeat in a return to a fight to the death between two slaves. In *Lolita,* the credit-title scene is reenacted within the text to mark both Humbert's submission and the turning point of the narrative, the beginning of the second part. In *2001* the alignment of the planets at the beginning and end of the film suggests the step ahead that the monolith's appearance has caused in both stages of humankind. In *A Clockwork Orange* the scenes in the second part consistently repeat actions that have been shown in the first part; the only difference is that Alex is the victim in the second part, while he was the "executioner" in the first part. In *Barry Lyndon* a duel caused by his desire for his cousin Nora sets Barry off on his journey; a second duel ends his life with Lady Lyndon and forces him to return to Ireland in exile. In both cases he has to fight members of a social class to which he does not belong and which is not willing to accept him, thereby emphasizing the defeat of Barry's endeavors.

Full Metal Jacket employs this ordering of the scenes and the similarities between them as a powerful signifying force. The film is structured in such a way that events in the second part continuously interact with previous events shown in the first part. The second part provides variations of situations or ideas previously presented. The credit-title music provides a popular song that seems almost to accept the inevitability of war and illustrates the passivity of the soldier being called up. "These Boots Were Made for Walkin'" accompanies the first shots of Vietnam in the second part and seems to denounce the destruction the Americans carried out in a country they were supposed to be helping. Hartman, the drill instructor, is the first part's representative of law and order in the army; he uses language as a weapon to debase his men and impose his bigoted ideology of nationalism and religion. In the second part it is the editor of *Stars and Stripes,* the newspaper for which Joker works, who becomes the embodiment of the military command, since in the rest of the section the soldiers lead their own platoons. The editor also uses language as a tool with which he manipulates the information the world is going to obtain about Vietnam: he defends the right "to be misinformed," as a sign in his office reads. Furthermore, Hartman's language is appropriated by the men in the second part. Joker's final voice-over commentaries share the same sexual bigotry seen in Hartman, and the language Eight-ball uses with the young prostitute the men are offered is close to Hartman's, too. If during the training of the soldiers the image of authority was the commanding officers and the dehumanizing task they perform through language, in the second part authority seems to be given to the media and to communication in general, as the appearance of TV reveals, as defenders of "the right, patriotic attitude."

The debasement of the recruits in the first part is paralleled by a scene in the second part in which Joker bumps into the lime-covered Vietnamese dead, suggesting that the loss of human qualities the Americans have suffered is also a partial death. In the first part the main character, Joker, develops a friendship with Pyle, the recruit who is bullied by the rest of the platoon to teach him the necessity to improve. Pyle becomes the proof that the soldiers are learning the military code, which demands the sacrifice of the weak for the benefit of the strong — the strong usually being those in command. Pyle is the reluctant soldier who, once "properly" motivated, can transform himself into what the instructor asks him to be. The second part introduces Cowboy as partly a mirror image of Pyle. Cowboy is the cheerful fellow who, without wanting to, becomes head of the platoon and has to lead his men against the sniper. He dies, like Pyle, and in the reaction of his companions we find the variation: now the aggressor is not the military establishment, as with Pyle, but the foreign sniper who must be annihilated. Pyle's and the girl sniper's deaths bear certain resemblances, too. In both cases it is more like an execution than a simple death, as both are shot in the head — Pyle even in two heads, since he dies in the "head" of the platoon. Both are good marksmen. Both deaths are, in part, encouraged by the dialogue uttered by other characters: Hartman's insults in the case of Pyle, the dialogue of the soldiers around the dying girl in the case of the sniper. In both cases there is a reference to Mickey Mouse: in the first part the instructor, awakened by the noise in the head, demands an explanation, referring to what has happened as "this Mickey Mouse shit." In the second part the sniper's death is quickly followed by the final scene, in which the soldiers march singing the Mickey Mouse song as if they were schoolboys. Both deaths suggest images of childishness, of immaturity, of conduct that the human mind cannot easily understand or assimilate. Moreover, both deaths conjure up the idea of suicide. The shooting of the sniper by Joker suggests the death of the feminine in him, of what made him feel sympathy for the weak and had shocked him in Pyle's death. Pyle's suicide is caused by the instructor and his fellow soldiers and represents the disappearance of the human feeling of compassion in those recruits who stay alive to serve in Vietnam. The sniper's death confirms the process of dehumanization at work during the film and suggests the complete annihilation of any possibility for understanding of the other in this war. Joker's voice-over reveals, with a vocabulary that has changed from the one he used in the first part, he now having adopted Hartman's diction, that he only cares about himself and can only be happy to be alive after what he has gone through. Joker has killed the sniper with a bullet in her head, which is a way of showing how the rebelliousness has been killed in his head, too, allowing him to live.

The idea of the girl representing the soldiers is also hinted at by the use of a similar composition to frame her as she is dying, as had been used to frame Hand Job when he died: they are encircled by the soldiers, who are shown from the point of view of the corpse on the ground. Also, the death of the sniper suggests the links between death and sex that the film has scattered around. In the first part Hartman made the recruits sing a song in which they referred to their genitals as their "guns"; in the second part the soldiers offer the prostitute rifles in exchange for sex. When Joker asks the rest of the men what they are going to do with the dying sniper, Animal Mother answers, "Fuck 'er." When Joker meets Cowboy's platoon, the men greet him and Rafterman by saying that they are killers and heartbreakers. The common origin of life and death that Kubrick had explored in *Dr. Strangelove* seems to be present in this film, too. *Full Metal Jacket* is only one example of the careful structuring of elements that Kubrick's filmography exhibits. Every element has a function within a system of parallelisms, similarities, and contrasts from which meaning springs out.

Other links are established by stylistic elements. Setting and mise-en-scène in general are useful means of creating links: the chateau with its decor and lighting link the initial Broulard-Mireau meeting with the court-martial scene in *Paths of Glory,* both being expressions of military cowardice and desire to thrive. The futility of Humbert's life is suggested by his return to the same setting where the text had started in *Lolita:* his quest has had no reward. In *2001* the monolith and the food are recurrent elements that mark the development of the narrative; also, the bone being hurled resembles Bowman's change into the Starbaby, both being signs of the development of intelligence. In *The Shining* the maze-dissolve into Jack's mind finds its counterpart in the real maze outside the hotel, where Jack will try to kill his son. The link suggests that Jack's mind is in a maze, about to break down; when Jack does break down he ends up frozen in the real maze: his tormented mind has been the cause of his death.

Camera movement is another element of style that usually establishes links in Kubrick's cinema. In *Paths of Glory* similar camera move-

ments link the attack scene and the ball scene when Dax meets Broulard to inform him of Mireau's order, contrasting the bloody way soldiers are supposed to fulfill their duties with the elegance and
sophistication that forms the generals' lives. This contrast is also conveyed through the different camera movements which accompany
Mireau and Dax when they move about the trenches: Mireau is shown
from the front, whereas when Dax appears the text offers us his point
of view. The initial crane movements of *Spartacus* resemble those that
close the film, suggesting the uselessness of the slaves' attempts to fight
Rome. In *The Shining* Danny's rides through the corridors of the hotel,
which represent his entering the dreadful past of the place, are shown
in tracking shots; similarly, his escape through the lanes of the maze,
the outcome of his daring insight into the depths of horror, is shown in
tracking shots.

The parallelism may exist not between elements within a film but
between elements in different films. Lateral tracking shots recur in *The
Killing, Paths of Glory, Spartacus, Lolita,* and *Full Metal Jacket.* These
shots attempt a quick description of the locale and the characters, serv-
ing as establishing shots. Tracking shots that show the character from
the front suggest the similar natures of the characters they accompany.
They appear in *Paths of Glory* (Mireau in the trenches), *A Clockwork
Orange* (Alex in the record shop), and *Barry Lyndon* (Lord Bullingdon
entering the club to demand satisfaction from Barry). The three characters are entering settings where they are going to find the object of
their exploitation: the soldiers, the young girls, Barry; and the camera
movement highlights the almost insulting confidence the characters
show. The composition of the shot that shows the character between
two backs suggests that the character is being pulled by two opposing
forces; it appears in *Lolita* in the ball scene as Quilty feels caught in the
middle between two women, and in *Dr. Strangelove* in the War Room,
where the president is being dominated by the events taking place in
the other two locales. The strategy in *2001* of including space from the
ground to the sky in the apes' shots reappears in the scene of Cowboy's
death in *Full Metal Jacket.* The strategy attempts to place the individual
in his natural context, showing the struggle between the context and
the individual. The reappearance of this strategy in *Full Metal Jacket*
suggests that human beings have evolved but are still the same animals
that kill their brothers on a meaningless impulse, the same impulse to
explore the unknown that makes humankind improve and develop.
Shots in which the reverse shot is withheld mark the passing to a more
important stage that is going to advance the narrative. They appear in
the Stargate sequence in *2001*, in the conversation between Ripper and

Mandrake in *Dr. Strangelove* where the audience learns about Ripper's madness, and in the meeting with the chevalier in *Barry Lyndon* where Barry is introduced to the kind of life he will try to lead in the second part of the film.

These parallelisms created between films by means of stylistic elements are the few cases in which we can refer to intrinsic stylistic norms common to Kubrick's films. These stylistic norms are present in a text without being motivated by the textual need to convey a portion of the fabula; they establish links between the fabulas of films, but their appearance seems to be motivated only by the textual desire to establish such links. Apart from these, Kubrick's cinema tends to present intrinsic norms that affect each individual film and are ultimately linked to the contents of the text. These norms acquire significance and convey ideas of the fabula.

Editing in shot/reverse shot and crosscutting are relevant in *Killer's Kiss*, since the former, a strategy of subjectivity, evolves into the latter, joining the two characters and the two locales where they work — in short, the two worlds. Focalization through shot/reverse shots is shown in *Killer's Kiss* to possess the capacity to create meaning not only by suturing space but also by leading the text into the crosscutting of events taking place in different locales and making them interact. Crosscutting is also a key stylistic feature of *The Killing,* where it establishes a dialectic relationship with the many long takes presented by the text. Crosscutting introduces an element of fragmentation into the film that the spatiotemporal continuity of the long take counterbalances. In this way the film creates a tightly constructed text with respect to time and simultaneously maintains the atmosphere of realism and coherent description of characters that are necessary to elaborate an appealing story. In *Paths of Glory* the movement of the camera is used in such a way, and accompanying such events, that an implicit confrontation with editing is suggested. The presentation of Mireau's resolution to take the Anthill by means of cutting seems to confer on editing the task of presenting injustice, suggesting that subjectivity (what editing has created in this scene) always contains the seeds of evil. The same scheme is kept in the rest of the film, where the failed attack that represents the death of a great number of soldiers is shot without much recourse to editing, contrasting with the virtuosity of montage during the court-martial scene, where the subjective structures set by editing reveal rotten military morality on the part of the prosecutors and incapacity on the part of the defense counselor Dax.

Lateral tracking shots in *Spartacus* appear during the slave-school section and in the fields while the free slaves train. They are intimately linked to the depiction of how the slaves prepare for fighting, which, according to the Romans, is what they were born for. The use of lateral tracking shots, both when the men are slaves and when they are free, suggests the illusory nature of their freedom. Lighting and characterization are salient features of *Dr. Strangelove,* where the invariable use of stark lighting in the three locales hints at the distance from reality shared by all the characters. Characterization is essential in the game of comic distortion imposed by the text and in the exploitation of artificiality the film exercises by using the same actor for three different characters. Depth of field is the main strategy at work in *Lolita,* where it allows the creation of different levels of knowledge and the irony the text uses against Humbert. Camera movement and the exploration of perspective are the stylistic options characteristic of *2001.* Both contribute to shaping space, which is turned into the expression of all the complexities with which the fabula deals. Mise-en-scène with the purpose of stylizing the world of the text is fully at work in *A Clockwork Orange,* where it attempts the creation of a reality disconnected from whatever notions the viewer may have about it. Zoom shots and mise-en-scène are outstanding in *Barry Lyndon;* they are the most important part of the general tendency of the text to present itself as textually "beautiful." The zoom shots in this film are close to a textual pattern working on its own, independently of the fabula it depicts. The text uses them as introductory elements in each scene, and the few occasions on which they are omitted mark a scene as relevant. This function of pointing out the importance of a certain scene is carried out, however, without any connection with the development of the fabula: it is a purely textual desire to mark the scene in such a way; it does not stem from the specific configuration of the elements of the fabula.

Camera movements acquire great relevance in *The Shining,* where the tracking shots recur in Danny's ramblings around the hotel and, most importantly, in the final scenes where the boy has to escape from his own father. These camera movements establish a link with the maze outside, suggesting that the hotel is another maze; when Jack's mind is associated with the maze we understand that his mental deterioration is linked to the locale in which he lives, and this leads us to the film's final acknowledgment that the hotel is haunted. Camera movements create links between elements of the text, facilitate the understanding of the film, and enrich the reading we may make of it. Camera movements in *Full Metal Jacket* are also given a prominent function. In the first part they accompany the men in formation in straight lines, which will turn into oscillating ones in the second part. The actual war of the second part has destroyed the perfection of the ideological code engraved in the soldiers' minds; they are not saviors but mere killers who do not quite understand what they are doing in Vietnam. This is reflected in the change of camera movements. In Kubrick, intrinsic norms are always linked to the effective depiction of parts of the fabula. There is not usually any attempt to create a purely structural pattern with no fabula-related connection at all.

As can be inferred from the previous pages, the notion of poetics outlined here is somewhat peculiar: it includes not only formal aspects of style but also their relationship to the contents those stylistic options suggest. In conclusion, it must be said that Kubrick's cinema does not repeat stylistic options as part of a strictly parametric narration.[6] It is, rather, a cinema that is somewhat consistent in its use of certain options, but these options usually have a specific effect in the configuration of the contents of the text: style tends to become part of the view of life the films express. The analysis has, therefore, constantly referred to the connection between certain textual options and meanings they inevitably create, or at least suggest to the viewer.

So far, the general conclusion that may be reached is that Kubrick's cinema presents a combination of classical and more "modernist" uses of stylistic options. Kubrick does not blatantly break away from the tradition of classicism, but from a tacit assumption of its postulates, he creates variations of the norm in a parodic game of alteration that always has a signifying function. Kubrick's films also establish patterns of recurrence that create stylistic patterns and are finally invested with meaning — for example, editing with foregrounded narrative force. They use stylistic strategies to mark fragments of the film that are particularly relevant (shot/reverse shots, fades, and dissolves). The films also emphasize the physicality of the image as meaningful (angle and distance of framing), together with the use of color, which tends to become metaphorical. Kubrick's films show a constant attempt at formalizing the texts, at making each element acquire a meaning relevant to the theme of the film independently of the meaning they may be used to convey in the first place (mise-en-scène). Finally, the workings of sound (music, voice-over narration) hint that Kubrick's cinema has gradually evolved from faith in the mechanisms of narration to distrust of them. This evolution is matched by an increasing tendency to use stylistic strategies as self-conscious organizers of the text, acknowledging that they are creating artificial illusions of coherence, since the most recent films tend to question the power of the text to provide a coher-

---

[6] See Bordwell (1985, 274–310). He explains his concept of parametric narration as one based on the development of strictly stylistic patterns.

ent view of reality. In the dialogues we see again an attempt to formalize, to make every part of the films acquire significance. This attempt to
show the complexity of reality is more apparent in the later films, where
the form of dialogue is more frequently exploited and where sound effects are more often used as substitutes for dialogue.

Finally, Kubrick's filmography exhibits a great awareness of the use
it makes of stylistic options to create large structures of parallelism and
symmetry. These large structures are capable of suggesting numerous
and complex meanings, as this has revealed.

Narrative Form

This part of the analysis will deal with the schemata that the text tacitly
or explicitly follows and that help the viewer's construction of the
fabula. It will also deal with the principles of narration, the textual manipulation of the fabula and its effects on knowledge, self-consciousness, communicativeness, causality, time, and space. All these aspects of
the narrative have been analyzed following the theories developed by
David Bordwell in his works on filmic narrative. Bordwell proposes a
model of film study that explores the different ways in which a viewer
makes meaning out of a cinematic text. Based on cognitive psychology,
this model assumes that people perceive and think through organized
clusters of meaning called schemata. People manage to make sense of
their reality because they are goal-oriented beings. Through the process
of socialization every individual undergoes we acquire certain routines
and patterns that lead us to construct sets of expectations and habits
that form the schemata. These schemata change and develop as individuals are confronted with new situations that they are expected to
understand and react to. Therefore, viewers have certain goals in mind
when facing data that they have to order and assimilate. Films offer the
viewer cues related to the schemata associated with narration. These
schemata are ideas about what a story is and the ways in which the elements of a story may appear; notions of reality and the connections
between films and a realistic portrayal of reality; and expectations about
different types of films and their generic classifications, stylistic options
taken by films, etc. (Bordwell 1988, 29–47; see also Janet Staiger,
1992, 63–68).

All of Kubrick's films adhere to the "canonic" story format, a
schema of fabula organization that, because of its high degree of codification and recurrence, can help the viewer fill in any information the
text may fail to provide. This type of story format presents texts divided
into several parts: the introduction of setting and characters, explana-

tion of affairs, complicating action, ensuing events, outcome and ending (Bordwell 1988, 35). Crosscutting seems to be the stylistic strategy
that most helps in the configuration of a canonic story. The alternation
among the different settings allowed by crosscutting privileges a type of
story that evolves by the confrontation between two ideas and has its
final resolution in a compromise between them. The main aim and effect of this narrative mode is the production of coherence. It establishes
identifiable schemata that allow the viewer to create expectations about
what is to come, therefore fostering a unified plot. The plot's potential
developments are restricted to a small number of possibilities, preventing surprises and preserving the coherence of the text.

The search for information the viewer carries out in the reading of a
film assigns each element of the text to a certain classification, according to the motivation the viewer can find for the inclusion of the element in the film. Kubrick's cinema shows a predominance of
compositional, transtextual, and artistic motivation over realistic motivation.[7] Kubrick's texts do not claim similarity to reality but keep to the
rules they themselves have set as part of the game. They aim to be fictional, to present us with an alternative to reality, and in their development the suitability of a textual or fabulaic option is weighed according
to its coherence with the rest of the text and to its capacity to suggest
meaning within the realm of the story.

Kubrick's texts often fall into clearly codified genres: films noirs, war
films, satires, science-fiction films, period films, pure fantasies, horror
films. Certain stylistic options contribute to shaping a text that the
viewer may interpret as belonging to a certain genre or to a certain kind
of narration. Shot/reverse shot sequences carry out a game of distortion that creates identifiable types, schemata that point to the distortion
of the text into satire or to the distortion of subjectivity. Crosscutting
creates the schema of a type of text that develops by the close interaction among its parts. None of his films, however, belongs exclusively to
one pure genre: under their apparent homogeneous generic codification they are finally revealed as examples of different generic conventions that are consistently subverted, transforming the genre in a certain
way. They offer a mixture of codified conventions and subverted
structures that create variations of the different genres to which the
films originally seem to belong. This subversion of generic conventions
is usually carried out by means of self-conscious manipulations. *2001*
takes to an extreme the convention of bright, ordered mise-en-scène,

---

[7] For a discussion of the different types of motivation, see Bordwell (1988,
33–40).

so that it comes to suggest destruction rather than hope for a better future — the meaning traditionally associated with the convention in science-fiction films. *Full Metal Jacket* is a subverted Vietnam War movie, since it alters the usual pattern of training followed by success in combat: training is here followed by chaos in the face of battle.

This self-consciousness is assimilated through artistic motivation: whatever signs the text gives about its artificiality tend to be accommodated as an essential part of an artistic text that tries to use that self-referentiality as a source of ideas. The schema related to artistic motivation is demanded by the formal option of the long take, which results in the exaltation of the text as such; the same is true in the cases in which close-ups create an emphasis on the physicality of the text. The inexpressive nature of actors, which leaves the creation of meaning to textual manipulations, demands a certain degree of artistic motivation. Similarly, the use Kubrick's films make of music clearly foregrounds the tendency to use the text as source of meaning. Finally, the strategy of color, changing from contributing to the creation of space into a vehicle of meaning in itself, demands a degree of artistic motivation, since it draws attention to the physicality of color.

A crucial strategy in the configuration of a film is the process of shaping the viewer's perception of the fabula carried out by the text. One important strategy is the control of the quantity of information to which the viewer has access; the kind of information, expositional or not; and the way in which such information is offered: it appears either at the beginning in a lump or distributed throughout the text.[8] Kubrick's films are divided into two groups with respect to these considerations. Several films present concentrated, preliminary expositional information and no gaps: *Paths of Glory, Spartacus, Dr. Strangelove, A Clockwork Orange,* and *Barry Lyndon.*. These are unambiguous narratives: action films, satires, and period films where the text attempts to analyze a portion or a phenomenon of reality or an institution (the army, slavery, nuclear war, modern violence, or prosperity and decorum in eighteenth-century society). They therefore demand a quick introduction of characters who embody ideas, and who will help the text to explain its points. In these texts we usually find a direct confrontation between the characters and the society of which they are a part.

Another group is formed by *Killer's Kiss, The Killing, Lolita, 2001, The Shining,* and *Full Metal Jacket.* These films show distributed, delayed exposition and the presence of informational gaps. They are films

---

[8] For an analysis of the different ways in which a narrative may arrange the presentation of its information, see Meir Sternberg (1978).

noirs, mystery stories, science-fiction, horror, or war films where the forces that threaten the characters are not distinctly revealed. Characters develop slowly and face inexplicable, illogical events that turn the narrative toward unexpected endings. Nothing is clearly perceived from the beginning; the true nature of characters or of reality is not presented to us: they change and surprise us, hinting at the ever-present difficulty of apprehending reality. They are usually ambiguous narratives; paradigmatic examples would be *2001* and *Full Metal Jacket*, as opposed to the more unambiguous *Paths of Glory* and *Barry Lyndon*. One strategy that is intimately linked to the creation of informational gaps, however, appears as often in films belonging to this second group as in those belonging to the first group: the withholding of the reverse shot temporarily hides something from us (Ripper's mad face in *Dr. Strangelove*, the chevalier's proud appearance in *Barry Lyndon*, etc.). This option creates expectation, surprise, and, perhaps, also suspense; but as we have said, it can be found in most of Kubrick's films. It underlines the ever-present tendency of Kubrick's cinema to govern the access of the viewer to the information the text holds, together with its tendency to use the informational gaps as creators of effects of surprise or suspense that will reinforce the presentation of the withheld information. This is particularly relevant with respect to the visual side of such a presentation, since Kubrick's texts usually place more force of signification on the physical presentation than on the meaning conferred on the element by its position and relevance in the sequence of the fabula.

Kubrick's films vary in the degree of knowledge they impute to the viewer: they range from omniscience in *Dr. Strangelove* to Humbert's restricted knowledge in *Lolita* or the partial knowledge the astronauts on the *Discovery* have about their mission in *2001,* both of which the viewer is made to share. With respect to communicativeness, the films are usually communicative: they tend to share with us all the information they have. *Lolita* and *2001* are the exceptions: they strive to withhold information from us — for instance Quilty's affair with Lolita or the real cause of the space travels in *2001*. Crosscutting and depth of field are the two main strategies associated with the communicative text in Kubrick. Crosscutting allows the viewer to obtain the whole picture of what is taking place in the different settings that comprise the narrative, as happens in *Dr. Strangelove* and *The Killing*. Depth of field creates differences of knowledge among the characters in a text, as in *Lolita,* but these differences are openly presented to the viewers, who can appreciate the irony of many scenes because they possess all the information necessary to make sense of the film.

The common and defining feature of Kubrick's cinema is its self-consciousness, which points to a narrative mode in which the textual side of the film is constantly emphasized, and in which all the elements of mise-en-scène, including the characters, are manipulated to create meaning. Sometimes this textual activity of meaning-creation leaves aside the exploration and consistent development of characters as agents of meaning and relies on textual manipulations of placement of characters, camera movements, voice-over commentary, and so on, to suggest ideas. Self-consciousness suggests a cinema in which the various elements that constitute a film are consistently turned into symbols of ideas and in which the development and interaction of those elements is used to explain the dialectical battle the film had set out to discuss. Cinema is understood as a dialectical struggle. Cases in which the films reveal awareness of their status as artificially constructed texts include the blatant distortion of a certain cinematic code. Shot/reverse shot sequences have been mentioned as one of the main objects of distortion in Kubrick's cinema: by withholding the reverse shot or by cutting the sequence to the rhythm of the music, sometimes to facilitate the rhythmic movement of the characters, as in the gambling-table scene in *Barry Lyndon,* Kubrick's films blatantly distort a highly codified structure.

These distortions destroy the effect of suture that shot/reverse shots achieve,[9] laying bare the artificiality of narration in an alteration of the traditionally accepted ways of creating space in cinema. Unclassical montage is also a source of self-consciousness, as the Christ-dance in *A Clockwork Orange* exemplifies, although greater self-consciousness is produced by depth of field. Depth of field makes possible the presence of self-conscious commentary in the form of titles that make remarks on the contents of the shot. Depth of field allows the texts to include in the same shot titles, characters, and other elements of mise-en-scène that can comment on one another, the titles usually providing information in the most self-conscious way. The title "Mind Your Step," placed above the stairs that lead to Rapallo's office in *Killer's Kiss,* suggests the danger Gloria and especially Davy are in since Rapallo has discovered their relationship. The titles behind Ripper's back in his office, sug-

---

[9] According to Jean-Pierre Oudart, shot/reverse shots provide a movement which helps narration construct space while effacing any sign of authorial intervention. In shot/reverse shots the first shot implies a space offscreen which is revealed in the second shot, therefore completing a view of the narrational space and revealing the absence of an enunciating agent (1977/1978, 35–47).

gesting a blind adherence to military codes, or on the books Turgidson takes to the War Room in *Dr. Strangelove,* pointing to the outrageous logic of human life exchange of which he is so fond, are only a few examples.

Three kinds of principles relate the text, or "syuzhet," as Bordwell calls it, to the fabula. The three of them are pervaded by narrative logic, according to which the viewers define phenomena as events at the same time as they construct relations among them. These relations inform the principles of causality, temporality, and spatiality. With respect to causality we perceive an evolution from the first films to later ones. The first films exhibit a tight causality, where scenes are linked through cause-effect relationships that lead us through the text, investing it with meaning. From *2001* onward we perceive a relaxation of such causality rules: in *2001* the relationships between one scene and the next are not so distinctly constructed as cause-effect. The ellipsis into the future suggests that the spaceship is the final step in the evolution of the bone as weapon, but the match-cut does not seem to provide us with a cause for such a development or for the elision of time. Later, the jump from the *Discovery* to the Stargate sequence seems to lack a cause, and its significance is, in part, difficult to grasp because of this lack of connection with the previous events. The film demands a great degree of participation by the viewer to fill in the causal gaps it scatters all around. Lack of causality is also apparent in *A Clockwork Orange* and *The Shining,* two films where the lack of motivation for violence confers on its presentation a great power to stir the audience's emotions. Causality seems to be restored in *Barry Lyndon* and *Full Metal Jacket,* however; the emphasis of both texts is on the process of change the characters undergo as an expression of the social forces that manipulate them. These two films explore the social relations in the eighteenth century and their effect on the life of an individual, and the process of dehumanization the Vietnam War meant for many Americans who took part in it, respectively. The two texts are concerned with causes and effects, with the moral value of certain codes of behavior, and with the reaction of individuals to such codes; a type of text is needed that places a great emphasis on the reasons why things are the way they are: a great emphasis on causality.

Several stylistic strategies are related to the issue of causality in Kubrick's films. We find many of them whose function is, on the one hand, to demand, and, on the other, to foster the search for causality that will provide the text with meaning. The alteration of shot/reverse shot sequences produces a search for causality that takes into account elements of generic conventions (what type of text is this?), as well as

the specific features of the characters and story (what are the links between the characters and between the characters and the action?). Editing, in general, cues the testing of hypotheses about causality between
fragments that are joined together. The viewer is asked to elicit such
causal relations or to perceive the existence of a formal structure that is
disrupted, as in the *Barry Lyndon* scene where the zoom shot is interrupted by a cut that takes us to a different locale. Fades also have effects
on causality. In *2001* they create a reading practice that asks the viewer
to provide a plausible account for "The Dawn of Man" section, since
the scenes that form this section are linked by fades. In *Paths of Glory*
fades mask ellipses and informational gaps that the text quickly solves:
the text does not allow us to hear the jury's sentence, which is replaced
by a fade out, but the preparations for the execution that follow it suggest that the men have been sentenced to death. Graphic matches demand a causal relation between the two elements joined, as in the
passage from bone to spaceship in *2001*. The dissolve from Jack's face
to the maze in *The Shining* is a similar case where the apparent illogicality of the transition demands an explanation that the text does not
explicitly provide but that the viewer may easily find when considering
the rest of the story.

The study of time in Kubrick's filmography reveals an abundance of
crosscutting, of simultaneous events that are presented successively,
corresponding to a type of cinema that explores the confrontation of
several forces and their development. They show a relative absence of
flashbacks and flashforwards. This type of temporal arrangement creates
texts that focus the viewer's attention on upcoming events (the suspense effect), closely adhering to fabula order; at the same time, they
encourage the primacy effect, which invests with authority and a feeling
of truthfulness what appears at the beginning of the text, since each action can be measured as a change from the first one we see.[10] With respect to frequency, several films show fabula events that are recounted
twice in the text: in *The Killing* parts of the holdup are presented several times, corresponding to the various characters' activities during the
robbery; in *Dr. Strangelove* the final explosion is presented through
several nuclear bombs successively exploding, in *Lolita* the credit-title
scene, where an anonymous hand paints a girl's toes, is reenacted later
to indicate Humbert's submission to Lolita and mark the beginning of
his fall. These repetitions are used to mark the significance of the re-
peated scenes within the plot, since they are usually the most important
events in the text. This repetition points to Kubrick's tendency to em-

---

[10] See Meir Sternberg (1978).

phasize the importance of parts of the fabula in a purely textual way, not in a fabulaic one that would follow the laws of plot development.

With respect to duration, we find the obvious reduction of fabula time in text-time characteristic of narratives. This is sometimes achieved in a self-conscious way, as in the fast-motion scene in *A Clockwork Orange,* or, more usually, by employing ellipses, such as the ones commented on in *Paths of Glory, 2001,* and *Full Metal Jacket.* Also characteristic of Kubrick is dilation through slow motion — for instance, in the fight between Alex and his friends at the marina in *A Clockwork Orange* — and repetition of the same event, as in the final explosion in *Dr. Strangelove.* All of these distortions of duration are emphasized as part of the stylization of the text, in order to demand the creation of logical explanations of the change from the first to the second linked element — bone to spaceship in *2001* — or in order to draw attention to the incapacity of the text to control the contents of the fabula, as in the ellipsis of the sentence in *Paths of Glory.* They are textual ways of drawing attention to specific fragments of the fabula. The self-consciousness of these devices foregrounds distortions of duration, the most typically classical of narrative temporal manipulations. By taking to an extreme these classical mechanisms self-consciousness lays them bare, implicitly questioning their claim to produce clarity and transparency.

Several stylistic strategies appear related to the function of time in the text. The expansion of textual time finds its most effective ally in crosscutting, since the alternation between different locales forces the film to show in successive scenes events that may have happened at the same time in the fabula. Montage compresses time and omits events that do not have a direct effect on the development of the narrative, as in the training scenes in *Full Metal Jacket,* or it may create textually impressive fragments by manipulating visual or aural material, as in the Christ-figure dance in *A Clockwork Orange.* Long takes, on the contrary, contain the theoretical possibility of preserving a temporal continuity where no dilation or compression of time is allowed. *Lolita* is a paradigmatic film in this respect, providing us with scenes where the text follows the characters' movements by means of camera movements, thereby preserving both a fabulaic and a textual continuity that contributes to the realism of the film.

The mechanisms of space production acquire meaning in Kubrick's films not only through the natural depiction of space they carry out but also through the textual arrangement of the elements that shape such a space, elements that in this textual attempt are given added expressive force. Shot/reverse shots turn into crosscutting, thereby producing omniscience, as in *Killer's Kiss,* while distorted spatial structures usually amount to distorted narratives as in *The Killing, Dr. Strangelove,* and *A Clockwork Orange.* Camera movements, which help the presentation of space, acquire the extra capacity to link scenes and, therefore, create ideas by suggesting similarities or contrasts, as we have noted in *Paths of Glory, Full Metal Jacket,* and *The Killing.* Depth of field also produces space with varied effects, as we saw in the section devoted to cinematographic properties.

Shot space in cinema is created through perspective, camera movement, movement of characters, lighting, and color. But several of Kubrick's films question these procedures. Perspective is questioned in *2001.* In the track scene we find oblique visual lines created by elements of mise-en-scène: the edges of the track cutting across the frame render a perspective that posits a vanishing point outside the frame. The completion of the composition is impossible, since its vanishing point is outside, and, as such lines are part of a full circle, such a completion of perspective by reaching the vanishing point cannot be shown within the frame. This play with space parallels the film's difficulty in reaching a satisfactory ending, which expresses the human inability to understand reality no matter how many artificial machines are used in the process. Human intelligence cannot understand the whole universe because it is only a small point in the universe. The whole picture (the whole cinematic space, the whole meaning of the film) can only be seen from the outside, from a totalizing position that human beings cannot occupy. The film suggests this by playing at not allowing the audience to occupy a totalizing position with respect to the apprehension of space in the film.

Camera movements are questioned, again in *2001,* in the spaceship dance sequence. The sequence exposes the audience's incapacity to know how this space is produced. We do not know if the dance is the result of camera movement, of movement of the ships, or of both movements at the same time. This ambiguity suggests considerations about the relativity of space in cinema, which the film links to the relativity of progress in intelligence. The importance given to spatial configuration in the "Dawn of Man" sequence, where the absence of dialogue confers on space a great signifying power, is reinforced by the spatial discontinuity offered by the match cut. This involves both a temporal and a spatial jump that the text suggests is also a jump in technological development: from here on, progress and space are related. The relativity of spatial directions is also laid bare in the flight attendant's scene: when she is reframed vertically the text dismantles the notion of verticality it had posited at the beginning of the scene.

Even though this may be a realistic depiction of zero-gravity conditions, it reveals that the typical presentation of verticality created by films is a convention based on the artificiality of the relationship between films and the position occupied by viewers with respect to verticality. This move suggests that the coherence of cinematic space is the result of artificial forces, of conventions, of cinematographic codes, and not the result of the faithful depiction of a reality that the film can approximate to us. The artificiality of the process suggests that perhaps the progression of intelligence that we see throughout the film may also be only apparent, since it relies on notions of intelligence that are, after all, devised by human beings. The final jump into the Starchild promises a human being capable of understanding the universe through an intelligence that can free itself from the constrictions of weak human thought.

In *2001* continuous space is only possible if it is deceptive, as the runway scene reveals. The track is a continuous circle along which the members of the *Discovery* crew run without end. A slight reframing of the camera, together with a tracking shot, allow the whole space of the track to remain onscreen without any continuity break. Such continuous space is only possible because of the mise-en-scène device of the track and the camera movement, laying bare the artificiality of the construction of space in cinema. The last scene in *2001* shows how subjectivity, expressed by means of shot/reverse shot sequences, appears as an element that links different portions of space, creating both spatially and cinematically a coherent process of Bowman's aging. Bowman sees different views of himself that show him get older. When the reverse shot of the sequence shows the older Bowman looking at where the previous Bowman was, the text reveals that the space corresponding to this previous Bowman is empty. The shot/reverse shot sequences are, therefore, not completed; they only offer us the illusion of their coherent existence. Only the deception created by subjectivity devices allows the apparent continuity of this space. The shot/reverse shot sequences impose a discontinuity that their strong codification renders irrelevant. Bowman's quick aging seems to lay bare this discontinuity; but the progression of the narrative, the logic of the appearance of this process at the end of the film, masks such discontinuity and makes the scene spatially acceptable, although baffling for the audience.

By means of editing, the text joins together pieces of fabula that are chronologically distant from one another. Each cut bridges a long gap of time, which is elided by the spatial juxtaposition of the shots, linked by eyeline matches. The depiction of progression and improvement of humankind is also rendered through spatial variables that mask ellipses.

Cinematic space can present such a progression coherently, a possibility that parallels the human being's discovery of that same progression. The signifying element in the text is, therefore, revealed to be mainly its spatial configuration, since the development of the themes in the film is intimately related to that configuration by the text.

Apart from these questioning processes, issues of space are made relevant to provide parts of the text with meaning. The Stargate sequence in *2001* is a progression toward the vanishing point of traditional linear perspective. The meaning of the text can be found in the textual strategies themselves. Since the text presents its meanings through a discussion of space, the issue of perspective becomes relevant. Linear perspectival systems are also employed to emphasize the visual side of the text: linear perspective orders the elements of mise-en-scène in space and facilitates the reading of the shot by the viewer. In *Barry Lyndon* this strategy helps in the aesthetically pleasing rendering of space for the enjoyment of the audience. The same use of traditional linear perspective is found in *Full Metal Jacket* in the prayer scene, where the lines of cots are presented as if fading into the distance: the emphasis this time is not on beauty but on the constricting power of such an organized view of space, suggesting the constricting nature of military life. Space may also become the expression of the subjectivity of a character, and the ways in which such space is created may produce metaphorical readings that can be applied to the character. For instance, in *The Shining* the tracking shots in the corridors of the hotel reveal a maze-like space that is later associated, by means of the maze-dissolve, with Jack's subjectivity and internal life. Jack's disturbed mind and its association with the hotel is suggested by a specific way of creating space: camera movement. Something similar could be said of *Paths of Glory* and the various "adjectives" which the military men are given through camera movement, as I have explained in the previous sections.

Scene from Paths of Glory: *the look of military arrogance.*
Kirk Douglas, Adolfe Menjou. © *1957 Harris Kubrick*
Pictures Corporation. All rights reserved.

2: Modifications of Accounts of Film as Narrative, Motivated by the Previous Analysis of Poetics

WE HAVE SEEN THAT IN KUBRICK'S CINEMA there exists a primacy of textual elements in the configuration of meaning. Formal parameters create meaning that usually reinforces the overall meaning of the fabula. Some of these formal parameters are involved in the creation of subjectivity. The style of Kubrick's cinema works hard to destroy internal subjectivity and replace it with external views. The examples of symmetry and parallelism discussed in previous sections are proof that Kubrick's films try to impose meaning through their textual configuration, and that this textuality demands from the viewer a great capacity to establish links between elements, to relate elements by similarity or contrast and infer a meaning from these relationships. Kubrick's cinema rarely demands identification to create meaning; this job is left to textual formal patterns.

A great number of formal elements of style evolve into external focalization. Shot/reverse shot sequences are distorted with the purpose of placing emphasis on one pole of the sequence over the other. The scene in *Dr. Strangelove* where Mandrake discovers Ripper's plan has become by now the prototypical example. In *2001* shot/reverse shot sequences evolve into external focalization when the object of HAL's eye is shown reflected on the surface of the eye, and therefore from an external position to that of the computer, not from the logical point of view of HAL. At times these sequences are used to stylize the reality of the film, as in the scenes where Mr. Alexander's frenzy is conveyed through stylized sequences in *A Clockwork Orange,* or to distort reality through characterization or acting, as in *Dr. Strangelove* or *The Shining,* which results in externality and detachment of the audience from the text.

Fades at times constitute parts of narratives that demand the viewer's "reading" practice of interpreting the text from an external position. In *2001* the "Dawn of Man" sequence uses fades that cue the viewer's hypothesis about what may have happened in the time between scene and scene and what the cause-effect relationships between the scenes may have been. In *The Shining* dissolves are capable of leading us into the characters' subjectivity, as in the maze dissolve where Jack's mental disturbance is suggested. But the text evolves toward dissolves that provide us with external views of reality, as in the final scene, where the camera approaching the photograph reveals an external agent, since the movement does not belong to any character. The text manipulates our final apprehension of the film.

Crosscutting is also partly an element of externality, since it shows the interaction of several fragments of fabula material before drawing us into the text through identification. It is a strategy that places the viewer in an obviously artificial all-knowing position that points to the external vantage point occupied by any decoder of texts. This externality is, nevertheless, highly codified and accepted within the classical model, because it allows the viewer's comprehension of the text and produces involvement in the action. Crosscutting produces omniscience, which confers on the viewer a privileged status of knowledge, favoring an attitude of external configuration of meaning as a prelude to one of involvement in and submission to the mechanisms of the text. Match cuts are another example of how editing strategies may derive into externality. The match cut in *2001* of the bone and the spaceship involves a shift from the subjective view of the ape to the externally portrayed view of the spaceships dancing for the enjoyment of the viewer.

The workings of reframings in *2001* reveal that the text is working with space but regardless of characters' intervention in its creation. The characters' subjectivity is not relevant in this game with space, which is staged for the viewer only. The meaning suggested by the reframings in the track scenes, while the members of the crew run along the endless circular track, is only offered to the viewer, the character being only one of the textual elements the film uses to shape that meaning.

Angle and distance of shooting in Kubrick have as their effect an emphasis on the image's physicality. This emphasis attempts to suggest the meaning of the character or mise-en-scène element by means of the exaltation of a visual side that is done externally, without taking into account the interaction of characters and events. Low-angle shots in Kubrick usually accompany a pervading distortion of the components of the text, sometimes with a satirizing effect, as in *Dr. Strangelove*. Close-ups are also relevant in the foregrounding of the image's physicality, which usually provides meaning by revealing the character's true nature. A good example is Barry's inexpressive face in *Barry Lyndon*, a hint of his incapacity to adapt to a new social status.

Depth of field evolves into externality in different ways. In *Lolita* it allows the creation of differences of knowledge that require a knowledgeable viewer and foster an external approach to the events of the film, which are perceived as clues to the solution of a mystery. The last scene in *2001* renders depth of field ineffective to construct point-of-view shots, thereby denying the device a connection with internal subjectivity that other films also explore. *Barry Lyndon* uses depth of field and mise-en-scène as aids to the exaltation of the physicality of the text. The text's beauty is more important than internal subjectivity, and even the inner feelings and attitudes of the characters are expressed by means of external views of astonishing beauty. In this film they also contribute to the establishment of a textual pattern of zoom shots whose final development is invariably a depth of field composition. Depth of field in Kubrick tends to work externally in its meaning-production process.

The composition of shots usually aims at such a perfect balance and symmetry that the engaging capacity they might have is destroyed. Perfectly balanced compositions in *Barry Lyndon,* for instance, do away with the capacity of the shot to elicit identification, since the viewer notices an attempt on the part of the text to formalize the elements of cinema so as to suggest an idea from an external position: the world of strict formality of the Berlin court. The text is privileged over the fabula, becoming the main mechanism for the creation of ideas. The stylization of acting in many of Kubrick's films also presents the text as more important than the fabula. The obviousness and self-indulgence of the acting in *Dr. Strangelove, A Clockwork Orange, Barry Lyndon,* or *The Shining* transform the activity of actors and actresses into one of the most important mechanisms of expression, always through the foregrounding of the text over the fabula.

The use of extradiegetic sound — mainly music — as commentary on the text shapes films that, again, demand an external attitude of interpretation and meaning-making on the part of the viewer. Music in *Full Metal Jacket* obviously needs a viewer capable of linking the meaning of the songs within the American context of the Vietnam War. In *Barry Lyndon* voice-over narration also provides commentaries that, in their irony toward the characters, create an external approach to the development of the action.

The externality of focalization is, therefore, often accompanied by a process of distortion whose aim is invariably to present the viewer with a striking visual rendering of the text. Externality is, therefore, linked to a certain emphasis on the physicality of what appears onscreen.

At this point I would like to introduce the notion of autofocalization. Focalization is traditionally understood as selection of information that helps in the transformation of the fabula into the text. Traditional theories of focalization distinguish between external and internal focalization; but ultimately, filmic focalization is always external, since the attribution of a shot to a character (internal focalization) is always carried out by an external organizing force that occupies the position of the camera. External focalization is demanded by film narratives:

> It is as if film narratives required a constant return to objective presentation for a better understanding of the internal gazes that occur in the text. . . . One reason for this is the difficulty that film has to present the mind of a character outside narration. In a novel, in a passage in internal focalization, the mind of the character can be shown without a change in focalization. The character can be focalizer and focalized at the same time, while keeping perceptual control over other characters or objects. In film, although, as we have seen, dreams, hallucinations, memories, etc., can be shown, it is problematic to express the characteristics of the vision while showing its object, hence the resource to shots in external focalization, in which the focalizer becomes focalized and in which we can analyse better how what he perceives affects him (Deleyto 1991, 170).

This external nature of focalization in cinema is parallel to the unmediated nature of iconic signs: cinema's language is less mediated than verbal or symbolic language; it is more mimetic. Filmic language cannot avoid its potential for signifying, while a symbolic language can control it, since it demands the reader's imagination to make up the coherent world the text wants to create. The text may, therefore, choose to control the quantity and quality of information given to the readers, which inevitably results in the control of their constructing activity. An iconic language does not need the viewer's participation so desperately, and cannot, therefore, decide to restrict the viewer's access to the information provided by the icon, the icon itself being all the information the viewer requires. Therefore, the signifying potential of cinema is more openly exposed than that of a verbal language, and this characteristic allows cinema to present in a single instance of focalization two focalizing trends: that of a character on something or somebody, and this something's or somebody's focalization on itself/himself/herself.

The strategies of focalization proposed by Deleyto and Branigan share the feature of strong codification. This feature implies a low self-consciousness that does not lay bare their status as diegetic mechanisms but, rather, emphasizes their status as contributors to a mimetic, unobtrusive narrative mode. The situation is different in literature, since the mediation of focalizers and narrators is essential to the coherent construction of a fictional world by means of the abstract, mediated medium of verbal language. In cinema, viewers use their vision to build up this fictional world. Vision is a medium that, owing to its nature as less mediated than verbal language, shifts the emphasis from the intermediaries (focalizer, narrator) to the object of perception itself. The essentially mimetic nature of cinematographic language turns the object of perception into the recipient of more functions than the fictional world created in literature. In cinema the image itself is capable of carrying out part of the focalization and of carrying it out about itself (García Mainar 1993b, 154–155).

Seymour Chatman has proposed a theory of focalization in which the points of view of characters can be shown by the mere portrayal of their attitude toward what they are doing. In a novel the characters' points of view would be provided by their thoughts; and the readers would have to use such data, since no others would be available, to create the "picture" of the action in their imagination. In film, however, the action with all its potential of signification is shown to us, and the iconic nature of photography shows things independently of human point of view. Film cannot avoid showing the attitude of the character who appears on the screen (1981, 135–136). It can, therefore, offer us two points of view at the same time: if there are two people on the screen, that of the person who looks and that of the person who performs the action; if there is only one person onscreen, this person can offer his or her point of view on what he or she is doing. In the latter case we would consider that the character is focalizing himself or herself. This I will call autofocalization.

The capacity cinematic signs have of focalizing themselves is potentially present in every sign, but certain stylistic options make this signifying power stand out more than others and can provoke the coexistence of traditional focalization and autofocalization in the same shot. This characteristic of the cinematic icon is potentially subversive, since it contains within itself the capacity to offer meanings that contradict those of traditional focalization. We find here a clear source for deconstructive readings of cinema. Kubrick's cinema exploits the possibility of autofocalization to the full, and the stylistic strategies employed by his films consistently favor the creation of this type of focalization — at the same time opening the disseminative potential of the texts. Autofocalization in Kubrick has two functions. It emphasizes the physicality of the text, its quality as image (icon), producing narratives that are conscious of their own status as texts. It also marks important parts of the fabula as relevant for the development of the narrative: frontal tracking shots, withheld reverse shots, and close-ups have been already discussed as elements that use the emphasis placed on the text to mark the scenes in which they appear as narratively relevant. It seems that Kubrick's cinema invariably considers the exaltation of the text a valid means of expressing fabula-related points.

Next, I would like to discuss several aspects related to the concept of narration outlined by Branigan in his *Narrative Comprehension and Film* (1992). For Branigan, narration is the overall distribution of knowledge that rules the way in which, and the time when, the spectator acquires such knowledge. Narration is the process through which the uneven relationship viewer-text with respect to knowledge of the fabula is balanced: through this process the viewers acquire the information the text has withheld from them (63–85). Narration is, therefore, carried out with the help of textual strategies, and among these the use of shot/reverse shot sequences is important. They offer us information but at the same time, point out that something is hidden from us, something that the sequence quickly discloses (the reverse shot). Shot/reverse shot sequences are a clear example of the game with knowledge to which Branigan's notion of narration points.

As I have already mentioned, several of Kubrick's films question this structural element of shot/reverse shot sequences. In *Killer's Kiss* we find a partial negation of one pole of the sequence, and in other films these sequences are distorted to various effects. These cases would seem to fall outside the scope of Branigan's account of narration. The disappearance of the reverse shot, or the delay in showing it to us, is a negation of the game of concealing/revealing that Branigan argues narration is. These distortions are fragments that do call attention not to their function as links of narrative material but to their physical nature, to themselves as visual material. Perhaps the narrative function of anchorage[1] is still fulfilled, in part, by them, but within the classical paradigm the dislocation clearly emphasizes this other property of cinematic language. Therefore, we must investigate the ways in which this antinarrativity affects the narrative flow in each film and the differences from classical cinema that it achieves. The first and most obvious effect is, therefore, the emphasis given to the physicality of the image — that is, its fostering of autofocalization; and the feeling of externality this produces, since it means the rejection of a typical strategy of subjectivity and identification.

---

[1] By anchorage I mean the process of establishing structural links among elements which for example the shot/reverse shot carries out. An element links another one to a certain structure by introducing it or by opening up the possibility for its appearance: the shot within a shot/reverse shot sequence promises the appearance of a reverse shot.

I would now like to link subjectivity and autofocalization with the issue of metaphor,[2] since in my opinion a great part of the richness of Kubrick's cinema lies in its capacity to create metaphors. This claim is a logical outcome of the previous analysis of poetics I carried out in the first chapter. There I constantly resorted to metaphors to justify and classify the various stylistic strategies I analyzed in Kubrick. Metaphor, therefore, seems to be inherent in the kind of cinema Kubrick makes. I will progress from subjectivity and autofocalization to metaphor since the notion of metaphor requires an externality in the act of narration and is one of the processes autofocalization produces, since metaphors demand both externality and emphasis on the thing presented on the screen.

In *Narrative Comprehension and Film* Branigan discusses the creation of narrative meaning in the chapters "Causality and Metaphor" (1992, 44–50) and "Subjectivity" (1992, 125–160). He develops his idea of narratives being created through the viewer's application of top-down schemata to the elements of what he understands as a variation of the idea of the text. He discusses the metaphorical nature of such a process of meaning inference. I would like to extend these ideas and introduce the notion of metaphorical framing. Subjectivity is sometimes achieved by linking metaphorically a portion of space to a character, a link that is not supported by any character gaze, and this kind of metaphorical linking also implies the creation of a metaphor in the space that is linked to it: since it has no connection to the character, the only connection will be the viewer's perception of a meaningful relationship between the character and what is shown in the other shot. Therefore, the attribution of an image to a character's subjectivity depends on the viewer's capacity to perceive and infer, which is shaped by the text and its evolving theme. And this process results in the creation of meaning through the appearance of a metaphor that joins a space to a character.

The metaphorical relationship is produced by the textual context; such a relationship is a product of the text, a meaningful creation that must fit the overall pattern of development of the text up to the point at which it occurs. Metaphorical relationship/subjectivity understood

---

[2] "Metaphor is usually defined as the presentation of one idea in terms of another, belonging to a different category, so that either our understanding of the first idea is transformed, or so that from the fusion of the two ideas a new one is created. This can be represented symbolically as $A+B=A(B)$ or $A+B=Z$" (Whittock 1990, 5). The convocation of ideas $A+B$ must involve some transformation; otherwise there is no metaphor. Instead, there is only simple analogy, or simple juxtaposition.

in this fashion would not allow for the existence of relationships not envisaged by the text, not prefigured within the text. This contention would seem to deny the film's capacity to suggest contradictory meanings or to create ambiguity.

Not all critics would agree with this position, however. According to Trevor Whittock's *Metaphor and Film* (1990), metaphors stem in part from the creation of a context that provides the individual sign with meaning. But the contexts created may be of many different natures: they may, for instance, be created by verbal language; by a symbolic language; or by the language of images, which contains a greater component of iconic language. Contexts created through symbolic language are more capable of fixing this metaphorical meaning, since the strong codification of such a language contributes to the establishment of coherent meaningful structures. But filmic language is not symbolic as verbal language is, and the iconic component of cinema is a potentially creative force that may work independently of the rhetorical grammar set by a given text during its signifying activity. The textual material of films, their highly iconic language, may evolve into a logic of spectacle, of the icon, which may establish alternative structures to those of a rhetorical grammar, therefore enlarging the signifying capacity of cinematic language.[3] Still, I agree with Whittock when he privileges the workings of context in the creation of metaphorical meaning. At the same time, if the capacity to extract meaning and metaphors is left to the viewers, then the meaning of these metaphors cannot be stable, since they depend on the viewers' capacity to interpret texts, and, therefore, on their cultural background. Therefore, the process of reaching meaning is unstable, and this situation seems to make cinema a suitable object of study for deconstruction. The viewer has to provide the connections, understand the overall meaning of the text, and test the possible options. The possibility for different, even contradictory, meanings is open, since the text usually offers only one pole of the metaphor, while the other has to be looked for by the viewer. The presence of only one pole is characteristic of cinema's metaphors, which are devised before the moment of the utterance. They are born as insights before their appearance in the text (Whittock 1990, 29). The similarity or relationship between two elements is not usually expressed through their presentation and confluence at the same time; cinema presents to the viewer the interaction between the two elements by only expressing the element that contains the result of the interaction.

---

[3] For a detailed discussion of this capacity of cinematographic language, see García Mainar (1991).

So, two birds may become the representation of a happy marriage; but neither a symbol of marriage nor the married couple need to appear in the same shot with the birds.

To summarize, autofocalization emphasizes the external side of cinema together with its physicality. This emphasis helps in the creation of metaphors. And the creation of metaphors has to be performed in a context that makes their creation possible, a context of contents that make the reference of a textual element to another element outside the text suitable. Therefore, the meaning of a metaphor is determined by its context, but a view of such a context can only be achieved from a position of externality from which the viewer can grasp all the general ideas of the text and test the suitability of a meaning for a metaphor. Metaphors, therefore, demand externality, and Kubrick's cinema characteristically provides this externality.

Having explained the idea of metaphor as aided by autofocalization and externality, I will now deal with the types of metaphor that can be discerned in the examples of externality in the Kubrick films mentioned previously. Whittock's classification of metaphors in cinema will be followed.[4] The distortion of shot/reverse shots to emphasize one of the poles over the other suggests a metaphorical meaning by disrupting the strongly codified form of the shot/reverse shot. The effect is usually the distortion of a portion of the text with the aim of suggesting that Ripper is the killer to which his name points, that Alex and his droogs are the artists of the new age, and that the excellence of man's nature is not far from what drives him to kill and destroy. The reflection of one of the members of the crew on HAL's eye during one of these shot/reverse shot sequences suggests that HAL is the main intelligence in the spaceship. Still within the field of editing, the role of fades in "The Dawn of Man" section in *2001,* which cue a reading practice of interpreting the text metaphorically, is also the disruption of the rule set by classical cinema that the linking of scenes will reinforce causality. The dissolves in *The Shining* either allow our entrance into Jack's subjectivity or lead us to external views of reality, for example, in the final scene. The dissolves establish explicit comparisons between Jack and

---

[4] Whittock's list of metaphoric formulas includes explicit comparison (A is like B); identity asserted (A is B); identity implied by substitution (A replaced by B); juxtaposition (A/B); metonymy or associated idea substituted (Ab, so b); synecdoche, where part replaces whole (A stands for ABC); objective correlative (O stands for ABC); distortion through hyperbole or caricature (a becomes A or α); rule disruption (ABCD becomes AbCD); and chiming or parallelism (A/pqr — B/pqr) (1990, 49–69).

the maze or between the whole film and the view of Jack in the 1920s party, suggesting that Jack's mind is a maze (his madness), and in the second case that the whole film is only part of the eternal process of fantasy in which the hotel lives. The understanding of the metaphors is ensured by the disruption of a cinematic norm: that dissolves will limit themselves to linking different portions of the text with differing spatiotemporal variables, and will not add extra significance.

Crosscutting can also produce metaphors by explicitly comparing the fragments of film it links. In *Killer's Kiss* the similarity of Davy's life with Gloria's is suggested by crosscutting: both characters are exploited through their physicality, through their bodies. They are like mannequins in the hands of other people, as the final fight between Davy and Rapallo, where they use mannequins as weapons, explicitly says. In *Dr. Strangelove* crosscutting suggests that although each locale is supposed to hold differing degrees of common sense, the War Room being the supreme power and, therefore, holding the most sensible people, in fact common sense is absent from all of them and madness is not exceptional but the rule. Each locale has its own Ripper figure. Match-cuts also establish metaphors by explicit comparison, the best example being the editing together of the bone and the spaceship in *2001*, which suggests that both are weapons and at the same time signs of the development of human intelligence (which has, throughout history, been used in negative as well as in positive ways). The workings of reframings in *2001* are disruptions of the cinematic rule that strange perspectives are not allowed since they disorient the viewer. This strange perspective cues meanings about the importance of space as a metaphor for progress. The development of intelligence is expressed in spatial terms, and the Stargate sequence's progression through space is the climax of that development.

Depth of field also constructs metaphorical meanings in several ways. The differences in knowledge achieved in *Lolita*, where the viewer is the most knowledgeable, create metaphors through a juxtaposition that emphasizes the difference between Humbert and Quilty. Quilty is the artist, the man who can devise deception and can spot it. Humbert is only the scholar who studies the artist and who, ironically, cannot perceive artifice, which is what he is supposed to study. He is unable to realize that Lolita is being seduced by Quilty and that Quilty is playing with him. The rendering of depth of field as ineffective to purposes of subjectivity in the last scene of *2001* involves the disruption of the strategy of point-of-view shots, which points at a metaphorical meaning of space: the ineffectiveness of depth of field to render subjectivity suggests that this final scene represents a step ahead in cinematic form as much as in human intelligence, and that this new stage of humanity cannot be communicated with the already existing devices of cinema. In *Barry Lyndon* depth of field emphasizes the physicality of the text. In this case the film creates a metaphor by means of synecdoche: the part replaces the whole; the beauty of the text stands for the law of decorum at work in this society, which privileges the external side of human relations — their appropriateness — rather than what the characters hide inside.

The composition of the shots also suggests metaphors in several films. The compositions that are perfectly symmetrical in the depiction of subjectivity or show two backs turned to us are obvious disruptions of shot/reverse shots, which suggest the film's rejection of subjectivity and the metaphor that in these worlds personal relations are not relevant for the characters (for instance in *Dr. Strangelove* and in *Barry Lyndon*). The stylization of the acting in most of Kubrick's films is an obvious case of metaphor through distortion: the first pole of the metaphor is replaced by the second, which appears distorted in a deliberate deviation from what is expected in the context of the film. The viewer expects non-stylized acting in cinema, since films produce a strong effect of realism that demands verisimilitude in the characters. The presence of stylized acting is, therefore, a clear sign of distortion in cinema, which makes it suitable for the suggestion of metaphorical meanings. In Kubrick's films this distortion extends to the whole text; a disruption not of the text but rather of the cinematic convention that qualifies the exaggeration of acting as exceptional. This distortion achieves various meanings. In *Dr. Strangelove* it is a metaphor for the distance between the characters and their reality, which they are not able to understand. In *A Clockwork Orange* it suggests the link between Alex and the world of art of which he is so fond, and the idea that Alex is also the product of the sophistication and sublimation of desire into art.

The workings of extradiegetic sound as commentary on the text are a clear example of metaphor through juxtaposition, when the sound contradicts the meaning conveyed by the visuals, or explicit comparison, when the sound means the same as the visuals. So the credit-title song of *Full Metal Jacket* seems to side with the political system that is forcing the young men in the visuals to join the Marines and lose their differences, as they are all shaved into similarity. It uses a typically cowboy tune to accompany a defense of American men's moral obligation to fight in the war. The credit-title song in *Dr. Strangelove*, however, shows the confrontation of tender music with the coldness of two airplanes in the act of refueling; out of this confrontation stem the metaphors of the planes as partners in the sexual act or as related as mother and child, both of which fit the film's tendency to argue that the origin of war and destruction is the same as that of life: desire. Finally, voice-over narration may be the source of metaphors in which the second meaning is implied by substitution. The author of the text is suggested by the identification the voice-over prompts: the external position and capacity to manipulate the development of the text and the ironic distance the voice-over often adopts suggest its connection with the authorial hand's desire to stress certain ideas over others. This situation occurs in the ironic voice-over in *Barry Lyndon,* where the skeptical attitude of the narrator about the human capacity to feel sympathy seems to coincide with the overall meaning of the text, since Barry is not allowed to live in a society to which he did not belong in the past.

These examples are mainly related to the metaphor that occurs as the result of the disruption, or sometimes the distortion, of a rule. Even though this metaphorical process is sometimes accompanied by other mechanisms of creation of metaphor, there is always a certain component of disruption or distortion that makes the appearance of meaning possible. But then, what rules are the object of this distortion? The classical cinema's rules or the rhetorical rules created by each of Kubrick's films? Are there disruptions of both types of rules? And are there metaphors that are created out of the disruption of a rule set by the individual text, which would mean a metaphor out of a rule that intends to be metaphorical, too? Is the potentiality for contradictory meanings inscribed here, in the very essence of Kubrick's cinema as externality aiding metaphor? Kubrick's cinema constitutes a deviation from classical narrative modes in cinema, and this deviation is performed consistently in each of his films; but his films also form rhetorical structures that the texts themselves alter.

We can easily find films that are complete deviations from classical stylistic rules for the whole length of the text: almost all of them are. And we can also find films that create their own rules only to break them. *Killer's Kiss* breaks the rules of shot/reverse shot and turns them into crosscutting. *Paths of Glory* sets up an opposition between camera movement and point-of-view shots that separates the generals from Dax, only to fool us into believing that Dax can save the men, which does not happen. *Lolita* seems to suggest Humbert's status as an artist figure by means of the sophisticated language and acting that accompany his image, but the text subverts this image by showing that it is, in fact, Quilty who is the artist and the one able to deceive; and this subversion is done by means of depth of field, which is apparently the tool of realistic cinema. *Dr. Strangelove* sets up a dynamic of satire, only to subvert it and transform it into a celebration of the text, into spectacle. *Barry Lyndon* creates a purely textual pattern of zoom shots and breaks it in the Bullingdon fight scene. *The Shining* tries to assign the fantastic part of the text to Jack's subjectivity, only to suggest suddenly that the fantastic is, in fact, real and that the film is not an account of a deteriorating mind but that the whole text is a fantasy. The square patterns of the formations in the first part of *Full Metal Jacket* change into rambling camera movements in the second, suggesting the difference between theoretical military action and the real thing, where the feelings of the soldiers are stronger than their training.

These considerations that the study of style and metaphor have suggested can be applied to the concept of focalization, which, in my opinion, will have to be reshaped to encompass the previous conclusion. An application of these partial conclusions would lead us to say that metaphors in Kubrick stem from the disruption/distortion of a rule, and that these rules are of various sorts in the various films. They include subjectivity devices, as well as other stylistic strategies. The effect is, as has been said, the creation of externality, the emphasis on the physicality of the text, which in turn helps in the appearance of metaphors. This externality is measured in terms of focalization; but the stylistic devices that create this externality are not only related to subjectivity, as the previous examples have made clear. Therefore, these reflections on metaphor lead us to reconsider the issue of focalization; and focalization should be explained as being produced by mechanisms that traditional accounts did not include, such as the stylistic elements of fades, dissolves, match-cuts, crosscutting, depth of field, composition of the shot, acting, extradiegetic sound, and voice-over narration. Traditional accounts of focalization understand it as the selection of fabula information created by the text. They do not accept that focalization may have an attitudinal aspect, that the attitude a character shows toward an element of the fabula or the text may be as important for the creation of focalization — and, therefore, for the internal textual coherence of the film — as the selection of information. If we understand that each attitudinal aspect has its source in focalization, however, then we will have to accept that in Kubrick's films this focalization may be produced by style. Thus, a new kind of focalization seems to appear: a focalization understood as the result of stylistic, textual elements. We will, therefore, have two types of focalization: one that is placed within the fabula/story (depending on the classification of levels we employ), as suggested by traditional focalization; and the textual or stylistic one, that I am proposing here on the basis of the notions of autofocalization and metaphor that Kubrick's films have introduced.

The creation of meaning by establishing a recognizable structure that will later be disrupted resembles the working of languages in general, and more specifically of symbolic language. This metaphorical process shows that cinema's language is partly symbolic, which leads us to propose that the symbolic signs of cinema are more elaborate entities than the iconic ones, and that a group of icons can produce a symbolic sign. This proposal implies that cinematic language is a mixture of icons and symbols, where icons group and give birth to symbols, revealing the complex nature of the signifier in cinema.[5] It is these disruptions of rules — the appearance of difference — that allows the text to create meaning. So disruption is essential to the configuration of language in cinema. And it is essential because cinema has no *langue*, in the Saussurean sense of a structured system of signs, and each text has to set its own rhetorical net to express ideas. The creation of meaning implies the disruption of the rules set by such a rhetorical net in each filmic text. This cinematic code, therefore, conforms to a kind of system that is similar to that of verbal language, where the meaning of each sign is obtained through the relationships of opposition among the elements of the system. These series of oppositions in verbal language are also disruptions of the rule of sameness and the introduction of difference in a system of prefigured elements. In this sense, verbal language and the rhetorical language of cinema are quite similar.

If we have a rhetorical language constructed to resemble symbolic verbal language, then we can say that cinema has two kinds of signifiers: those of rhetorical structures that use the icons as their material, and the icons themselves as signifiers, since they do not provide reality but only a system that is not as close to reality as it seems, as I have shown in "Kubrick's *Doctor Strangelove:* The Logic of Spectacle" (1991). This is so because the icons are also capable of creating rhetorical structures through color, expression of characters, settings, etc. The division into two kinds of signifiers does not mean that the capacity of the icon to create rhetorical structures is denied, which would be nonsensical since the basis of cinematic language is partly the icon. But one can still hold that the icon at times works as raw material for the stylis-

---

[5] James Monaco suggests a similar classification of cinematic signs. To the symbol and the icon he adds the index (1981, 130–140). Peter Wollen used the same classification in his classic *Signs and Meaning in the Cinema* (1972). There he described the icon as the sign that represents its object mainly by its similarity to it, the index as the sign that designates by virtue of an existential bond between itself and its object (as in the case of medical symptoms). Finally, he equated the symbol to Saussure's arbitrary sign (120–125).

tic strategies (rhetorical structures) that involve camera movements, editing, or other elements of style where the force of the icon is produced in part by the effect of these rhetorical structures or by the disruption of such structures.

Now, the specific characteristic of Kubrick's cinema is that it shows a great consciousness of the existence of these two levels of signifiers, since it uses rhetorical structures that not only allow the films to suggest ideas but also emphasize the iconicity of the icons. This tendency of cinematic language Kubrick's films exemplify can be used to propose theoretical concepts that should be applied to existing accounts of cinema. Autofocalization is only the application of the idea of the two levels of signifiers to subjectivity, but it should also be applied to other areas of theoretical study. In fact, the whole experience of cinema seems to rely on the existence of this double system of signifiers. Cinema is a more conservative medium than others, and particularly than verbal language, because it requires that the audience identify a minimum of information, that provided by the icon, before the viewer can proceed to unravel the complexity of its codes. Here lies the key idea to understanding classical cinema: classical cinema possesses a code that quickly and unambiguously presents to the viewer a recognizable form and recognizable events, characters, genres, etc., and then elaborates this material in various ways to create films with specific characteristics, although still within the classical norm.

Experimental cinema refuses to present the audience such a basis of recognizable events through a recognizable style, and it therefore demands greater attention from the viewer. The text promises to create partly new codes that, if not well presented and developed, usually fail to come across to the audience. Within the basic codes classical cinema possesses we can include external focalization, the use of traditionally accepted representations of ideas (home as the family in melodramas, stark light signaling ambiguity in films noirs, bright color in musicals), a chronological organization of scenes, a coherent representation of space, and more or less causally motivated development of sequences. All of these basic codes are explored by Kubrick's cinema: they are primarily set by icons that later form rhetorical structures; these structures question their own status as creators of subjectivity, coherent representations of space, etc., and one of the ways in which they do so is by emphasizing the iconicity of the text. This emphasis draws attention to the particular "double articulation" of cinema and, in a way, subverts it since it suggests that the icon may work in more ways than as a component of a rhetorical structure, and that one of these ways may be just the emphasis on itself, which may work in directions other than the establishment of rhetorical structures (for instance, by creating alternative structures of its own). From this point of view Kubrick might be considered a figure standing between classicism and experimentalism, since he experiments on the basis of classical devices, having understood that experimentation can only exist on the basis of a norm that is transformed.

From this new perspective, Bordwell's theories about cinema can be revised. To the division fabula-syuzhet will be added a third division, called style, which will be the realm of rhetorical structures; the syuzhet will be the realm of icons, the intermediate level between the rhetorical elaboration and the raw material. The syuzhet is the stage where the fabula events are transformed and reshaped according to narrative demands. This transformation is, in cinema, inevitably presented through icons, which hint at the original state of the fabula through iconic strategies: calendar pages falling indicate a temporal ellipsis, for example. The spatial, temporal, or narrational changes operated by the syuzhet are mainly represented by icons, and this is why I have chosen to link syuzhet and icon.

The concepts of knowledgeability, communicativeness, and self-consciousness have to include one aspect devoted to rhetorical structures and another to the icons. Some texts may be more knowledgeable, communicative, or self-conscious about their own rhetorical structures than others. The construction of space typically follows the rhetorical rules of shot/reverse shot, which, as we have seen, sometimes emphasize the components of the structure as icons. A reconsideration of the construction of space will have to take this fact into account. The construction of a perfect perspective also has as its purpose the drawing of attention to the beauty of depth in cinema, to foreground the icon. All the variables that help in the construction of shot space can evolve into emphasis on the icon. *Barry Lyndon* is a good example of a film where atmospheric perspective, familiar size, light and shade, and color are stressed as part of the emphasis on the space of each scene that the reverse zoom shot and the long-held shots create. Also, the temporal configuration of the text will be altered by the distinction between icons and rhetorical structures: an excessive emphasis on the icon may result in passages that seem to stop the development of the fabula; similarly, rhetorical structures that, for instance, reorient the viewer's attention from the succession of events to the evolution of a stylistic paradigm will result in an expansion of textual time and a halt of fabula time.

Christian Metz is the traditional point of reference in discussions of cinematic semiotics and the functioning of cinematic language. In his

Film Language (1974) he says that cinema has no first or second articulation, that the image is always speech and never a unit of language (61–67). But we have seen that there is a division into an articulation of icons and of rhetorical structures and that the latter uses the former as raw material. Metz thinks that the creation of meaning through paradigmatic relations in cinema is almost non-existent. The filmic image assumes meaning in relation to the other images, which could have occurred at the same point in the chain of signifiers only to a slight degree, he says (68). But if we assume that cinema creates rhetorical structures, then we are also assuming that the meaning of the structures lies in their codification, and this implies that a change in them is going to alter the meaning (and produce a different meaning). Therefore, paradigmatic options do create meaning, they exist in cinema.

Metz stresses that there may be certain paradigmatic meanings but that the attention is always directed toward the image and not toward the device (camera movement, etc.). Metz rejects the existence of a langue because he does not consider the workings of the images, of the icons in relation to the rhetorical structures that show them to us. The meaning of a distorted shot/reverse shot sequence lies not only in the distortion of a rhetorical structure but also in the effect on the configuration of the icon that the distortion has. The low angle, stark lighting and smoke that surround Ripper in *Dr. Strangelove* are partly an effect of the distortion of the shot/reverse shot sequence through which he is presented. Therefore, although our attention is directed toward the object shown, this object has been modified in its iconic nature by the rhetorical device that has been used in its presentation. We can, therefore, say that the configuration of the icon also stems from the workings of paradigmatic relations.

For Metz, connotation is homogeneous with denotation in cinema; film language is mainly connotative. The image predetermines to a great extent the connotation, whereas this is not so in more arbitrary, distant languages, such as verbal language (1974, 82). But if we assume that cinema has two kinds of signifiers, one of which uses the other as its raw material, then there will be a certain distance from the reality the text wants to connote at the level of this second type language (of rhetorical structures). So cinematic language will not be so close to its reality, after all. Even Metz admits that crosscutting imposes an alternation that makes clear that the signifier is not always analogous with the signified, since the signifiers are presented alternatively and the signifieds are simultaneous (in the case of a chase for instance) (103). So even Metz agrees that cinema has certain structures that in their textual endeavor separate from the signifieds they denote.

For Metz, cinematographic signification is always more or less motivated, never arbitrary, since there is always some relation between the sign and the reality it represents (108). This consideration will only be applicable to the level of the icon, however, since the signifiers created through rhetorical structures do not necessarily have to establish such a close relationship with reality. They may stand for abstract concepts such as freedom or solidarity, signifieds that do not easily bend to the requirements of what Metz seems to consider a strictly iconic language.

I will now resume the discussion of the previous sections by introducing again the distinction icon/rhetorical structures in the scheme of narrative. The icon/rhetorical structures would be included within both the syuzhet and the style levels. The rhetorical structures formed on the basis of icons are stylistic strategies that shape the creative activities of representation, narration, focalization, space, time, and character in a film. I will, therefore, apply my conclusions on the distinction between icon/rhetorical structures to the study of syuzhet components.

Icons/Rhetorical Structures:
From Creation of Meaning to Spectacle

In previous sections we have seen how icons and the rhetorical structures they could create were engaged in the creation of meaning in Kubrick's cinema. This creation of meaning might involve the establishment of syuzhet structures (parallelisms, repetitions, etc.) and the presentation of metaphors. Now I would like to move to a more general level and discuss the potentiality inherent in such icons and rhetorical structures to draw attention to themselves as icons, as visual material to be enjoyed not for its capacity to signify but for its beauty or spectacular nature.[6]

At the same time as he proposes the scheme fabula/syuzhet/style, Bordwell admits, following Kristin Thompson, that in a film there may be elements that are not narrational, elements that attract the viewer's attention because they stand out perceptually but do not belong to any narrative or stylistic pattern (1988, 53). He calls these elements textual

---

[6] Susan Sontag introduced this discussion, which follows the ideas of the realist film theorists, into the realm of contemporary criticism in her *Against Interpretation* (1964). See mainly 3–14.

excess.[7] I would now like to discuss the possibility cinematic language possesses of offering such excess, and of turning it into one more artistic possibility for film texts. In doing so I will draw extensively on ideas I expounded in "Kubrick's *Doctor Strangelove:* The Logic of Spectacle" (1991).

The arrival of psychoanalytic theories in the realm of contemporary film criticism has meant a major step forward in the reconsideration of the activity of the viewer. Using the concepts proposed by Sigmund Freud and Jacques Lacan, film theorists have attempted to account for the overflow of emotion spectators experience, which appears in the form of a strong identification with characters, events, or ideas presented in films. The passage of the individual from the union with the mother to the discovery of, and confrontation with, the rest of the world is a key area of study for psychoanalysis. This discovery introduces an external figure in what had so far been the omnipotent world of the child; the discovery of the other constitutes the beginning of its process of socialization, which will entail the repression of the feelings of omnipotence. The child's recognition of the world is carried out through representations, which Lacan links to the signifiers of verbal language. For Lacan the socialization of the individual is a traumatic entrance into a set of laws that restrict the power of the individual and that are erected on a linguistic system.

Christian Metz has applied these notions to the experience of the viewer watching a film. For Metz, the system of signs used by cinema causes in the viewer an awareness of the artificiality of the coherence-making process at work in watching a film. Viewers identify themselves as carrying out such a process; furthermore, they experience a desire to identify with the images projected on the screen, with the signifiers. These two processes coalesce into the enjoyment of the text as artificial, as signifier, as structure and fantasy. The viewers try to regain in their perceptual process the lost unity by identifying with the signifier (1979, 49–59). But the signifier is precisely the mark of the absence of the signified; the presence of a signifier is an implicit acknowledgment of the absence of that for which it stands. Signifiers or structures are always elements of fantasy, since they acknowledge an absence that is essential to their existence.

The motor force of these processes of identification is the viewer's desire. The separation of the subject from the primeval union creates the desire to return to such a state. The entrance into the world of lan-

---

[7] For an analysis of the concept of textual excess, see Kristin Thompson (1981, 287–295).

guage introduces an intermediary around which the position of the subject is going to be built. For the subject to desire someone or something, desire must be organized around a separation of the object from the subject. Language provides this separation and, therefore, produces desire (Cohan and Shires 1988, 158–159). This type of desire is the motor force that leads the viewer to proceed through the film. If the desire for the signifier is so essential to the experience of cinema, then we can conclude that the presence of the signifier as such is the motor force of cinema. Films contain, in the very essence of their language, reverence for their fantastic side, for the structures on which they are built. This idea is relevant if we want to consider the force cinematic signs contain in themselves, independently of their inscription into a narrative.

Once the sign is placed within a narrative there are other tensions at work in films that may emphasize the materiality of the signifiers. Such an emphasis is sometimes the result of the film's lack of coherence or unity. The realm of characters may become an area of such a lack of coherence. The special nature of characters, who are impersonated by real actors and actresses, produces a confrontation of meanings that at times makes the film's attempts at shaping unambiguous meaning fruitless (Dyer 1986). The connotations brought into films by the actors/actresses impersonating characters may clash with the meanings the film has decided to attribute to such characters. The difference between the two sets of meanings may be so irreconcilable that the characters become hard to believe, and incoherence appears. Characters will then be understood as elements of artistic indulgence that the viewer will accommodate as being motivated by merely artistic, never realistic, demands. They will become part of the enjoyment of the artificiality, of the fantasy, the film may offer. This enjoyment may also be produced by the intertextual connotations the characters may introduce: the links with other characters in other texts that a specific text may establish.[8]

The temporal structure of cinema may evolve into the creation of a purely formal syuzhet logic that will lead the viewer toward desiring and enjoying the ending. One of the most typical temporal and spatial organizations of films is crosscutting. It works by offering the viewer a fragmented and deferred version of the fabula. Crosscutting distends

---

[8] Judith Still and Michael Worton analyze the theory of intertextuality in their introduction to *Intertextuality: Theories and Practices* (1990, 1–44). Also, for a practical application of their ideas, and of Dyer's, see García Mainar (1994, 67–82).

syuzhet time in a self-conscious manner, while manipulating the rhythm of presentation, of evolution, of the events. Crosscutting transforms the viewer's search for fabulaic meaning into a search for the completion of the artificial structure set by the film. This process has been analyzed in depth by Roland Barthes, who understands narratives as the strategy of setting structural systems whose completion and final coherence is privileged by the reader/viewer over the coherence of the fabula.[9] He therefore sees in the closure of narratives the structural element that provides the whole narrative with meaning, since it means the final rounding off of structure.

Peter Brooks (1984) links this quest for structural logic to the effect of narrative desire. For him this type of desire is always desire for the end, but it has to stop at the signifier, since the direct contact with reality is not possible through a symbolic language (52–56). Narratives, therefore, work by manipulating their signs, distending them, creating suspense, delaying in multiple ways the final moment when the desired meaning is going to emerge, although this meaning is always a merely structural one. In my previous work on Kubrick (1991) I studied how *Dr. Strangelove* established a structural system that the film strove to resolve until the end. The structure the film set was based on the iconic nature of cinematic signs, which created a logic of excess and spectacle that the film was forced to maintain and improve up to the moment of closure.

One of the main ways in which films justify the appearance of material is subjectivity. The inclusion of views of characters or portions of space is introduced by the syuzhet with the help of characters' gazes, which point at the presence of something outside the sides of the frame. Focalization is, therefore, a major force in the construction of coherent cinematic narratives. My "Kubrick's *Doctor Strangelove*: The Logic of Spectacle" (1991) defended the idea that the two types of focalization, internal and external, might fulfill different functions with respect to the creation of meaning subjectivity carries out in cinema. Internal focalization, in which the new view is attributed to a character previously shown by the film, helps the syuzhet fix meaning, since it justifies the appearance of such new views. External focalization, where the new view is not attributed to any character, is, on the other hand, more susceptible to creating incoherence, since the presence of the new view is not justified in any way. External focalization was, therefore, more active in the process of exaltation of the icon that took place in

---

[9] See his "Introduction to the Structural Analysis of Narratives" (1989), *The Pleasure of the Text* (1975) and *S/Z* (1994, 67–82).

the case of *Dr. Strangelove*. The film showed signs of constantly distorting internal focalization and transforming it into external to favor the effects of the iconic logic of spectacle.

The elements of representation and mise-en-scène are also capable of favoring the logic of the icon. Films may establish a type of narration that evolves following the rules of a structural logic of stylistic devices. This type is what Bordwell calls a parametric narration (1988, 288–289), where elements of style establish an intrinsic norm that is maintained throughout the film, shifting the viewer's attention from the development of fabulaic events to the evolution of stylistic options. This stylistic logic may be completely devoid of narrative relevance, and on occasions it may become completely redundant, always remarking what other aspects of the syuzhet are stating. In these cases this excessive material resembles what Barthes has called the third meaning, the meaning that appears as excess because it does not provide any new meaning, therefore appearing artificial and self-conscious (1989, 326–328). This third meaning may disrupt the system of meaning established by the narrative and is, therefore, potentially subversive and capable of adding emphasis to a structural logic of the icon the film may establish.

I have tried to show that, given that narratives are the result of establishing structural systems that are always looking for internal coherence, films may establish structures that use as their "raw material" the icon rather than rhetorical structures. The icon is capable of creating its own systems, independently of the workings of rhetorical structures. This capability is what Kubrick's cinema reveals to us and is its most original feature.

The Influence of the Disseminative Icon on Rhetorical Structures

This section will apply the conclusions offered by the relevance of the icon and by the distinction icon/rhetorical structure to propose a classification of elements of style according to their capacity to create formal or meaning coherence. This classification will later be the object of a discussion that will study its suitability to reconcile formalist and poststructuralist views of art.

The self-reflexivity of the icon, its tendency to point at its own physicality, is only natural, since it constitutes the essence of cinema: a medium that presents short-circuit signs with which it aims to refer to reality in a more appealing manner than verbal language by calling attention to the truthfulness of its rendering of reality. But the self-reflexivity of rhetorical structures is not so common. In Kubrick, rhetorical structures point at their own artificiality as such structures and at the physicality of the icons that constitute them. It is this structural tendency to emphasize the icon on which I would like to concentrate, since it represents the introduction of the illusion of reality (and of disseminative power) into a system of signification that attempts to be symbolic. All the narrative aspects that use a symbol-like organization will, therefore, be examined and the influence of this iconicity of the icon on their functioning studied. This analysis will involve a more profound application of the concept of spectacle than the mere suggestion that it provokes dissemination of meaning. The study will undertake an analysis of narrative under the new light of iconicity and spectacle, one stemming from the workings of rhetorical structures that emphasize the icon. I will analyze the ways in which these rhetorical structures that emphasize the icon work in the construction of the various narratological concepts, apart from their already discussed capacity to draw attention to the text as spectacle.

The organization of space in a film narrative follows intrinsic norms to which the previous analysis of the icon may bring new relevance. Space in classical cinema is usually created by means of establishing shots, which introduce a great part of the space that will be shown, in a more fragmentary way, in the course of the scene, following the narrative demands the syuzhet encounters. The fragmentation of space is usually controlled by the demands imposed by focalization and subjectivity. The order and manner in which the space is fragmented depend on the perceptions of the characters whose development the camera follows. Therefore, establishing shots and those shots that contribute to the more fragmentary presentation of space will be creators of spatial coherence.

On the other hand, long shots do not seem to be so related to the establishment of a coherent space. Certain rhetorical structures involved in the construction of space emphasize the physicality of the icon, and this emphasis seems to be linked to a certain externality, as has been seen in the discussion of autofocalization. Long shots will be most capable of expressing such iconicity, since they present the most external, general view of the scene's space. The other fragmentary views of space pay more attention to relationships between characters and less to space.

The long shot contains a greater potential both to create meaning through metaphor and to disseminate meaning, the two potentialities of externality. This potential means that a communicative option — the long shot — may also become unnarrative, and also prone to the construction of metaphor. The long shots of Monument Valley in John Ford's films have become metaphors for the frontier life. At the same time they are employed as aesthetic mechanisms that exalt the spectacular beauty of Western landscape. The views of open outer space in *Star Wars* suggest metaphors about the immensity of unknown reality, while they also emphasize the spectacle of a beautiful, impressive view of infinity.

Close-ups can be argued to be the paradigm of iconicity-spectacle, even though they apparently do not belong to structures of externality: they are usually part of structures that work at a more particular level. They undoubtedly provide a strong aesthetic impression, however, which is employed to suggest ideas or simply shock the audience through their beauty, their emphasis on stylistic variables, and so on. Moreover, the proximity of the element of mise-en-scène shown by close-ups tends to do away with cues about its spatial position, contributing to a certain spatial disorientation on the part of the viewer. Formal spatial coherence is replaced by a striking view that emphasizes the physicality of the icon so as to produce meaning or simply to attract the audience's attention. Von Sternberg's films include many examples in which a close-up of Marlene Dietrich serves this purpose.

If we accept that the fragmentary renditions of space that occur after an establishing shot tend to be governed, and their appearance cued, by characters, then focalization starts to become relevant. Scenes are divided into several shots that follow either the subjectivity of the characters or their psychological intentions, cutting away, for instance, to the origin of a sound the character has heard. We have, therefore, been led back to the issue of focalization, which, as has been said, can be of various types, if we accept the value of the notion of autofocalization. Focalization may be the basis of metaphor (communication) and of dissemination of meaning (lack of communication). Now, if we follow the same rule of discarding generalizing concepts as able to provide us with a core of unalterable coherence, then we will have to conclude again that external focalization will be less preferable than internal. So our argument seems to be narrowing down to an emphasis on the importance of each individual character's look for the coherent construction of space.

But this logical development seems to contradict the first of our presuppositions, that externality and detachment were the elements that produced meaning by favoring metaphor. It now seems that we are to take character (the antithesis of externality from the point of view of space) as the element that makes spatial coherence possible. So, are meaning and coherence not equivalent? Or are they only not equivalent with respect to space? The creation of a coherent space is not any help for the configuration of complex meanings. This seems obvious. Perhaps the configuration of complex meanings does not amount to spatial coherence. We therefore see a double pull at work in the text: meaning and coherence (both in spatial terms), which have traditionally been understood to be complementary (meaning or creation of ideas related to the depiction of space stemming out of spatial coherence), are now rendered not to be so.

This conclusion about the subject of space suggests that it is in the internal interaction of individual elements that formal coherence is to be found, and that the most basic elements of meaning lie there, too. This internal interaction amounts to the workings of the fabula, to the development of events and characters.

The same tension between elements of generality and elements of particularity can be found in the strategies that constitute characters in films. The physical appearance of actors and actresses is an element of generality, which can be found in different texts and which demands from the viewer the recognition of a real person outside the rules of fiction. The iconic elements that define the specific meaning of the characters in each film (props, make-up, costume, movement, facial expression, etc.) are elements of particularity. The elements of generality are again the source of meaning that may develop into dissemination of meaning. In this case it is the links that actors may establish with other roles they have played in previous films. This generality is the source of intertextuality,[10] or the possibility for dissemination of meaning. We will, therefore, need to turn to the elements of particularity to find those aspects of character that contain the most specific, internally coherent portrayal of characters.

We can also distinguish this double code in the area of the temporal arrangement of films. Within rhythm, elements of generality are processes such as slowdowns or pauses, which may evolve into a description whose narrative relevance can best be accounted for from an external position, outside the narrative's dynamics of identification. Elements of particularity are ellipses, which constitute the basis of cinematic narratives, and scenes, which are also seminal elements of film narratives, since both usually accompany the cause-effect relationships typical of narratives, which allow the interaction of characters. Within order, the clearest element of generality is the strategy of crosscutting, which has

---

[10] For a discussion of intertextuality, see the previously mentioned introduction to *Intertextuality: Theories and Practices,* edited by Michael Worton and Judith Still (1990, 1–44).

been analyzed above as capable of favoring spectacle over ideas in Kubrick's cinema. One of the most representative films with respect to
crosscutting is D. W. Griffith's *Intolerance* (1916), which is traditionally acknowledged as a film of spectacle rather than as a film of ideas.[11]
The main element of particularity is achrony, on which many classical
films are based. Within achrony the use of flashbacks has become one
of the defining features of classical cinema, from the plurality of flashback sources in Joseph L. Mankiewicz's *A Letter to Three Wives* (1949)
to the film noir complexity of Michael Curtiz's *Mildred Pierce* (1945).

The activity of narration as we have defined it previously can be ascribed to generality in the case of extradiegetic voice, and to particularity in the case of intradiegetic voice. Voice-over narration may provide a
consistent and constant attitude toward the contents of the fabula,
fostering a detached comprehension of the text. Kubrick's *Barry Lyndon* is an example of a text where the extradiegetic narration creates a
consistently ironic and detached attitude of the viewers toward the
material that is presented to them. On the other hand, films such as
Full Metal Jacket and *A Clockwork Orange* use intradiegetic narrators
who offer us essential clues for the comprehension of the characters'
attitudes, relationships, and, consequently, actions. These intradiegetic
narrators help in the coherent construction of the fabula: they fulfill a
more internal and restricted function within the text than extradiegetic
narrators and are more prone to the establishment of attitudes that pervade not only the fabula but also the process of its apprehension by the
viewer.

Focalization includes external focalization as an element of generality, as the source of enunciative power in Benveniste's terms; and internal focalization as particularity, providing internal coherence among
portions of space. Autofocalization, since it can appear together with
both types of focalization, can be the creator of metaphors (meaning)
and the creator of dissemination of meaning, and can coexist with both
external and internal focalization.

The stylistic strategies of representation are those related to mise-
en-scène. They can be both general and particular depending on the
film's decision to present setting, props, characters' movements, performance, etc. as general or as particular. For instance, lighting may be
directed at distortion, as was argued in the case of *Dr. Strangelove* in
"Kubrick's *Doctor Strangelove:* The Logic of Spectacle" (1991), which
involves a general aim to alter the norms of the text, an aim that in its
consistency gives away its generality; but it may also be, in each indi-

---

[11] Cf. David A. Cook's *A History of Narrative Film* (1990, 97–101).

vidual scene, a contribution to clarity and spatial coherence. Mise-en-scène elements may oscillate between conceptions of generality and particularity, even in the same text.

Narrative elements are, therefore, created in films by stylistic strategies that are of two kinds: generalizing and particularizing ones. The generalizing strategies contain potential for the creation of rhetorical structures and metaphors, but also of dissemination. Particularizing strategies contain a greater capacity to create coherence at a formal level. But here we find a contradiction. Generality appears to be the dominant category in the creation of meaning, and meaning would seem to be produced by formal coherence. Generality should be the locus of formal coherence. Yet it appears that formal coherence is mainly possible through the elements of particularity. The production of meaning is, then, somehow different from formal coherence. This idea coincides with Stephen Heath's discussion of subjectivity. He says that subjectivity is produced by the fragmentation of space rather than by technical devices, such as the long take. The externality offered by the long take does not amount to a greater coherence of subjectivity, which finds its most coherent device in the use of editing, an element of particularity. Heath argues that fragmentation of space produces a continuity that is in part responsible for the creation of coherent spatial structures that produce subjective views (1981, 43).

Heath's remark is only one proof that the question of generality and particularity is at the back of a great part of contemporary film theory. This distinction can help us establish a new tool to define the characteristics of classical cinema, on the one hand, and a new kind of cinema represented by Kubrick's filmography, on the other. If we have arrived at the confrontation between meaning and formal coherence, then the whole discursive line suggests that richness of meaning does not necessarily result from formal coherence. Therefore, the whole basis of style, whose purpose is to create meaning through a supposed search for coherence, falls down. A traditional conception of style becomes shaky, and we need a new conception of style that admits that it has different effects: metaphor, dissemination, and formal coherence. The elements of style related to particularity create narrative concepts that possess coherence but not a full potentiality to signify. Therefore, a new conception of cinematographic narration is also needed here, one that includes this difference between generality and particularity and is capable of including those aspects of generality within a scheme of narration that encompasses all the disseminative potential of the icon, as well as its metaphorical potentiality. One must also acknowledge the capacity of generality to create coherence of meaning by installing an external viewer who creates a coherent meaning of the text as text. This double/triple potentiality of generality will be the defining feature of a new tradition of cinema that Kubrick's films represent, a revision of the postulates of classical cinema that stems from the evolution of the American cinematographic tradition itself.

The previous discussion can help to propose a new distinction between classical cinema, based on an internal kind of interaction and formal coherence, and a new cinema of which Kubrick's films are one representative, a cinema based on a coherence of meaning imposed from the outside and, to a certain extent, independently of the fabula's contents and development — a kind of cinematographic mode that, although not only represented by Kubrick's films, is not common in its attack on the precepts of classical cinema.[12] This new definition of classical cinema can be made by applying the notions of the icon and of rhetorical structures. Classical cinema tends to favor the creation of a realism à la André Bazin, where stylistic strategies privilege the presence of the icons. Other types of cinema are characterized by the greater presence and importance of rhetorical structures: it is a cinema prefigured by Yasuhiro Ozu and Ingmar Bergman, the French New Wave, Bresson and Dreyer. A new tradition emerges, characterized by the dissemination of meaning through the icon, which is emphasized through rhetorical structures that redirect the viewer's attention toward the icon, and by the exploitation of the double nature of externality as safeguard of meaning and as disseminative device. For an example of this last tradition we can turn to Griffith's cinema: a full use of the metaphorical structure of crosscutting also renders spectacle in *Intolerance* (1916), while autofocalization of characters is present in the same film and in *Broken Blossoms* (1919). This tradition, explained through the double side of externality, has been present from the beginning of cinema, which reveals the essential nature of such internal processes.

The main advantage of the theory proposed so far is that it is a scheme of formalist structures (stylistic structures) that is at the same time able to include in itself a distinction among the various strategies that accompany the creation and dissemination of meaning, and those that accompany formal coherence. This structuralist scheme is, therefore, able to accommodate all those antinarrative/antimeaning strategies that define the various poststructuralisms: deconstruction, feminist criticism, metafiction, and others. And it will, therefore, be useful for

---

[12] Noël Burch has studied the centrality of formal elements for the production of meaning in Japanese cinema, a meaning-production activity that uses style in a similar way to Kubrick's cinema (1979).

the analysis of the Kubrick films that will be carried out in the second part of this book, which will be approached from this perspective: as examples of the new aspects Kubrick's films bring in — the different varieties of antinarrativity/spectacle.

Can we derive all the narratological concepts and stylistic devices from the notion of focalization? The elements of particularity tend to be associated with the representation of characters. And this representation of characters tends to depend on the workings of focalization as a means of linking space, creating temporal order, and introducing the workings of mise-en-scène. If we accept that all phenomena come down to focalization, then the introduction of the notion of auto-focalization will mean the capacity of both internal and external focalization, and also of the elements of particularity and externality, to draw attention to themselves. This concept of autoreferentiality may be useful in yet a different way.

The scheme of generality/particularity is capable of reconciling formalism and poststructuralism, as was suggested above. These two tendencies are used by modern critics to organize the discussion and questioning of the various attitudes toward the study of artistic forms. I would now like to choose two works by two authors that are representative of two tendencies in contemporary criticism. Noël Carroll represents the disregard of textual form as capable of containing critical material to explain viewers' readings and ideological attitudes; Tzvetan Todorov praises the text's capacity to contain such material. Carroll understands the text as mere perception of reality, while Todorov allows it the possibility of being charged with self-reflexivity and ideological connotations. In my opinion, both tendencies can be combined by the scheme of generality/particularity outlined above.

Carroll, discussing contemporary film theory in *Mystifying Movies* (1988), distinguishes between a realist criticism that shows an implicit belief in the essence of reality, and modern film critics who use too many badly applied metaphors in their conceptualizing processes, and are unable to account for the viewer's actual experience of watching a film. Todorov studies various conceptions of the symbol in his *Theories of the Symbol* (1982). He distinguishes the symbol in classicism, where it provides access to essence, acting as a transparent filter within which scholars perceived both a literal and a transposed meaning. On the other hand, the symbol in romanticism only provides access to the symbol itself: the symbol is intransitive, and the whole experience of art concentrates on charging this intransitivity with artistic pleasure.

Carroll's book explores the major critical trends in contemporary film criticism to prove the inappropriateness of most of their theoretical assumptions. Carroll dismisses the critical practice of mixing Marxist and psychoanalytic theories, which is best represented by the Althusserian-Lacanian model of interpretation of the experience of cinema (1988, 53–88). He explains Althusser's concept of ideology as the system that places individuals in their reserved place without allowing them to realize that they are not free but manipulated through cultural and social laws. The positioning of the individual as subject in society is carried out by means of the interpellation the system directs at him /her. Such interpellation describes the subject as part of the structure of ideology. This construction of the subject is explained by resorting to Lacanian psychoanalysis, a theory that mixes Freudian ideas, Ferdinand de Saussure's concept of the linguistic system, and Claude Levi-Strauss's anthropological discoveries. Narratives — fictions — are taken as examples of the Other that promise a return, through imaginary identification, to the realm of unity with the mother. Carroll criticizes this Althusserian/Lacanian model because it implies that unity is linked to autonomy, to freedom, whereas construction, the Symbolic, the Other, is the realm of oppression. He, on the other hand, resorting to a more empirical analysis, argues that the human being is able to experience both unity and construction at the same time and that the distinction that holds the Lacanian system's idea of oppression as ideological effect is no longer tenable (1988, 80).

Carroll deals with realist theories, too (1988, 89–146). He divides them into those of the followers of André Bazin, who say that in watching a film the viewer mistakes the image for its referent, and those of critics who defend the idea that the cinema is not reality but is nevertheless capable of creating the illusion of reality. Both types of theory claim that this aura of realism as illusionism is a strong asset for the ideological activity cinema carries out. They understand cinema as a medium through which ideology is spread. A conception of cinema's illusionism is used by critics to present cinema as the process of placing the subject at the center of the experience of cinema and in this way creating the feeling of a unified subject who is utterly ideological. Carroll disregards these theoretical positions, arguing that they imply that cinematic language is coded. For him, film images are understood by spectators without reference to a code. Cinema's signs are pictorial representations that the viewer can perceive and understand without reference to a code, because they are not conventions: they are inventions. Human beings adopted strategies of looking, such as perspective, because they seemed to work in the representation of spatial relations among objects; but this decision was not arbitrary or free, it was made because such a system seemed to help in the representation of space.

Carroll thinks that film theorists have made a mistake: they say that if something is coded or conventional, then it is a cultural production, which is true; but the inverse is not true: that if something is a cultural product, then it is an example of coded or conventional phenomena (1988, 142–143). For Carroll, cinema's images are not conventional but inventions, and people can understand them because people can identify objects from the start, without any special training or a code.

He also discusses conceptions of cinema as narrative (147–181). He attacks the attempt to translate to film criticism Benveniste's theory of enunciation, arguing that in film it is problematic to distinguish the three categories (first-, second- and third-person narrators) that Benveniste established. He does not believe that in the absence of enunciating marks the viewers might feel that they are the enunciators themselves, and he sees this hypothesis as just one more attempt of film criticism to reinforce the theory of the unity of the subject (Althusser-Lacan) as proof of the ideological nature of cinema. Following this line, he criticizes Stephen Heath's proposal of narration in *Questions of Cinema* (1981). For Heath, narratives are collections of events posing an equilibrium that is destroyed and quickly regained at the narrative's resolution.[13] The story events and perspective are elements of coherence. When the coherence produced by perspective — its capacity to create understandable space — is threatened by camera or character movement, the coherence of the story events counteracts this threat and restores coherence for the subject to be rendered unified. Carroll says that there is no evidence that movement creates perspectival disturbances; and that if these disturbances existed the coherence created by the story would not counteract it, since they are two different concepts: space and story events.

Carroll proposes his own theory of narrative, with which, he admits, he only wants to explain mainstream cinema: narratives are organized around a set of questions opened by the text, whose answers are withheld until the narrative finds it suitable to reveal them. This theory accounts for the feelings of expectation, surprise, and suspense the viewer experiences. It is an account that attempts to explain narration through the spectator's activity of comprehending a film, and in this respect it resembles Bordwell's theory. Carroll discusses the concept of suture proposed by J. P. Oudart (182–225). For Carroll, Oudart and his followers use suture as a means of presenting the text as the mechanism of subject positioning that uses the viewer's desire for the Absent One as a

---

[13] See Edward Branigan's *Narrative Comprehension and Film* (1992) for a similar account of filmic narration 63–85.

way of inscribing the subject into the text and, through the shot/reverse shot structure, concealing such an inscription, such an ideological move. For Carroll, the strategy of suture is a theoretical array with no data at its basis: nobody has proved that the feelings of desire for the Absent One in a shot/reverse shot exist in the viewer; everything is based on non-verification. Carroll finishes his account of cinematic narration: the posing of questions and answers creates expectation and desire to know, the viewer's search for knowledge is governed by textual strategies called indexing, bracketing, and scaling. Camera movements point at what the viewer should know (indexing), the frame excludes what it is not interested in showing (bracketing), and camera movement plus zooms and other cinematographic properties change the dimensions of the objects (scaling), thereby attracting or not attracting the attention of the viewer.

Carroll's attacks on contemporary film theory are based on what he considers general misconceptions. Its central concepts are ambiguous because they are metaphorical in nature, they are constructed by using metaphors taken from different areas of study, and they are not capable of throwing light on the complex processes they are supposed to explain. In these theories the viewers' desire is understood as the force that leads them in the apprehension of a film text. But all kinds of desire are explained in the same way, making no distinctions, which has produced inaccuracy. The theories are too totalizing: they try to be applicable to all kinds of films, and generality makes them uninformative. Besides, they all rest on the assumption that cinema is an ideological process, an assumption that Carroll tries to disprove.

The proposal of a new scheme of cinematic signification, based on the existence of various levels of generality and particularity in film narratives, can in some cases provide Carroll's theory with more arguments, while in other cases it can help us modify some of his conclusions. Carroll says that film images are understood without reference to a code. Cinema's signs are pictorial representations. The model outlined above is able to refute Carroll here, because I propose that such pictorial representations in the end form rhetorical structures that are symbolic in their workings. Carroll suggests, with his disavowal of cinema as coded, that films are never the bearers of ideology, of cultural prejudice introduced through the code. The new model is able to introduce into the scheme of film theory an area of symbols that will open the way for the possibility of ideological constructions in cinema, allowing post-structuralisms into it.

The presence of a symbolic code allows for a concept of the subject as the privileged decoder, a process of placement that inevitably carries ideological connotations: the place reserved for the subject is imposed on one by the dynamics of the code — it is not the result of a free choice — in the process making the subject implicitly accept views and attitudes that belong exclusively to the system of the code. The rejection of a coded system by Carroll denies the presence of such ideological process. The proposal outlined above, however, allows a symbolic code that, at the same time as introducing the possibility of ideological connotations, presents the critic with a system to be exposed and challenged.

Carroll's description of Heath's theory of narration evolves into criticism by showing that it is based on loosely applied, ambiguously inaccurate metaphors. This is his way of attacking notions of cinema as narrative, which he thinks are attempts to place the subject as the great decoder, thereby defending the possibility of the unity of the subject and, implicitly, the ideological nature of cinema. Heath poses a narrative that constructs a double system of creation of coherence: the story events and perspective both try to create repetition as source of homogeneity and coherence. Both try to preserve the subject unity of the spectator by creating a coherent narrative. The fluctuations of perspective caused by camera movement or by the movement of characters are counteracted by the coherence of the story, which works to establish equilibrium and balance between disruptions, whether perceptual or diegetic. As we have seen, Carroll thinks that there is no evidence that movement may cause perspectival confusion and that the effect of story coherence on perspective is not tenable, since the former affects events and the latter the perception of space. They are different concepts. I agree in part with Carroll, since in the scheme the capacity of the fabula to create coherence was admitted. This coherence was formal coherence and not meaning coherence, which seemed more reserved to generality.

In Kubrick the repetition that according to Heath leads to homogeneity and coherence is the source of external meaning (related to the elements of generality), which is not the same as formal coherence (in my scheme being produced by the elements of particularity). The redundant presentation of the chateau/trenches confrontation in *Paths of Glory* helps the viewer obtain a clear meaning of the relevance of both worlds in the story that is being told. The typical division of Kubrick's texts into two or more interacting parts is another example of repetition, in this case with difference, whose purpose is to create meaning. In both cases the externality of the meaning-production process is evident, since the repetitions are part of the text's consistent and all-pervading strategies to suggest ideas. Carroll says that repetition does not create coherence, since the spectator does not perceive the text as closed but as a development. I agree with Carroll, but I would also like to introduce the idea that there may be a coherence at an external level of creation of meaning, different from the character or fabula-related one. And I can therefore propose that Heath's theory about perspective being secured by coherence can still be maintained if we understand the essence of coherence to be in some texts the external activity of metaphor, of meaning creation carried out through the elements of generality. This idea will be more widely explored in the discussion of *2001:* in this film perspective and metaphor help each other in the construction of meaning. This external coherence of meaning would present us with a stabilizing effect that in this case would not be the defining feature of the realist text: Kubrick's texts seem, rather, to propose another kind of style in which the overt creation of meaning is acknowledged by the text; they seem more proximate to postmodern creations that take this overt activity of meaning-shaping as their main theme.

Heath argues that the equilibrium model proposes a process of transformation-substitution-repetition as the means by which the narrative of the film secures intelligibility (1988, 182). The model proposed above reveals that these repetitions create coherence and meaning externally. Carroll's model of narration holds that the main link between scenes is an internal process of questioning and answering. This seems rather a process that in my model is carried out by the fabula events. It therefore seems that the new model is able to reconcile Heath's model, which proposes a subject unity to be achieved through textual/syuzhet coherence, and another, Carroll's, which rejects the idea of a subject unity as the aim of a text since he rejects the idea that texts may be ideological and proposes a more cognitive theory that starts from the spectator's perceptive activity. My model reconciles these two models of narration, since it sees in style room for both possibilities and is able to reconcile an idea of the text as ideological (=poststructuralisms) with an idea of the text as mere formalist construction (=structuralism, Bordwell's cognitive theory).

This acceptance of cinema as both a coded system that attempts to place the subject at the center of the decoding activity and a collection of signs that attempt faithfully to represent reality through icons takes us back to another of Carroll's discussions of contemporary film theory: the matter of Althusserian-Lacanian models of analysis. Carroll rejects them, as we have seen, because they imply that the subject may be either united, before contacting the outside world, or constructed, once it discovers the existence of the others. Carroll thinks that both experiences can coexist, that they are not mutually exclusive. I agree with

Carroll, since my theory is capable of including both the possibility of a unified subject, where the icon is almighty and there is no trace of rhetorical structures, as well as of a constructed one, where the icons are organized into rhetorical structures that work similarly to symbolic languages and where the presence of a code allows considerations about its potential to manipulate the subject in ideological ways.

Carroll's proposal of a new theory, which is born out of his criticism of contemporary film theories, can be easily assimilated into a new model that reveals that what Carroll finds incoherent or incompatible in those theories is not incoherent or incompatible at all if we adopt a wider theory, with which he implicitly agrees when he says that unity and construction are not incompatible. Besides, the model he proposes does not seem to me coherent enough with his move away from any system that may be taken as a code: in fact, his ideas of indexing, bracketing, and scaling imply textual structures that gain their relevance by their difference from, and opposition to, other alternative structures the film might choose. His scheme implicitly acknowledges the importance of rhetorical structures. His claim that cinema is only a set of images that are naturally, without any training, read and understood by viewers, and whose analysis only requires basic notions about the way films allow viewers access to their information, is not tenable.

All of his objections to contemporary film theory all but disappear if we adopt a model of analysis that can include the possibility of film language as, first, a level of icons, where the relationship with the reality they denote is more direct and, therefore, they do not involve the decoding of a sign, and that would coincide with Heath's concept of cinema's language. But the new model proposed here is also capable of including a second level formed by rhetorical structures, where the icon is used as raw material for the creation of structures that create a code to be decodified in a similar way to verbal languages. This second level allows the presence of notions of construction and, therefore, of ideological manipulation and, accordingly, of the possible subversion of such ideological systems.

Todorov's *Theories of the Symbol* (1982) offers the reader a different classification of criticism, but one that at bottom proves to be similar to the one we have seen above. Todorov sees in St. Augustine the beginning of Western semiotics and reflection on the symbol. Augustine distinguishes two types of meaning according to the nature of the symbolic relation: a proper meaning and a transposed one. A sign is transposed when its signified becomes, in turn, a signifier for a different signified. The proper sign is based on a single relation, the transposed sign on two successive operations (1982, 51). This division of the sign is related to my thesis: on the one hand, it establishes the difference between literal meaning and metaphor, at the same time including them within a system of what Todorov calls classical approaches to the topic; and, on the other hand, it helps support the idea of the "double articulation" of cinematographic language: icons as basic units that constitute rhetorical structures. The double function of the icon as representation and as part of a symbolic structure is similar to that of the signified that becomes signifier for another signified: the icon is a signifier that becomes a signified for the symbolic structure, which then becomes the signifier.

For the German romantics, however, the term *symbol* will be taken to designate the capacity of art to signify itself, to express its own artistic nature. For the romantics the nature of art consists in constituting a modification of nature from the artist's perception of it and wish to change it. Art is intransitive; it does not aim at portraying reality but at posing a filter that may transform itself into the recipient of the artistic content (1982, 147–221).

The division of cinematographic language into icon and rhetorical structures corresponds to the distinction that Todorov makes between classical and romantic notions of the symbol. Classical theories distinguish a proper meaning and a transposed meaning of words, the latter being more metaphorical, establishing links with other areas of signification different from those of the proper meaning. In this respect this second, transposed meaning or symbol (or metaphor) is similar in its mechanisms to the workings or rhetorical structures, which extract meaning from the icons by following a similarly metaphorical process. Moreover, the romantic notion of the symbol as an intransitive entity seems closer to the idea of the icon. The icon is close to its referent and is, in a way, intransitive until it becomes part of a rhetorical structure.

On the other hand, the division icon/rhetorical structures is parallel in its workings to the division literal/transposed meaning: in both the first element of the division acts as basis for the construction of the second. From this point of view the classical approach to the symbol, and therefore to art, can be included in this part of my scheme. The romantic notion of intransitivity and art expressing the artist's transformation of reality can also be accounted for in the same scheme through the notion of spectacle. The capacity the icon/rhetorical structure division has of drawing attention toward the iconicity of the icon, of displacing the weight of the work of art from the signification of a fictional world to its own expression, is similar to such a romantic conception to art. Therefore, my scheme and the capacity it attributes to Kubrick's cinema are able to reconcile these two approaches to art.

Furthermore, the romantics see in literature, in the symbol, an intransitive element, which designates itself infinitely: the romantic conception of art, and consequently the spectacle part of my scheme, can be linked to modern poststructuralism's emphasis on the power of the text to explore the construction of the subject in society, but a construction that is parallel to that of the text, one in which the poststructuralists seem to be most interested.

In fact, the possibility the scheme that has been proposed offers for the reconciliation of Todorov's two stages of literature in history is similar to the possibility it also offers for the reconciliation of realism and poststructuralisms as depicted by Carroll. My theory also suggests that Carroll's criticism of poststructuralist criticism (the Althusser-Lacanian method) may be refuted. Carroll denies the existence of a process of subject unification through identification, and of the process of coherence-making that suture carries out. This denial is invariably based on a criticism of specific processes linked to the perception of the text by the viewer, which, Carroll argues, do not correspond to the experiences attributed to the viewers (of union, of coherence) by critics. I agree with Carroll that the idea of the unity of the subject is not incompatible with the feeling of being constructed, and I also agree that the coherence produced by suture does not necessarily amount to intelligibility (1988, 199); but I also think that if we understand the ideas of unification, construction, coherence, and intelligibility at a more general level, taking into consideration the whole text and not individual examples of technique, we will have to agree that unification, construction, coherence, and intelligibility do exist and that the text helps produce them. A text sets up strategies to control the viewer's understanding of the fabula. These strategies require from the reader/viewer a certain external position from which to perceive and make choices. This external position is provided by elements of externality. So, construction, but also unification of the subject (since the subject gains access to knowledge that was not possessed before), coherence, but also intelligibility (since the aim of the text is to provide the viewer with all the clues to understand a text), all of them exist and are a product of the text's workings.

We can, therefore, take Carroll's argument further by saying that perhaps the individual experience of the viewer when watching a film is unified and constructed at the same time, but that this does not mean that the metaphor of the individual being forced to adopt a subject position pre-established by the text is false. The notion of externality supports this view, since it emphasizes how viewers may apprehend the text as a whole, something implied in the discussion of the metaphorical activity of Kubrick's films, where viewers were placed in an external position from which they could establish links among textual elements. It is a process of apprehension and understanding that works by providing the viewers with all the information: placing them in a position of all-knowing power that turns them into decoders and masters. So a more general, external view of the cinematographic text helps us realize that the processes that Carroll understands not to exist but to be the product of critics' misapplication through metaphors of other concepts unrelated to the experience of a viewer's watching really do exist as a product of the text. The more external approach enables us to reincorporate Althusserian-Lacanian poststructuralisms into the realm of a formalism-based theory of cinema.

The notions of externality and generality can explain concepts that Carroll finds inadmissible in contemporary film theory, at the same time as it provides proof for some of his arguments. The scheme reconciles the capacity of the subject to feel imaginary unconstructedness and symbolic constructedness from an external position of the viewer perceiving the text. While agreeing with Carroll's theory of mainstream cinema, the scheme also hints that this process places the subject in a certain position that is ideological, therefore approximating the ideas of poststructuralisms (Althusser-Lacan) that Carroll rejects. The innovation brought in by my scheme is that it is able to produce two possibilities for the positioning of the subject: one at a particular level, another at a more general one. The subject can be placed outside the text, as being conscious of the activity that is performed (the understanding of a fiction). Carroll seems to understand only the activity of the viewers at a particularizing level, denying, therefore, their capacity to be aware of their own status as viewers and of their own processes of cognition.

This idea is also applicable to Todorov's distinctions. A text that fosters an external decodification is able to posit a reader who understands the intransitive text as being somehow transitive. A consideration of a text from an external position involves the reader's appreciation of the self-consciousness inherent in any narrative process. The understanding and acceptance of self-consciousness opens the way for an easier consideration of the intransitive text as, in fact, describing an object, the text itself, therefore becoming a transitive text. Also, the autoreferentiality that autofocalization reveals regarding focalization has been found in all the textual phenomena of cinema. Therefore, focalization and the idea of autofocalization, which are the origin of the theory I have proposed here, provide us with a useful metaphor for the whole process.

3: *2001: A Space Odyssey* (1968); or, A Journey toward Ambiguity

THE FOLLOWING REFLECTIONS WILL SERVE AS AN introduction to the analysis of three of Kubrick's films: *2001: A Space Odyssey* (1968), *Barry Lyndon* (1975), and *Full Metal Jacket* (1987). They will justify what might otherwise seem to be an arbitrary choice of three texts, as well as expound the relevance of their analysis.

The previous notions of generality/particularity will be placed in a new context that will become the area of discussion in this second part of the book: this context is the debate about language and its capacity to signify, together with the contribution of deconstruction, which argues that language ultimately only refers to itself and that meaning is never stable because it is the product of a play of signifiers. The previous discussion has, in fact, reached a concept, generality, that coincides with the results advanced by deconstruction: the same mechanisms that produce a meaning can be used to dismantle it and produce alternative meanings, which finally results in the absence of a stable meaning — signifiers referring only to other signifiers, and meaning being just the product of a random play of signifiers.

Recent analyses have, however, laid bare the intrinsic illogicality of certain basic pillars of deconstruction. One of the pillars that has been the object of close scrutiny and has been found guilty of inaccurate logical development is precisely the notion of language as a play of signifiers. John M. Ellis, in his *Against Deconstruction* (1989), criticizes deconstruction's description of the nature of language. He goes back to the principal motivation of deconstruction in this area: the analysis and criticism of Saussure's theory of language. For Ellis deconstruction has misread Saussure and misapplied his concepts. According to Saussure, the phonetic shape of a word is arbitrary, but what is more important — and something that deconstructionists tend to forget — is that the concept to which the phonetic element refers is also an arbitrary creation of a language that decides to organize meaning in a certain way. The structure of the concept is an arbitrary creation that does not necessarily exist outside language. Ellis cites the concept *warm*, whose reference to temperature and relationship to *hot* and *cold* is the result of a division into concepts, a division or structure that is arbitrary: what for the English language is warm need not exactly coincide with other languages' concept of this intermediary state between hot and cold.

The organization of this concept, called *signified* by Saussure, is constantly ignored by deconstructionists and is the origin of their assertion that the only things provided by signifiers are facts about language itself. The signified becomes the basis of the signifier, since it provides the latter with a definite portion of reality to name; but the signified also has its origin in the existence of a reality it decides to portion in a certain way. Therefore, the signified remains a link between the pure abstraction and arbitrariness of the signifier and the presence of a real fact of nature. It is, therefore, difficult to affirm that language, which is for Saussure the union of a signifier and a signified, only offers examples of itself, since the signified is intimately linked to the reality it patterns. Ellis says:

> the fact that *warmness* as a concept is a creation of the English language does *not* mean that warmness has nothing to do with reality or that statements that include reference to warmness are only statements about the English language, not about the world. On the contrary, variations in temperature must exist and be perceptible to allow the contrast between *warm* and *hot* to *mean anything*. If the words only told us something about English without also telling us what the actual conditions were that made the use of one rather than the other an appropriate and correct use of English, then they could not tell us anything about English either: English would not exist. It works both ways: the word *warm* gives us information about our language only given our recognizing temperature variations. And the word *warm* gives us information about the world only given our ability to understand and use English. *It is just as wrong to say that warmth is simply a fact of nature as it is to say that warmth is simply a fact about language;* and the greatest error of all would be to assume that the falsity of the first of these alternatives required us to turn to the second (1989, 47–49).

This assumption is, in fact, one that deconstruction makes. Therefore, the notion that signifiers only tell us about themselves is untenable.

Deconstruction's idea that meaning is unstable because it is the result of the infinite play of signifiers also stems, according to Ellis, from a misreading of Saussure. Derrida transforms Saussure's system of differences and contrasts, which is based on *specific* differences between signifiers, into a flux of play where differences are not specific but infinite; meaning also becomes limitless. For Ellis, this notion is illogical, since, following Saussure's concept of language, if terms could play indiscriminately against all other terms, endlessly and indeterminately rather than specifically, the result would be no specific contrasts that produce meaning, no difference forming a system. For Saussure, a language was a system of demarcating an infinite landscape of differences, so that in turning into arbitrarily defined units a perceptible contrast could be perceived on which meaning would be built. If such a system is now infinite the basic idea of a system of differences disappears, and we have no difference, no meaning (1989, 53–54).

Therefore, the capacity of languages and texts to include a wide variety of effects on meaning, which is one of deconstruction's tenets, is now rendered a capacity to portray the illogical development of the deconstructive processes previously outlined. I would like to present the three Kubrick texts I have chosen to analyze as stages in one of deconstruction's most important statements, in order to see if the films may help us propose a way out of the dead end at which Ellis has placed deconstruction. In the process I will return to the ideas of generality and particularity, especially to the notion of generality as producer of various possibilities for meaning and, therefore, in a way close to deconstruction's idea of the infinite play of signifiers. The statement of deconstruction I would like to discuss in this way is the idea of the plurality of meaning, which results in ambiguity, as opposed to that of a single meaning. It is, in fact, a version of the opposition language as play of signifiers/language as direct, stable vehicle of meaning.

The analysis of the films that follows will support the thesis that each film represents a different attitude to the creation of meaning. *2001* is based on the plurality of meaning and on the notion of ambiguity. Generality is in this film the creator of ambiguity, which functions by opposition to the idea of a single meaning, and also of multiplicity of meaning. Ambiguity closes off any possibility of a stable reading. Ambiguity stems from the film's use of a certainly nonclassical narrative mode that builds a mainly visual experience, where the power of signification of the visual sets off different interpretative systems and even threatens to discourage any meaning-making attempt on the part of the viewer. *Barry Lyndon* is a mixture of classical and parametric narration, where generality shows the expansion of the classical code in its process of shaping clear meanings, aided by the exploration of a traditional code of cinema: its pictorial basis. *Barry Lyndon* presents generality as creator of clear meaning by mixing two narrative modes that seem irreconcilable (classical-parametric) and by exploiting a classical code (the pictorial code) through the recourse to self-consciousness that the zoom shot means for the creation of perspective. There seems to be a progression from generality as creator of ambiguity in *2001* by exploiting the irreconcilable nature of diverse processes of meaning to generality as creator of clear meaning in *Barry Lyndon* by mixing two narrative modes that seem irreconcilable with the rest of the narrative forces in the film.

This progression sets a difference between the two films, which become representatives of the opposition generality-as-producer-of-plurality-of-meaning (*2001*) / generality-as-producer-of-a-single-meaning (*Barry Lyndon*). This dynamic follows the typical development of deconstruction's arguments, according to Ellis's description of them. For him, deconstruction always deals with pairs of opposites. One pole of the opposition is provided by the traditional account of the issue being discussed, and the other pole is its exact opposite, provided by the deconstructionist as an alternative to the traditional idea, a good example being the previously described oscillation from language as a fact of reality to language as a fact of itself. For Ellis, deconstruction is at this point the victim of its constant attempt always to state the opposite from what is understood and accepted at first:

> Paradoxically, it would seem that deconstruction is a victim of the restrictive binary logic that it likes to denigrate: it thinks in terms of subverting and undermining traditional views, but that excludes the really progressive possibility of just *departing* from those views, their emphases, and their terms. It is surely that kind of departure that provides real progress (1989, 81).

This tendency of deconstruction produces several misconceptions and illogical developments of the issues presented for discussion. The two films by Kubrick seem to be good examples of how this polar opposition can also be found in filmic texts through an analysis of how generality functions. But can we find any alternative to this oscillation between two such opposed systems of meaning-configuration? *Full Metal Jacket*, the third film to be analyzed, provides such an alternative. It combines the ambiguity of *2001* and the clarity of *Barry Lyndon*. It exemplifies the double side of externality: the ending fixes meaning, somehow disavowing the plurality of sexual positions entertained previously and explained through the politics of masochism. The ending is part of the institutional tendency to make endings accommodate the traditionally accepted ideals of the institution, but the text as a whole includes the two possibilities of externality in this case: fixed sexual position and multiple sexual positions. *Full Metal Jacket* may be seen as a progression in Kubrick's filmography in its attempt to include both tendencies of generality.

Moreover, *Full Metal Jacket* sets a limited range of possible meanings (here sexual possibilities of identification): it is not a limitless number of possibilities for meaning that are offered in the text, as an application of the theory of the play of signifiers would hold, but a set of possibilities that in their restricted nature contain their value as liberating and original concepts. Their limited nature makes them part of a really meaningful system, where alternatives exist and can be communicated to the audience. It is precisely this act of offering different available possibilities within a systematized whole that I would like to stress as the most significant contribution of *Full Metal Jacket* to the theoretical context set by the other two films. The film seems to be a rejection of the deconstructive notion that the opposite of a single meaning — infinite meanings — is the result of the attempt to dismantle a privileged ideological position or reading by asserting its polar opposite. *Full Metal Jacket* shows a different kind of subversion in offering variety but still within a restricted system, which makes it more fruitful than notions of limitless difference, since the film shows that an alternative to the abolition of the code proposed by deconstruction is an intermediate path consisting in the presentation of a variety of alternatives to the position privileged by the text. The existence of these alternatives within a limited system favors their availability, since they become comprehensible, something the extreme attitude of deconstruction refuses to admit in its assumption that the only possible alternative to an idea is its polar opposite.

Full Metal Jacket is the only film of the three that is set in the present, and the only one that deals with sexual definition: the present time seems the time of most complex reality, and the time when human beings seem most capable of understanding such complexity; and, the complexity is the more astonishing since it is present in the realm of sexual identity, one of the most intimate and, therefore, delicate processes in the life of human beings. *Barry Lyndon* deals with the confrontation of the individual with society, a past society whose strict norms are oppressive but allow the individual a possibility of fighting them. *2001* is about the future, where the ambiguities presented are assimilated by the viewer through the distance imposed by the text, a distance that allows an intellectual position. The individuals in the text are so absorbed in their technological world that they remain unaware of the mysteries of future intelligence. *Full Metal Jacket* gets the closest of the three to the intimate nature of the individual while dealing with issues that can be recognized as topics in present-day society.

The analysis of the three films also provides conclusions with respect to the action of generality: generality helps us to understand the textual processes at work in each of the films. The elaboration of multiple meanings, of a single one, or of a combination of the two tendencies can be clearly dissected through the tools the concept of generality offers the critic. The common activity in the three films of shaping meaning by arranging macrostructures that set contrasts and similarities is also analyzed at this level of generality, in this case achieving not only meaning but also formal coherence. Generality, closely associated with the idea of externality, becomes the best definition of Kubrick's cinema, a narrative mode that constantly attempts to separate the viewer from the contents of the film in order to elicit a reflexive attitude. Generality, through the wide range of effects it may help us to analyze, becomes the best tool for analyzing postmodern films. Its capacity to explain the creation of meaning and its dissemination approximates generality to the textual practice of postmodern films, which try to present the viewer with different possible readings and contesting internal forces. Generality will even become a tool of analysis in the most innovative and original case we will study: *Full Metal Jacket*. This film will offer us the new possibility of alternative meanings without reaching the extremist position implicit in the notion of dissemination. *Full Metal Jacket* provides several possibilities for its textual fulfillment, but these possibilities remain within the limits of a comprehensible system, refusing to abolish the potential of the code as dissemination threatens to do. Generality, therefore, appears as the analytic concept that enables the understanding of all these possibilities, as the main textual concept related to the formalist, deconstructive, and feminist critical theories we will employ in the forthcoming chapters.

In the analysis to come we will see how the elements of particularity, which are the most basic source of formal coherence, are gradually but consistently turned into help to the elements of generality, to the extent that the construction of formal coherence begins to be apprehended from an external, all-knowing position provided by generality. This process will be commented on, whenever it becomes apparent, in the analysis of *2001* and *Barry Lyndon*, but it will be omitted in the analysis of *Full Metal Jacket* because it will have become obvious by then. The analysis of the three films will show us how the formal coherence of particularity tends to be taken for granted, and how the handling of meaning resorts to concepts, such as repetition and contrast, that demand a formal coherence that pervades the whole text and demands a detached apprehension of the film. These new strategies present us with a formal coherence more proximate to notions of generality, which will become the guarantee of a great amount of signification in the three films. All this is done through the exploitation of the code in order to present the viewer with material to decodify and shape into meaning from a position that rejects identification and fosters reflection.

The plot of *2001: A Space Odyssey* takes us back to the prehistoric past, in which a tribe of apes lives in constant fear of predators while quarreling with a neighboring tribe for the possession of a water hole. One day they wake up to see a black monolith. After the apes approach and touch it, one of them becomes able to use a bone as a weapon to kill other animals for food. The apes later use bones to defeat the rival tribe. An ellipsis of four million years transports us to a world of outer space and spaceships. Dr. Heywood Floyd arrives on the moon to investigate a similar monolith that has been excavated and is emitting signals in the direction of Jupiter. Another ellipsis introduces the spaceship *Discovery*, which has set out on a voyage to Jupiter. Two astronauts, Bowman and Poole, with three other hibernating crew and an infallible computer, HAL 9000, inhabit the spaceship. The computer causes the death of Poole and the three hibernating men when it discovers that the crew plan to disconnect it. Bowman manages to disconnect the computer and is forced to continue the journey alone. In the last section of the film Bowman approaches Jupiter and is drawn into a new dimension where human laws of space and time are no longer applicable. He finally arrives at an elegant room, where he sees himself age until his dying self again meets the black monolith. Bowman is reborn in the form of a new, transcended human being who competes with the majesty of the other planets in outer space.

The study of *2001* will be divided into two sections. Section one will discuss the ways in which the film creates meaning through metaphor and the use of space. The section will end with a discussion of the mixed kinds of narration present in the film, which reveals the high self-consciousness inherent to the text. The externality of the process of creation of metaphor and space will be analyzed in section two, together with its double nature: it may become both a safeguard of meaning and a possibility for the instability of meaning. The metafictional dimension of the film will be analyzed, as well as the possibilities the code set by the narrative offers for its own deconstruction.

The disruption of shot/reverse shots in the last section is one of the best-known scenes in the film. It is an example of the change from the particularity-coherence of subjectivity to generality-metaphorical meaning and later deconstruction produced by the alteration of the sequence of shot/reverse shots. The following analysis of *2001* has to be placed within the context of the ideas presented in the first part of the book, in their consideration of elements of particularity and generality.

Formalist Analysis

This section will include a description of the process of meaning-making through metaphor and through the alteration of spatial variables. Both involve the configuration of a text that demands the active participation of external elements, an idea that will be used to suggest the existence of paradigmatic relationships in film language, since external or absent elements are necessary to create signification. The section will end with a discussion of the self-conscious nature of *2001*, a conclusion reached by discovering traces of several narrative traditions that are made to coexist in a complex textual web. The externality of signification plus the self-consciousness inherent to the film will pave the way for the deconstructive reading in the second section.

The analysis of the film from a formalist point of view demands first of all a careful study of the many devices the text uses to create metaphorical meanings. We will also see how metaphor helps certain formal structures, such as subjectivity or externality, to work and therefore suggest meaning, too.

The alignment of the three planets at the beginning of the film is quickly transformed by the dynamics of the text's contents into a warning that a leap for humankind is about to take place. The monolith might also seem the cause of such a change. A later scene shows the ape touching the monolith as a mark for the beginning of the race's development. The monolith might be interpreted as an entity that provides the apes with a primitive form of intelligence that will lead them to use bones as weapons, to survive by killing their kind. This hypothesis is confirmed by the appearance of the monolith at the moment the ape starts to use the bone as a weapon.

The "Dawn of Man" section demands that the audience consider it a particularly metonymic attempt to advance the narrative. The audience is asked to interpret the events in this section as a brief, paradigmatic example of the evolution of humankind from prey to killer. This change results from the development of their intelligence to use objects for other purposes than those for which they are primarily supposed to be used. The apes are substitutes for an abstraction of the human race, and their actions are to be understood as hinting at the larger, complex process of evolution.

The match-cut on action that separates section one from section two links a bone with a spaceship traversing outer space. For Whittock, this is an example of explicit comparison between two elements whose similarities and differences are made to meet. Matching action is usually employed to make an unobtrusive join. Here the difference between the two objects is not unobtrusive but startling, the cut forcing the viewer to hypothesize the meaning of the textual decision to place such elements together (Whittock 1990, 51–52). The spaceship is made to acquire undertones of weapon, hinting at how the forms of aggression have changed and have turned more subtle although no less dangerous, as the computer HAL will later prove. It also suggests that the spaceship is the expression of human intelligence, even though this intelligence is not yet capable of understanding the mystery of the monolith. The outer-space dance in which the spaceship is introduced, to the accompaniment of Strauss's "Blue Danube," suggests the perfection of the life created by technology, at the same time linking art to such a technology through music: both are expressions of human refinement. In this case we face an example of synecdoche, where one part — the artistic beauty of dancing to the music — stands for another side of beauty: the beauty of technology and science. Another scene links Floyd's floating fountain pen to a previous external view of the spaceship in which he is traveling. The explicit comparison reinforces the idea that both pen — language, and by extension, art — and technology are proof of human development. Both are the product of human intelligence, and human creativity, and both share the same source: curiosity. What drove the ape to approach the monolith, and consequently to kill his kind, is now presented as also the origin of art: the curiosity that leads one to approach an already known reality from a different angle lies at the basis of art.

Once Floyd reaches the space station's hall he is framed in long shot, the frame including fragments of setting all around the character. This shot resembles those in the "Dawn of Man" section, where the apes appeared surrounded by their wild environment. The strategy of parallelism suggests the similarity between Floyd and the apes, stressing that, despite all its development, humankind is still contained and constrained by its environment, on which its life depends. No matter how much humans use and improve their intelligence there will always be phenomena they cannot understand, that remain larger than they are. The white color of the setting on the space station points in its consistency to the significance of white as a symbol. The connotations of purity traditionally associated with white are here modified, since, once we realize the cold personal relationships among the characters, it turns into expression of lack of humanity: the "dark" side of the perfect, flawless nature of emotional life. In the conversation with the Russians the viewer is given a brief example of the status of verbal language, which stands for the function of verbal language throughout the text. Such a vehicle of communication and expression of human feelings has become a mere object of empty formalism that only enables a superficial contact with other people. The conversation is a mere collection of greetings and a brief example of how Floyd uses language to conceal information from the Russians.

The lunar expedition to the monolith's crater leads to a view of Floyd approaching and touching the rectangular form in a way similar to that in which the ape did earlier in the film. Again, the parallelism describes Floyd as the representative of the evolution of humankind. The following cut to section three links Floyd to Frank Poole and David Bowman, as if passing on to them the function of representing the developed ape. Inside the *Discovery* we are given a shot of HAL's eye, on which we see reflected one of the men coming into the circular corridor through another door and corridor. This view of the man on the surface of HAL's eye provides the indication of HAL's capacity to focalize. This image is, however, provided by an external focalizer, the creator of the film's diegesis, which allows us to enter the world of events. Later, HAL is given the capacity to focalize internally, offering us wide-angle shots of the men that are meant to represent the distorted view of its circular eye. Although shots of the men externally reflected on HAL's eye are quickly replaced by internal focalization from HAL's position, its presence at the introduction of the machine suggests that the manipulative, external and cold way in which HAL is going to handle the men also exists in that first external focalizer that is the film creator of the diegesis, the extradiegetic narrative force. The link established between this external focalizer and the machine indirectly qualifies external focalization as an expression of dehumanization.

In a later scene the two men enter one of the ship's pods and cut off all communications with the computer HAL: they suspect a computer malfunction and decide to disconnect it if it continues to fail. The conversation is, however, being lip-read by HAL through one of the pod's windows. The shots that make clear to us that HAL is reading their lips are not wide-angle shots, as HAL's point of view has been presented so far, but shots of ordinary angle width, which points to the externality of focalization since they are supposed to be point-of-view shots from HAL's position. The machine is in control of the men because it is capable of being inside and outside itself, of thinking to itself and of saying a different thing to the outside in order to fool the crew. The machine withholds information from us and from Bowman, and focalization hints at the capacity of the machine to be uncommunicative. It also points out the capacity of two types of externality to suppress information: the externality of narration in film texts, and the externality that threatens not to allow us to discern the intricate meanings of *2001*.

The disconnection of HAL at Bowman's hands is a moment fraught with metaphorical meanings. The red chamber that contains HAL's brain units introduces a color we had only briefly seen in the ape's first carnivorous meal. Red, the color of blood, is intimately linked to bodily functions, in the case of HAL suggesting the presence of a more human kind of life than we had imagined. HAL's fear of disconnection is equated to the human fear of death, revealing the machine as capable of human feelings and reactions. HAL's disconnection makes it impossible for Bowman to continue his journey aboard the *Discovery*. He is forced to use a small pod in section four, where he will enter a world devoid of logic. HAL's disconnection, therefore, means the end of logic as we know it (Youngblood 1970, 140), Bowman's trip being one beyond logic, where no human mind can understand what is happening. The Stargate sequence provides an example of a metaphor achieved through the distortion of a given textual parameter. The way in which Bowman travels toward the infinite is staged through a hyperbolic rendering of perspectival lines of changing colors. Bowman's journey is presented as if its aim were the vanishing point of perspective, a point in an infinite dimension of space. The final shots present the symbol of the new baby, the Starchild. It represents, within the chain of meanings associated with previous metaphors, the possibility of a new human being possessing a new intelligence that can understand the new illogicality of space and time because they are perceived as changeable, rather than as coherent or immutable parameters.

The symbolic richness of the text has led critics to propose meanings for almost every element that appears in it. David Austen, in an article written the year the film was released, sees a reference to space in the "Blue Danube" theme: space is not blue but black in the film, and only the fantasy demanded by art can paint it blue for us. Richard Strauss's "Thus Spake Zarathustra" is the musical accompaniment for the alignment of the planets: the theme's title makes reference to Friedrich Nietzsche's theory of the arrival of the superman, whose coming would replace the old gods. It seems that the crucial moments when this music appears mark the steps toward the birth of a new human being who will be able to live in a world unknown to us. Accordingly, the film abounds in images of sexual/biological undertones, in images of copulation and giving birth. The film's title is for Austen a clear reference to Ulysses' voyage, suggesting theological connotations that are confirmed as the viewer proceeds through the text (1968, 24–27).

A relationship of similarity can be established between two components of a film through metaphor. This similarity may be suggested by various methods: for instance, by substituting one for the other. In *2001* it is not similarity but difference that is implied by substitution. We are given a multiplicity of parameters and rules associated with science in the film. Science has displaced romance, and this difference would seem to constitute the theme of the film; but in the end we are led to the mystery posed by the final scene, which has to be solved by proposing a metaphor. The final scenes in which we see Bowman looking involve the rupture of a textual rule that is capable of suggesting a meaning in the process. The structures of shot/reverse shot are altered here, creating a gap in the film's attempt to suture all traces of self-consciousness. This alteration works as a call to the viewers to elicit their active participation in the creation of meaning. We see how Bowman ages each time he looks offscreen: he sees himself gradually older in the shot that provides the object of his gaze, but the expected reverse shot in which we should see, from the standpoint of the new shot, the younger Bowman still looking at his older version shows no trace of the younger character. The subjectivity that is attributed to Bowman and that helps place the viewers with respect to such a production disappears, leaving the viewers as the only agents who have to place themselves. The text places the viewers in this active position because it wants to elicit a metaphorical meaning from the sequence's arrangement of variables: Bowman is undergoing some kind of transformation or development as a human being, which involves a change in his subjective capacity.

Another metaphorical process involves the production of meaning through the alteration of a rule previously established by the text. The new arrangement will first surprise the viewers and it will later ask them to explain it by providing it with a meaning. Section four of *2001* represents the disruption of the rule of objectivity that pervaded sections one and two, section three being an intermediate step toward the presentation of subjectivity in the last part of the film. The first two sections present the evolution of the apes and Floyd's journey through space from a distance, never allowing the viewer to share the perceptual position of the character on the screen. The last section places us in the position of Bowman as he traverses color-changing corridors into a new dimension. The scene in the room presents the film's turn to self-reflexivity. It reveals that traditional modes of focalization are not enough to understand that experience, and it therefore forces the critic and the viewer to search for metaphorical meanings: the scene expresses the human evolution to a new dimension where space and time have different natures from what we know.

This textual use of a metaphor implies that metaphor exists beyond the realm of comprehensible subjectivity, since the organization of shot/reverse shots the scene gives us is not coherent according to the rules of cinema. Metaphor transcends the strictures of the code of subjectivity. This insight can be linked to the assertion made in the first part of this book: that subjectivity always needs a certain metaphorical intervention to take place. This sequence is, therefore, only an attempt to expose the metaphorical nature of subjectivity and focalization. At the same time, it suggests that it is only by analyzing in depth, and by improving, the mechanisms of subjectivity that we can progress in the understanding of reality — of ourselves. Metaphor is confirmed to be a textual element that contributes to the effective configuration of subjectivity and meaning.

The final scenes inside the room mean a break with the previous coherent depiction of space and time. They reveal spatial and temporal ambiguity, since every new shot in the chain of shot/reverse shots introduces us to a new time — Bowman is older each time — and to a new space that does not include the character in the previous shot. The viewer's comprehension of the spatiotemporal variables is not complete, because they do not provide the coherence for which the viewer is constantly looking. This lack of coherence is, in fact, only a trace of the entrance into an illusory world, no longer understandable as possible (McKee 1969, 206). While the textual arrangement of the other sections helped in the construction of possible realities, we are now offered a section where the rules of space and time are different from the ones cinema has traditionally established. We are asked to infer that Bowman is now in a completely new world, for which we have no mental patterns that can aid our understanding. It is by creating this context that the idea of a jump into a new age of intelligence is conjured up. The lack of verbal language is also a rule that the text disrupts. In fact, the whole film contains so little dialogue that it represents a major divergence from the conventions of mainstream cinema. But even within the film the last section strikes us because of its complete lack of any kind of verbal language, not even the primitive collection of grunts the apes of the first section used to threaten the enemy. This fourth section is far more ambiguous than the other three, using ambiguity to allow viewers to posit their interpretations. The absence of language contributes to shaping a filmic fragment that demands a metaphorical interpretation in an attempt to create an open experience.

Another important method the text uses in its process of meaning-creation is the alteration of spatial variables, which suggests ideas about the relevance of such a narrative element as space. These ideas also derive from a metaphorical process of understanding the cues set out by space.

Certain scenes in the film create ambiguity about the origin of movement.[1] Narration is in part the creation of space; therefore, the origin and the workings of narration are rendered ambiguous. In the "Blue Danube" scene the camera movements and the movements of spaceships within the frame are staged to the rhythm of the music. Camera movements alternate between movement to the right and to the left, always showing the earth or the moon in the background — or tilting from one to the other — plus the spaceships usually moving in an opposite or oblique direction to that of the camera. At times it is difficult to distinguish whether it is the camera that is moving or the spaceship, when the background is the black backdrop of space. This difficulty produces ambiguity about the origin of movement and, therefore, about the origin of the creation of space through movement parallax. If narration is, in part, the creation of space, then the origin and the workings of narration are also ambiguous. The introduction to the following scene is similarly ambiguous. It starts with a fade-in from white. Something seems to be moving, but we do not know whether it is the camera panning or something in the mise-en-scène moving: it is a flat, plain white surface. In the end it turns out to be a sliding door that lets Floyd into the station.

During the trip to Clavius, and again to the music of "The Blue Danube," cinematic space is rendered relative. The flight attendant walks around the spaceship carrying food trays for the crew and the passengers. At one moment she walks along a corridor that places her upside down. She then walks into the cockpit this way, and the camera rotates upside down to place her in an upright position, the position the pilot and the copilot occupy. The "right" position of verticality is, therefore, questioned: the notion of verticality is relative in cinematographic space, it can be created and disrupted by the film's textual strategies.

During the *Discovery* sequences the artificiality of space in cinema is again pointed out. In one scene we see one of the characters shadowboxing as he runs along continuous circular corridor. A traveling movement of the camera, combined with slight reframing movements, keeps the man on the screen all the time. There is a certain divergence between the movements: of the man and that of the camera. The continuously progressing movement of the character can be rendered by a

---

[1] For an analysis of the film's ambiguity of time and space, see Falsetto (1991, 126–147).

slight movement of the camera. Continuous space can be rendered by cinema only as long as such a continuity is deceptive. In this case, the use of a continuous circular corridor and reframing create spatial continuity. Cinema's look of spatial continuity is only an illusion, made possible by restricting the reality it can offer us. The self-consciousness of the scene is evident, clearly laying bare the artificial nature of cinema's construction of space.

In the same scene the views resulting from such a placement of the camera render a frame crossed by oblique lines — the frame includes the continuous circular corridor — where the perspectival lines do not fade into the distance but seem to continue outside the sides of the frame. This is most important, since the rejection of single-source lighting creates a flat space that has to hand over to mise-en-scène and camera movement the creation of perspective. This scene introduces a variation on traditional linear perspective, while the Stargate sequence presents us with a flight toward the center of perspective, toward the vanishing point, in a metaphorical reference to the origin of everything, where humanity is going to travel beyond the infinite into a new dimension. Dave Bowman is reaching the source of everything, the eternal continuity, the vanishing point from which all space — equated to all life by the film — can be gazed upon.

Space is a major parameter in the configuration of film narratives. Together with time, it constitutes the basic pillar on which most accounts of cinematographic narration rest. Edward Branigan's *Narrative Comprehension and Film* (1992) outlines a view of filmic narration understood as the movement of reconciliation carried out by the text between the levels of screen and diegesis. Light and sound create systems of space, time, and causality that work on two levels: on a two-dimensional screen and as movement among objects in a story world (33–34). For Branigan narration is mainly a top-down phenomenon that relies on top-down processes of apprehending screen data followed by the viewer, processes that help organize screen material into story material, creating temporal and spatial systems: temporal continuity, ellipses, simultaneity, chains of spaces, spatial gaps, and so on. Top-down schemata are hypotheses set by the viewer about the development of the narrative in all its aspects; the confirmation or non-confirmation of these hypotheses helps the viewer make a coherent whole of the film. They are top-down because they work from the top, from the external activity of the viewer's attempt to understand the screen data provided by the film at the bottom. Impossible space is that which does not fit any of the spatial patterns, which cannot be justified as existing wholly within the diegesis. Impossible space produces perceptual problems of a kind that force the viewer to reconsider prior hypotheses about time and causality (39–43).

The previously discussed distortions of spatial variables that *2001* presents are, in a way, modifications of the kind of space usual top-down patterns accommodate within the viewer's set of expectations. They therefore produce alterations in the viewer's capacity to reconcile the systems of two-dimensional patterns of light and sound with the system of the story world, of the diegesis. They question the viewer's configuration of a coherent diegesis from the basis of screen data. The considerations about space and perspective in *2001*, and mainly its final attempt to reach the vanishing point of space, are an attempt to deconstruct such a notion of narration, since finding, or promising to find, such a vanishing point means the destruction of the perspectival pattern. This system of perspective assumes that lines within a shot should direct the viewer's attention toward a certain point, but they should not reveal such a point as proximate or knowledgeable. The existence of such a vanishing point is only useful inasmuch as it helps organize and distinguish the different planes of depth. The vanishing point is not important in itself; what is important is the organization of mise-en-scène elements it helps produce in the shot. The film's decision to open the possibility that such a vanishing point may become knowable and reachable is a tendency whose anti-narrative potential reveals the film's disruptive attitude.

The workings of space in *2001* make a self-conscious reference to the strategies of narration as exemplified by the more particular case of spatial configuration. They all point to the ambiguity and artificiality of narration and implicitly force the viewer to provide explanations for such divergencies from the traditional classical model of filmmaking. The film's handling of space draws attention to the development of such a variable throughout the film, making the subtitle *A Space Odyssey* relevant in its literal sense. The familiar, easily understandable spaces of "The Dawn of Man" section are quickly replaced by spaces that pose difficulties for the viewer's understanding and for the film's unobtrusive pretensions. If space is so relevant, the viewer is led to ask, in what ways does it create meaning? The answer is: by resorting to metaphor. The ambiguity and relativity of space exposed in sections two and three will be interpreted as the film's realization that in the world of technology human beings are only newcomers and that they have not yet grasped the intricacies of the new science simply because they lack the intelligence to do so — the intelligence to avoid being puzzled by an ambiguous space or by spatial positions that are not familiar. The new intelligence that is born in section four will be capable of accepting such ambiguities and relativity and, by exploring the origin of such spatial configuration (the vanishing point of perspective), will enter a new dimension where previous notions of space will be abandoned because they are old-fashioned.

The previous paragraphs have laid bare the film's internal structure of suggesting metaphorical meanings as its main source of signification. Metaphors usually require the breakdown of pre-established categories or patterns in order to signify. The rhetorical patterns set by individual films have to be altered in order to create a distortion that the viewer is asked to interpret metaphorically. Metaphors, therefore, express portions of reality that have not yet been explored by the film, where no set categories or patterns exist. Metaphors are necessary once a certain reality evolves and new signs are needed to denote it. A leap forwards in development demands new metaphors that can express the new situations (Whittock 1990, 7). In *2001* a new age of intelligence is born, its process and its result being conveyed to the viewer by means of metaphors of varying difficulty and subtlety. It is the unexplored nature of the new dimension the human being enters that most strongly needs metaphors in order to be patterned and understood; metaphors are needed to name the unnamable.

We have seen that metaphorical processes become important allies in the effective narrative workings of subjectivity, externality, space, self-consciousness, and, in general, in the creation of meaning. These textual strategies demand metaphorical processes that provide them with formal coherence and elicit a meaning. I would like to use this idea in the considerations that follow, as well as as a basis to be subverted in the second section, which is devoted to the deconstruction of the formal codes outlined by the text.

2001 is a peculiar film with respect to its consideration of metaphor. It is generally agreed that metaphors in cinema can be of many types, but that they are of such a nature that the audience's failure to identify them would not disturb its understanding of the film. Cinematographic metaphors are, therefore, supposed to be highly unobtrusive (Whittock 1990, 39). *2001* is a different case, since the demand for the viewer's activity of proposing metaphorical meanings is made in a highly obtrusive manner. The audience cannot fail to perceive the match cut from bone to spaceship, the strange presence of the monolith, or the distorted shot/reverse shots of the final scene. If the viewer does not propose meanings that provide the text with coherence, the film may become ambiguous or difficult to understand.

According to Branigan, narration in the visual arts consists in a process of positioning the viewer with respect to a production of space, subjectivity being the production of space attributed to a character (1984, 177). For him, a change in the elements of representation of subjectivity is to be interpreted as the appearance of a new level of narration. The disappearance of the origin of the gaze in Bowman's scene obviously cues the presence of a new level of narration where the viewer is asked to take part by proposing meanings such an alteration may suggest.

Daniel Dayan and Stephen Heath have written texts that have become emblematic in the field of subjectivity and its ideological connotations. Dayan's "The Tutor-Code of Classical Cinema" (1974) is a classic of film theory in its study of suture, and Heath's *Questions of Cinema* (1981) devotes a chapter to the same concept and its connections with Lacanian theory. Both agree that suture is the process of constructing a place for the subject by eliminating traces of self-consciousness in subjective sequences. Through the placement of the individual in an ideological system, the threat of self-consciousness that would do away with the illusion of reality and would highlight the manipulative potential of the cinema is avoided by introducing a new element that did not exist in the first shot: a second shot that justifies the presence of the previous one. Similarly, a stylistic structure whose meaning is not clear, which produces ambiguity and, therefore, runs the risk of being self-conscious, usually demands the intervention of a new element that provides it with meaning. This new element may be provided by the text or, in some cases, by the viewers' inference capacity, using their ability to create metaphors, and therefore meaning, from the textual material. In all of these cases the recourse the text demands is an element that has not been introduced yet, a new and external element. Therefore, meaning always derives from externality. Therefore, the ideological construction of texts always depends on externality, too: externality is a major force for the construction of ideological positions in texts. In *2001* this externality is present in the film through the metaphorical process demanded by the text.

For Christian Metz, connotation is homogeneous with denotation in films; the image predetermines the connotation to a great extent, whereas this is not so in more arbitrary, distant languages such as verbal language (1974, 82). The relationships *in praesentia* are so rich that they render the strict organization of *in absentia* relationships superfluous and difficult (69). The language of cinema is so rich that it contains its referents in the same denotative intention. What Dayan and Heath have said, however — Dayan said it in roughly the same years that Metz stated the previously mentioned ideas — is that the film text tends to resort to absent elements when it fails to provide itself with coherence. Such absent, external elements are quickly rendered internal and present in some cases, such as the second shot of a suturing shot/reverse shot sequence, but at other times the external elements remain external, as in the recourse to the viewer's capacity to elicit metaphors: the viewer and the last meaning suggested by the text are not present in the text. It seems that Metz's idea has to be reshaped to accommodate the possibility that an absent element might be essential for the construction of the text. This is the case in *2001*.

In Metz it seems as if the disregard of absent elements and the privileging of present ones is an argument that proves his more pervasive idea that film language lacks a language system. For him, films have realizations of language — present ones, in the text — but not a language system that, as do all linguistic systems, produces meaning by contrast between what appears in the text and what might have appeared (paradigmatic relationships), by the influence of what is not there in the text but belongs to the same category as what does appear, making it signify. I think the discussion of suture and my introduction to the interpretative function of the viewer reveal that absent elements are necessary for a coherent understanding of narrative films. The nature of these absent elements is not, in some cases, so close to that of the present elements as in the case of paradigmatic relationships in a linguistic system, but they are, nevertheless, absent elements giving meaning to present ones. In the case of the second element of a metaphor the difference is evident: the first element appears in the film — it possesses a materiality — while the second element only exists in the viewer's mind.

Therefore, structures such as suture and, in general, patterns that avoid self-consciousness, together with structures that elicit metaphorical meanings, create a certain linguistic system in film texts. This system is not as regulated as in the case of verbal language, but it is based on the same general principles. If *2001* presents us with a linguistic system based on absent elements, then this will involve the capacity of the system to be precise about its meanings through paradigmatic difference. But it will also involve the possibility that the constantly changing absent elements — in cinema the absent elements create rhetorics, not grammars — may destroy meaning. The change of context provided by those absent elements will produce a change of the meaning of the present ones, since meaning is produced by context. The discussion of absent elements has, therefore, revealed the nature of the cinematographic code: it possesses a capacity to systematize the production of meaning that is proximate to that of verbal language.

The study of metaphor, which has revealed its dependence on external, absent elements, is a proof of the concept stated in the first part of this book: the elements of generality are capable of creating meaning through metaphor, as well as of showing the instability of meaning. This concept will be further explored in the second part of the analysis of *2001*.

The function of metaphors is, therefore, in part to elicit the viewer's creativity and participation in the text. The degree to which a cinematographic text produces such an effect, together with the degree of ambiguity it exhibits, are two important parameters that contribute to defining a film as part of a specific narrative tradition. I would now like to undertake a brief discussion of the film as containing elements from diverse narrative traditions, with the resulting self-consciousness this diversity involves. *2001* lacks the depth of psychological definition of character, the presentation of the clear origin of its conflict and the unambiguous resolution of the plot classical films possess. Unlike in classical films, stars are not the principal causal agency, since the characters are impersonated by relatively unknown actors and actresses. Classical films are organized around a deadline, which produces a temporal pattern where the end is going to provide meaning and narrative coherence to the whole film. *2001* moves forward, but it is not until the end that we learn what the aim of the mission is; and the end remains ambiguous or allows for multiple speculations. The various sections do not provide the viewer with enough information to discern any deadline, since events evolve without any apparent aim. It is usually after the events take place that their possible aim is suggested. The linearity of classical films is altered by several leaps in time, one marked by a match-cut, others by titles that introduce the individual sections.

Narration in *2001* is omniscient and self-conscious but not highly communicative. The classical style presents a narration where film technique is only a vehicle for the transmission of information. In *2001* film technique is not only a vehicle, it becomes itself the object of attention for the viewer — film technique becomes spectacle. In classical narration, style encourages the spectator to build a coherent time and space for the action. In our film, style at times works to make the construction of such a space and time difficult. This is because temporal and spatial ellipses sometimes confuse the viewer about the true temporal and spatial coordinates in which the story is taking place.

Classical style is geared to the depiction of characters and their actions. Shot format, three-point lighting, continuity editing, etc., are all meant to privilege the construction of character and action. *2001* seems more interested in the machine, in long shots and long takes, flooding light and shining colors. It seems to be consistent with its own rules of perspective, space, and style, rather than with its thematic patterns. *2001* contains traces of art-cinema narration. It admits and depicts the ideas that the world may not be knowable and that personal psychology may be indeterminate — here it is overwhelmed by the machine. It attempts to depict both climactic and trivial moments in the same manner. A great deal of time is devoted to actions that do not seem to have much narrative relevance: the replacement of the malfunctioning unit on the *Discovery* takes up a great deal of screen time, for instance. The realism obtained is of a different kind from that of classical narration. Here we find a text that confers a great importance on the performance of actions, no matter what those actions may mean. The strategy seems to hint at the film's pervading enthusiasm about film style in itself.

The tight causality of classical narration is replaced by a more tenuous linking of events that is even emphasized by the presence of causal gaps. Viewers are not allowed to know the real causal connections among the sections, or even the cause of many events that they see evolve on the screen. The monolith provokes a causal gap throughout the text, one the viewer is asked to bridge by providing the slab with a meaning. The bone-spaceship match-cut does not provide a causal link, either, and the cause of the *Discovery*'s mission is not hinted at until HAL is disconnected and the videotape informs us and Bowman of it. The partial absence of deadlines does away with the possible temporal tightness and coherence they produce.

Omniscience and knowledgeability — basic pillars of classical narration — are here subverted. The text focuses on the limitations of character knowledge, which is also made extensive to the audience, not allowing the viewer to realize the full meaning of the text. The main theme of the film is the imperfect nature of human intelligence, which is conveyed by restricting both the characters' and the audience's access to the real meaning of the quest we are shown.

Style gains a prominence typical of art-cinema narration. Mise-en-scène is a clear example, where the spectacularity of special effects manages on its own to present the viewer with an interesting visual experience. Style is also foregrounded in the case of the focalization techniques used in the last section. Overt narrational commentary, containing a high degree of self-consciousness, is present in these cases, shaping a text whose artificial status is constantly laid bare. Consequently, the textual demand for explanations from the viewers elicits their process of understanding about the way in which the textual material has been shaped. Self-consciousness about the communicative process is evident in *2001*, where the development of the text does not seem certainly to direct us to clear-cut conclusions. The open end, therefore, finally confers on it an aura of irresolution. The staging of the movements of spaceships and planets to the rhythm of "The Blue Danube," and the impossible shot/reverse shots of the final sequence are other examples of the film's self-consciousness. The art-film aspects of this narrative demand a high-level interpretation that can solve the problems of causality, time, and space posed by the text: in this case this higher level demands a metaphorical interpretation.

2001 also possesses features of historical-materialist narration. It treats the text as both a narrative and an argument, narration turning into rhetoric. The signifying intention of every element we have discussed so far is proof enough of the way in which this film uses its elements to build up arguments. The match-cut is a good example of how the film suggests the viewer's reflection on the evolution of the human being and of that being's capacity to create and use tools. In the course of the film the characters lose the uniqueness characters have in classical or art-cinema narratives and become prototypes of groups. The apes are a clear representation of primitive humankind, Floyd of the human being in charge of technology, and the *Discovery*'s crew of that dominated by it, both types of modern humankind being, in fact, unaware of the real implications of the systems they have created.

The film makes extensive use of intellectual montage. The "Dawn of Man" section, the scenes with the monolith, and the final section are examples of how editing serves the purpose of placing side by side images that may elicit ideas or propose arguments in the way the text wishes to present them. The film follows a typical structure of *roman à thèse,* portraying the human being's apprenticeship, which is also a typical feature of historical-materialist narration. We are shown how the human moves from ignorance to knowledge and from passivity to action until Bowman finally enters the new dimension of intelligence, the acquisition of this new intelligence being presented by the text as the culmination of the human process of improvement. Viewers are also included in the apprenticeship, since the film withholds information and prevents their complete understanding of its plot and meaning. The ending seems to promise such a clarification, but the demand on the viewer's participation is so strong that the film's final meaning becomes a matter of mere supposition. As I have already remarked, the text's rhetorical aim allows it to defamiliarize classical norms of space and time in an attempt to produce meaning. The narrational process becomes quite overt as the film employs tropes that suggest meanings through metaphors or similes: the bone and the monolith have already been analyzed with this function.

Finally, *2001* also contains certain formal aspects that qualify it as, in part, an example of parametric narration. The lack of dialogue cannot be missed by any viewer accustomed to traditional narratives where dialogue is an important element to transmit information about characters and events. The radical divergence in this respect from such traditional narratives — in *2001* there are even two sections that do not use any dialogue at all — makes the appearance of dialogue acquire a saliency that the text chooses to employ to mark the relevance of certain fragments. Thus, Floyd's verbal interchanges are foregrounded, as well as the conversation among the crew members and HAL aboard the Discovery. Apart from the signification we may perceive in these scenes, they are clearly made to stand out because of the presence of verbal language. The film's attempt to foreground these middle sections suggests comparisons with the sections devoid of verbal language: the really important changes in the history of humankind are portrayed in the sections where verbal language does not appear; it seems as if the expression of human contact and affection verbal language allows is not considered important for human development.

The fact that the film contains so many elements that can be ascribed to narrative traditions different from classical cinema transforms the text into a self-conscious exercise, constantly eliciting the viewer's activity of distinguishing its intricacies and subtle meaningful differences. This process of constant address to the viewer contains strong ideological connotations. According to Bill Nichols, such processes place the subject in the position desired by the text, making the viewer accept the ideological assumptions implicitly or explicitly expounded in the film. This process is the way in which the social system attempts to tie the subject to the relationships that most favor the interests of the system (1981, 34).

Perspective is one of the most powerful mechanisms cinema possesses in order to establish such an ideological system. Through the setting of perspectival lines the text places the subject in an ideal position for the apprehension of the image. Perspective is an active strategy in the ideological process of inscription of the subject (Nichols 1981, 52–57). Ideology represents subjectivity as a state of continuous self-apprehension in order to subject the individual to meanings that perpetuate the social structure (Cohan and Shires 1988, 133–136). The final scene of *2001* destroys such a continuity of subjectivity, laying bare the system of formal design necessary to create it. The last scene is, therefore, revealed to be ideologically subversive.

Subjects are ideologically sutured to the text by placing them in a position created by the text. This position is not occupied in the text by the viewer but by a signifier (Cohan and Shires 1988, 162). In the last scenes of *2001* this signifier — Bowman — disappears and is transformed into the object observed. The disappearance of the signifier shatters the ideological workings of suture, revealing the ideological process at work in subjectivity and hinting that in the new dimension of subjectivity it will be more difficult to dominate subjects through textual mechanisms. The process of suture is exposed, laying bare the artificiality of narration and breaking the ideological illusion that sustains the state of affairs set by the text. A way out of ideological attempts to oppress the subject, therefore, starts by creating a certain awareness in the viewer about the formal structure of a work.

Narratives explain, and in the process solve, contradictions, usually through the interaction of their formal elements. The arrangement of events amounts to their explanation, in the sense that they provide reasons why the final events are the outcome of earlier actions (Nichols 1981, 76). This takes us back to the Hegelian idea that a work of art's form is able to recover the lost harmony that stems from the contents or the social place of such a work in its historical time (Eagleton 1976, 73). *2001* says that human beings are unable to understand the universe because of their restricted knowledge. This lost capacity cannot be recovered by the film's formal design, in part because analysis reveals that such a formal design is at times subverted. These considerations will lead us to alternative approaches to the film, as we will see in the second part of this analysis.

As a conclusion, it can be said that the analysis of metaphor has disclosed its importance as both creator of meaning and support for formal structures. Subjectivity, externality, space, and self-consciousness demand the intervention of a metaphorical process that can provide them with consistency. Self-consciousness has led us on to the study of the film as a reflexive text, in its mixture of various narrative modes and traditions. The self-consciousness inherent in metaphorical processes in this text lays bare its ideological intentionality. The analysis of formal structures was based on metaphors, whose self-conscious nature has been revealed as a hint at the pervading self-consciousness of the film, with the ideological connotations this suggests. Section one has, therefore, contributed an exemplification of the workings of elements of generality.

Self-consciousness, Deconstruction

This section is a continuation of the study of the text stemming from the basic conclusions reached in section one: that the film privileges elements of externality/generality. In section two the study of subjectivity, space, and the instability of meaning will reveal how the film is invariably based on elements of generality. I will first discuss the implications of self-consciousness understood as the internal reflection of the film on its own narrative mechanisms.

The considerations of perspective of *2001* suggest a discussion of narration, since the arrangement of elements in the frame, following the dictates of perspective, allows the creation of coherent space where the narrative is to be developed. In cinema coherent space is a central tool of narration, since it allows the viewer quickly to acquire information about the positions of the characters in the space they inhabit. The search for the center of perspective is a search for the origin of narration, narratives, or texts. The film tells us that the origin of narratives lies precisely in what they search for, in the element outside the narrative they try to reach and around whose search the complex structures of narrative evolve and map out the backbone of a story. The rest of the story is filled in by distensions and retardations (Barthes 1989a, 288–292).

It is the search for what cannot be reached that moves the narrative onward. *2001* entertains the possibility that such a goal may be achieved but only in an unknown dimension, where time and space are understood differently. *2001* links this final reading of the goal with the passage onto a new stage of human intelligence, hinting that in this new stage narratives as we know them will have been left behind because they will no longer have the impossible goal as their motor force: Bowman will then be capable of living without narratives, because he will know everything. This idea is suggested by attacking the origin of coherent space, an attack on an element of particularity in order to suggest a metaphor, a product of the effect of generality. Space is transformed from an aspect of particularity into an aspect of generality.

The reflection on perspective is linked to the reflection on subjectivity the film carries out in its development from sections one and two to four through three, which the film's dynamic transforms into a reflection on the necessity of narratives in the dimension of a new intelligence. In section four, the text demands a great active participation of the viewer to propose hypotheses about the meaning of the altered shot/reverse shots. The subjectivity of the Stargate sequence ends up in this alteration. The text reflects on the necessity of subjectivity for the creation of narratives, especially in the case of cinematographic narratives where focalization is a major way of creating meaning. The culmination of the film's process with respect to subjectivity really occurs in the Stargate sequence, where Bowman's eye reflects the changes of color of the space he traverses. The viewers' perception of such a change of color provides them with the real meaning of the experience: the change of humanity as it enters a new space of unknown tonalities. The following altered shot/reverse shot sequence points to a new stage of subjectivity that this new dimension demands. In this new dimension the function of subjectivity as an element that provides temporal and spatial coherence will have to be changed, suggesting that narratives will not be necessary. Bowman's fast aging is only a hint at the transformation of narrative and, therefore, of subjectivity in the new dimension. Again, the change from the spatial coherence inherent to subjectivity is changed into a disruption of space that renders subjectivity self-conscious, therefore claiming for it the status of creator of metaphors. This is another example of the textual attempt to transform elements of particularity into elements of generality.

The process of resorting to metaphors that was traced in previous pages, following the demands made by the text on the viewer, also foregrounds the process of creation of narratives. As has already been remarked, filmic narration relies on a constant dynamic of proposing metaphors to bridge the meaning gaps with which the texts present the viewer. It has also been mentioned that even the process of subjectivity is ultimately the metaphorical process of attributing an image to a character's gaze, the viewer providing the link with the aid of the text's formal parameters.

The fact that the last section of *2001* can only be accommodated into the viewer's schemes by providing a metaphorical meaning for it is proof of the film's refusal to include the possibility of the text's own redundancy and destruction — which is what this fourth section suggests. The insistence on providing a text with meaning points out the essential function of meaning as cover for structure, content appearing as a mechanism that conceals the workings of structure (Barthes 1980, 107). The use of metaphorical meaning by the viewer provides the sequence with a meaning, however ambiguous it may seem. The process of accommodating the fragment within a possible interpretation of the whole film is, in fact, a self-conscious process of justifying the presence of a structure of space and looks that seems strange to the viewer. If the viewer were not capable of investing the structure with any meaning, this would be highly obtrusive, since the film clearly plays with space and shot/reverse shot rules in ways not advanced by previous cinematographic narrative modes.

The constant positing of hypotheses for metaphors is the result of human curiosity, which needs information to be satisfied. This curiosity is in *2001* the origin of technology, art, and also of death. It was curiosity that led the ape to touch the monolith, that turned the bone into a weapon, that created technology and finally art and language — remember the metaphor of the fountain pen. The film is telling us that such a curiosity is inherent to human beings, and that it is at work in all aspects of their lives since narratives can only exist when the subject lacks some knowledge and wants to acquire it. The new dimension without narratives will also involve the lack of curiosity, but a lack of curiosity because the human being will be more knowledgeable than it is now. The text exemplifies how even in those cases in which a narrative wants to express the death of narratives and, therefore, a new step into non-representation, the text has to use the traditional tools and resort to the traditional force of narrative: the viewer's/reader's curiosity.

Space, as has been previously discussed, is relative in the film, and only continuous because cinema can manipulate it and restrict the reality it offers us. Those scenes in which we analyzed the relativity of film space reveal the cinematographic manipulation carried out by film to create the illusion of continuity. Continuous space in cinema is always the product of masking and joining discontinuity. *2001* lays bare this process of creation of continuous space. In fact, this self-consciousness is only part of the reflection on narrative, now associated with the creation of space. The self-consciousness of the device reveals to the viewer that space is a tool the text uses to reflect on narrative and narration. The search for the origin of space will, therefore, be the search for the origin of narration, as has already been seen. And the spatial discontinuities of Bowman's last scenes will be marks of the disassembling of traditional narrative modes in the passage to the new dimension.

In the process of understanding of narratives the reader/viewer oscillates between the configuration of an illusion of coherence and the breaking of such construction. If the readers were to achieve a balance, they would obviously no longer be engaged in the process of establishing and disrupting consistency. The inherent lack of balance is a prerequisite for the very dynamism of the operation. *2001* is a film where such a balance is not clearly accessible to the viewer even at the end of the narrative, since the text does not provide a completely trustworthy meaning-making closure.

Bordwell's account of the viewer's activity of filmic perception is helpful at this point, since it describes such an active function of the viewer in the understanding of films. For Bordwell, perceiving and thinking are active, goal-oriented processes. The subject acquires and constructs a series of schemata that help and direct the subject's processes of inference making. Inferences may be obtained through what he calls bottom-up processes, where conclusions are reached on the basis of perceptual data, or through top-down ones, where the organization of data is determined by expectation, background knowledge, problem-solving techniques, and other schemata. Perception in cinema consists in the identification of a three-dimensional world on the basis of cues. The search for information and its accommodation work by including each new element as part of a certain kind of textual motivation: compositional (relevant to the story), realistic (similar to reality), transtextual (elements typical in a genre), and artistic (for its own sake) (1988, 33–40).

2001 is a film text that constantly draws attention to the workings of this perceptual process and the schemata set out by traditional films. The film may, however, be argued to be more than merely self-conscious, since it possesses elements that point to themselves with an explicit or implicit intention of suggesting a reflection on the mechanisms of narration. The film, in its rejection of dialogue and its privileging of visuals, is, in fact, privileging spectacle; but in a way this self-conscious rendering of the fabula also draws the viewer's attention to the spectacular nature of cinema and criticizes it. Such spectacular visuals are qualified by the text as only an extension of the bone-weapon used by the ape: humankind has not evolved in any other way toward understanding; it is still unable to understand itself or the universe that surrounds it. Such a questioning of the film's components is typical of metafiction. Metafiction self-consciously draws attention to its status as artifact and in providing a critique of its own methods examines the structures of narratives, at the same time exploring the possible fictionality of the world outside the fictional text (Waugh 1984, 2).

Such textual reflection on its own narrative components is present throughout. The last scenes, in which we see the alteration of focalization structures, attack the conventions of filmic realism. If realism is understood as a medium that conceals the mechanisms of oppression, naturalizing them, this last sequence is self-consciously destroying such an ideological process. This sequence is asking viewers to question themselves about the ways in which illusionism works in cinema, making us accept the irrational by demanding that we provide it with meaning. Also, it exposes how cinema constructs subjectivity as a key element to dominate the subject ideologically, making the individual adopt a predetermined place. In the process of showing us Bowman's aging as a conscious process for him, we also become aware of how such a process is imposed on us as viewers, how the presentation of a text demands our participation, and how in that participation the seed of naturalized oppression may also exist.

The lack of an authoritative omniscient author contributes to creating a world where eternal verities no longer exist, but only a series of constructions, of temporary structures. The film's almost exclusive reliance on the visual side of cinema, together with the lack of verbal language, leave the viewers alone to discern the relevant information out of what is offered to them. The scenes in the "Dawn of Man" section, for instance, stage actions that the viewer is asked to decodify without the help of verbal language. The process of evolution the apes go through has to be understood and explained by interpreting the visual cues offered by the film.

2001 is self-reflexive in its strict dependence on visual material, yet it demands from the viewer the capacity to propose metaphorical meanings, thereby making the viewer explicitly acknowledge the self-reflexive nature of the text. The paradox of metafiction is that the metafictional text is both self-reflexive and still oriented outward, toward the reader/viewer (Hutcheon 1991, 7). *2001,* being a fantastic film, is intrinsically metafictional, since fantasy constantly elicits the reader's/viewer's act of imagining the world, of giving form to the signifieds suggested through the symbolic, iconic language that makes up the text. The demands for temporal and spatial coherence made by the fantastic text are, in fact, paradigmatic of the imaginative leaps in time and space required in the understanding of any fictional work (Hutcheon 1991, 76–81). This particular film, however, makes strong demands on the viewer in the construction of space, time, and logical causality; and its reliance on visual language, with the ambiguity it produces, extends these demands to limits unusual even for fantastic texts.

The "Dawn of Man" section shows how apes have to use bones for purposes different from those for which they are primarily created. They have to recognize in the bones a different function from the usual one. This process is the same the text demands from the viewer, who is asked to interpret the section metaphorically, not for what is presented but for what it means. In this sense the section is enacting the same process it demands from the viewer. The section is aware of its belonging to a code that needs decoding in order to signify.

I will now attempt to dismantle the structural forms that were discussed in section one. Here, other structures will be seen to appear, while those that existed (metaphor, externality, space) provide clues that offer a different perspective on their capacity to signify. This part should be taken as a discussion exemplifying the possibilities for deconstruction offered by the construction of meaning effected through the elements of generality. Such a construction of meaning is based on an external element, the viewer, that simultaneously brings about the instability of meaning.

2001 contains elements that reveal the textual attempt to create a purely structural logic that the film is going to follow. The use of space in the text is an exploration of all the possibilities offered for its configuration. The film varies from the natural space of the "Dawn of Man" section to the artificiality and cinematographic construction of sections two and three, where settings and complex special effects create a perfect space out of technology, and finally to the impossible space of the shot/reverse shots in Bowman's last scenes. The text seems to have engaged in a dynamic of exploration of the different possibilities available for the shaping of space. The textual evolution seems as important as the contents it partially helps to depict.

The four parts of the text are separated by temporal ellipses. These ellipses are gradually shorter, culminating in the final Stargate sequence, which starts almost after the third section ends. It seems as if these gradually shorter ellipses are fulfilling a logic of their own that is going to culminate in the last scenes. The shot/reverse shot sequence of the aging Bowman is a mixture of short and long temporal ellipses, taking us to a new temporal dimension where time is both long and short at once. Bowman gets old in each shot, but the logic of suture demands a spatial contiguity that seems to secure temporal succession, too. This sequence means the culmination of temporal expectancy for the end. Ellipses are paradigmatic of particularity-coherence. Here they are made to suggest such long or illusory passing of time that they are turned into the source of metaphorical meanings: the first ellipsis takes us from the primitive human to the age of spaceships, the film implying that the time is different but the relationship of human beings to its tools is not, since machines are still likely to react against them. The second ellipsis introduces us to the *Discovery*: while we understand the relevance of the machine, HAL, we are not offered information about the purpose of the journey, and therefore we are not allowed really to understand the meaning of the computer. The third ellipsis is again supposedly leading us to the resolution and final understanding, while in fact it only opens the door to more ambiguity. The alteration of temporal structures results in meaning. Yet the reference which is made here to ellipses returns them to their status as creators of temporal coherence, a coherence that is, however, only structural.

Sound also contains a certain structural logic. In the first section the apes make noises while eating. The last section shows how Bowman eats: we hear him eating proper food again. It is this logic of sounds produced by bodily functions that is created and fulfilled by the text. The return to the sound of eating suggests our need to retain our human nature in order to cross to the age of new intelligence. The loss of human nature seen in sections two and three is not an asset for the development into the new dimension. Also, dialogue is absent in sections one and four, but present, although scarcely, in sections two and three, confirming again that verbal language has become, in the internal code of the film, a sign of mere formality among people, not of real human contact. Verbal language separates speakers instead of bringing them together.

A similar development can be perceived in the use of props the men handle, tools that help the men with their everyday tasks. From the ape's use of the bone as a weapon we have to wait until the end to see the old Bowman eating with a proper knife and fork. Sections two and three show men who only handle machines, panels full of lights and buttons with no direct effect on the most human aspects of their lives. If we look at figure expression and movement, the crouched posture of the apes does not reappear until the final view of the Starchild. The logic of repetition is fulfilled at the end of the film.

So far we have found several elements of the text that create a structural logic fulfilled before the text finishes. According to Roland Barthes, the text creates its own logical time, formed by structures that aspire to close themselves and that admit distensions and inserts in the process, therefore extending the length of the narrative. The most important process at work in the text is the opening and closing of formal structures, what he calls the adventure of language (1989a, 295). *2001* is a film where the setting out of formal structures is evident, as has been briefly discussed above. We can perceive that there is a logic of formal elements that in a way parallels the narrative of contents.

In *S/Z* (1980) Barthes argues that creating a story does not involve conveying contents but elaborating a textual form that maintains the mystery and curiosity throughout the story. Narration consists in the organization of form so that it maintains the necessary suspense (51). Denotation is not the truth of discourse, it is not outside structure, but it has a structural function similar to the other elements. Denotation is superimposed on the narrative structures, and justifies the rule of structure. The search for meaning manages to draw the viewer's attention away from the workings of structure. Does this happen in *2001*? Yes, it does, but not completely. The difficulty posed by the text with respect to its meaning conceals the workings of the magnificent visual material that is presented to us, but at the same time such visual material is emphasized.

Barthes studies *Sarrasine* as the disappearance of paradigmatic op-posites, which create meaning. The absence of opposites in language, in gender, and in the economy of the body makes representation impossi-ble (180–181). In the last scene with Bowman the character is both ob-server and observed, something impossible within the system of cinematographic subjectivity outlined in shot/reverse shots. In this sense he is also the representative of the destruction of opposites. The system of representation of point of view — focalization — is subverted here, laying bare the incapacity of cinematographic language to express this new stage that leads to a new development of humankind. This fi-nal scene can be linked to *S/Z*, since both share a similar destruction of opposites that questions representation. At a more general level we can say that *2001* breaks the distinction between traditional narrative and spectacle: the brilliant nature of the visual spectacle becomes the real content of the text. Viewers are baffled by the difficulty the text pres-ents, by the constant textual demand that they propose metaphorical meanings. The enjoyment of the purely visual/aural side of the text seems easier, once the text shows that the signifier is just as important as the signified. For Barthes the pleasure of the text consists in the shifting of the emphasis from the contents to the form, the signifier be-coming preeminent. This emphasis on the signifier may become dis-ruptive for language if it destroys the consistency of the text and the metalanguage that gives authority to the text. *2001* may be seen as part of a textual dynamic that privileges the signifier over the signified, where visual richness becomes the rule of the text.

This turn from the text as set of structures to text as the realm of spectacle can be proved through a study of the capacity of the film's textual visual/aural material to disrupt the construction of meanings through metaphors. The accumulation of special effects that build up a perfect world of outer-space life creates in the viewer the expectation that the text will continue to astonish the audience through a wonder-ful display of mise-en-scène artificiality. The film addict usually remem-bers this film as a difficult text with respect to its meaning, but also as a brilliant collection of surprising images opening a window onto the mysterious beauty of space. The film privileges long shots over other methods of presenting space. Long shots favor an external view on the contents of the frame, presenting them as prone to metaphor and dis-semination of meaning. The baffling visual/aural experience makes it difficult for the viewer to pay attention to the proposal and development of metaphors. The amount of information is too large for the viewer to be able to concentrate on everything.[2]

Certain metaphors, the film suggests, are easy to grasp by the viewer, particularly those that imply an explicit comparison between two elements (match-on-action bone-spaceship, pen-spaceship), synecdoches (lack of human contact stands for lack of human feelings, the "Blue Danube" dance), objective correlatives (HAL as logic), symbols (alignment of planets, color white, color red). Other metaphors are, however, too problematic to be apprehended unambiguously: those that stem from parallelisms face the difficulty that the great amount of spectacular information might not allow the viewer to realize the aspects that are made the object of parallelism. The long shot of Floyd is difficult to associate with the apes in section one, and the link Floyd-ape as both touch the monolith is also difficult since the screen-time separation between the two actions is quite long.

Metaphors that are created through rule disruption and distortion are also problematic, since they depend on the viewer's awareness of the rule to be later disrupted or distorted. The disruption of the rules of suture, of a coherent expression of space, of dialogue (lack of it), of objectivity, all depend on the viewer's capacity to realize the difference once a new state is introduced. Furthermore, these more "difficult" metaphors do not work with specific representations of objects or men as much as the others do. Previous metaphors depend to a great extent on the physicality exhibited by the images. This physicality makes the signs of those metaphors more prone to establish a logic of spectacle based on the beauty, the technical perfection, the eeriness of the images. The "difficult" metaphors are much less prone to such spectacular dynamics. Therefore, the "easy" metaphors are more dependent on the visual quality of the material, more prone to spectacle even though they may be understood unambiguously; while the "difficult" ones may create ambiguity as to their meaning. Both kinds of metaphors are therefore problematic, since a sign embedded in a chain of spectacle does not secure its final arrival at the exact meaning it may want to communicate.

For Cohan and Shires (1988), a text creates meaning through oppositions, producing metaphors, metonymies, and sets of oppositions. But a linguistic system may be altered by discourse and context, there-

---

[2] Other films seem to owe to *2001* part of their attempts to present a striking view of an impossible world through the use of special effects, long shots, etc. The *Star Wars* trilogy, the *Alien* films, *Blade Runner,* and in general all modern science fiction and futuristic fiction of the Arnold Schwarzenegger kind.

fore being unable to fix meaning, or creating other meanings not expected by the text. Accordingly, this study of *2001* includes two parts, one where the sets of meanings created by structures (including a formal study of the film) are provided, which have been explained in the section on metaphor, and a second one, which follows, where the ambiguities and alterations the text may produce are explained.

The potential failure to understand the full meaning of the match-on-action bone-spaceship may cause difficulty in understanding the relevance of the parallelisms between section one and the rest of the sections. It prevents an understanding of the relevance of technology as both aid and weapon that may rebel against humankind. If viewers fail to understand the connection between the pen and the spaceship they miss all the dimensions of technology as related to art, plus all the self-reflection inherent in the text. The failure to grasp the rule-disruption metaphors leads the viewer to miss the implications of the last section, the view of the Starchild as the first specimen of a new dimension of human intelligence. If viewers do not understand the parallelisms they are bound to miss the idea that the human race, for all its technology, has not evolved as much as we think from the times of the ape. Finally, the symbols also convey essential meanings. Otherwise viewers would miss the meaning of the monolith as warning, as giver of intelligence: they would miss the idea of lack of humanity in spaceships plus the presence of humanity in the computer HAL, which represents the culmination of dehumanization, a state that has to be remedied by the jump into the new dimension.

In fact, this possibility of lack of understanding exists because the whole system of signification set by the film relies on the proficient work of an external agent: the decodifying viewer. This is an aspect of cinema that has already been commented on several times here, but *2001* makes such an extensive use of it that the whole meaning and structure of the text is made dependent on an external agent to such a great extent that its status becomes especially relevant for our study. Eagleton uses Macherey's idea that the task of the critic is to analyze what the text says and what it silences in order to expose the conflict inherent in the text and how it is produced by its relation to ideology (1976, 34–35). In *2001* we have a textual demand for the participation of the viewer to give a meaning to the text. This is, in fact, a way of inscribing the viewer into the ideology of the text. The emphasis on the visuals and the privileging of spectacle may, however, be understood as a way of shattering this ideological construction.

Jacques Derrida has defined a term that can be used to explain this phenomenon: the parergon. The parergon or frame is what bounds the picture and makes what is inside acquire a significance by contrast with what frames it. It is a concept that comes close to that of the signature: it needs repetition to ensure its capacity to signify. But repetition itself reveals the absence of a signifying intention (Brunette and Wills 1989, 108). In the case of suture, as we have already remarked, the presence of an offscreen character needs to confirm itself repetitively to be meaningful. Its absence creates a disruption of the code that is inherent in the workings of such a presence of a character. It contains disruptiveness in its very essence.

Paradoxically, what is outside confers a meaning on what is inside, since in the case of *2001* it facilitates the arrival of the textual possibilities of meaning. The intervention of the viewer is so often demanded that it becomes a key figure in the narrative organization of the film. Such an external element, the viewer, is in this case subject to many variables and possible contexts, which make it difficult to assure that the understanding of the film is going to be coherent or unique.

I would now like to discuss the relevance of the multiplicity of meaning and of the ambiguity that, in my opinion, are present in *2001*. The outside position of the viewers constructed by the film is mainly achieved, as we have said, by the constant demand that they propose meanings. The instability produced by the possibility of plurality of meaning is, therefore, derived from the idea of the parergon applied to *2001*. The text makes use of its dependence on the viewer for the configuration of a final meaning, exploiting it and laying such a dependence bare by suggesting several possibilities for the ending. I will now study the ways in which the film suggests such a plurality of meaning, in an attempt to explain the deconstructive force the text contains — deconstruction being understood as the denial of a single meaning. Also, the film's occasional evolution into ambiguity is another way of destroying meaning, since it seems to deny the possibility that the viewer may obtain an ultimate meaning from the text.

According to Robert Phillip Kolker (1988), *2001* has two sides. It is a spectacular experience in which the viewer is assaulted by an endless array of visual data, and it is also a cold inquiry into the implications of technology and the future of the human being. The first side of the film produces ambiguity, since the text makes no demands on the viewers for them to suggest possible meanings. It lures the audience into a world of enjoyment of the beauty and perfection of technology, relieving the viewer of the responsibility to understand it. The visual is perceived as attractive but lacking in accessibility to its ultimate origin or meaning. Ambiguity, therefore, provokes passivity, confirming the viewer's secure subject position by suggesting that there is nothing to be understood in the text. The second side of the film produces multi-plicity of meanings or open-endedness, requiring that viewers be able to pattern and unify the text according to the clues they are given. It demands that viewers place themselves in various subjective positions and that they recognize the formal processes of textual construction, an activity we have already discussed. These textual demands on the viewer construct an emotionally distant subject, more attentive to form and patterns than ready to identify with the characters (115–116).

The film's potential to suggest ambiguity is easily discerned, since most viewers' first reaction to the text is an enthusiastic involvement in the richness of visual detail and the complexity of the technology it presents. The scarce narrative information, the lack of verbal language that might clarify the relevance of what appears on the screen draws audiences to become quickly engaged in the enjoyment of its spectacular depiction of space and technology. Also, the contents that may be inferred through this scarce narrative information seem to suggest the human subjection to a higher power that leaves no room for individual, uncontrolled action. The abandonment both to the existence of a superior entity controlling humankind and to the overwhelming visual experience may lead the viewer to think that the film is not capable of providing a meaning and may, therefore, discourage any search for it. The film ends up being understood as an antirational approach to the mysteries of space, technology, and the future.

This consideration of the film suggests its proximity to other concepts outlined by Derrida. The many long descriptions of actions that do not resort to ellipses in screen time point to their status as distensions, delays set by the text in its formal process of patterning toward closure. Brunette and Wills would see similarities between these distensions and the delays that they describe as the cause of adestination. Communication is carried out through discontinuous texts. Cinema — in its mixture of verbal, visual, and sonic languages — is a good example of such discontinuous nature. It depends on the arrival of the information at its destination (1989, 181). The delay caused by the distension whose intention is to build up a spectacular world in detail produces some sort of adestination: the film risks adestination, which becomes an asset of the ambiguity we have previously mentioned.

For instance, the Stargate sequence is astonishingly long if compared to the amount of information it gives. For many viewers the sequence becomes unbearably distended, to the point of causing boredom. The spaces through which Bowman progresses in his pod offer a constant change of color, texture, and spatial design, which catch the viewer's attention at the same time as they suggest Bowman's journey into the unknown — beyond the infinite, as the title has promised. The reverse shots of his color-changing eye suggest Bowman's gradual acquisition of a greater consciousness; they suggest that his development requires a change in the subjective parameters of understanding space. This implicit information, however, is contained within a sequence that extends for a longer time than the viewer needs to decodify it. The sequence becomes foregrounded in its spectacularity, and viewers feel at a loss once they realize that the text does not offer a possible reading for the length and repetitiveness of the spectacle. The viewer is discouraged from any further reflection on the sequence, and the wealth of color, texture, and spatial design even becomes boring because it is repetitive. The meaning of the sequence is, therefore, questioned by the formal presentation the text has chosen for it.

We can even deconstruct the notion of positionality of the subject carried out by the text through the notion of adestination. If the message does not arrive at its addressee, then the process of communication lacks the consistency it requires. Therefore, the position built for the subject will be altered, since there is nothing to be communicated. In the case of an ambiguous text this is possible because ambiguity questions understanding. The subject will be constructed in a position where one will not be asked to inscribe oneself into the text by accepting the textual construction of form. The new subject will be asked merely to enjoy such a formal design, turning the text into mere entertainment.

But *2001* is also an open-ended narrative. The film refuses to be highly communicative about its real meaning, as I have said. The traditional methods the text might use to explain itself as it develops are not present here. Verbal language might have provided links between scenes, advancing what is to come and clarifying the respects in which what has passed was relevant. But here verbal language is almost nonexistent. The text presents the viewer with a multiplicity of cues that may lead to various readings and conclusions.

The film is interested in offering its reflection on the future through the analysis of its form. The cinematographic representation of the future has traditionally been based on the depiction of cleanliness, order, and austerity found in films from the fifties. Settings and costumes are uniform, showing straight lines and geometrical forms. The materials of the future are metal, glass, and plastic. Spaces are never crowded, and human figures occupy areas in an orderly arrangement. Darkness exists only in outer space; interior spaces are always brightly lit (Kolker 1988, 118). The impression these features suggest is one of calm and order, where efficiency pervades every human action. The same external appearance of the future also, however, accompanies a more pessimistic view of development in certain films. Kolker mentions Fred M. Wilcox's *Forbidden Planet* (1956), in which the world of order and efficiency is inhabited by creatures who forget about their unconscious drives; those drives then become personified and destroy them. Such contradictions are not questioned and the code of order and neatness standing for the future remains. For Kolker, *2001* explores these conventions and the assumptions about the future; he concludes that the film questions the direct relationship between future and efficiency/progress by exaggerating the extremity of conventional images (119).

The film combines the traditional view of cleanliness and geometrical form with an extraordinary fondness for detail. The lack of verbal language is counterbalanced by the great amount of information that appears through screens and graphics — for instance, during the death of the hibernated crew. The film is filled with words presented in a type called Helvetica, an expression of order and uniformity. The complete organization of visual form in the text suggests its ideological content, confirming that "clean and orderly" does not only mean future but also emotional and intellectual death in a world ruled by machines, a world that has turned men into part of technology: the men are only cold and distant circuits fulfilling a specific function, as if they were machines (120–122). It therefore seems that the human beings in the film are controlled by a superior force that has turned them into a mere part of its mechanism.

Kolker outlines two possible readings for the text. One would say that history is controlled by a godlike power, that the monoliths are its transmitters and that they teach humankind the use of weapons that will lead to technological perfection. Men are passive because they are only elements that serve a higher plan. Only a machine — the HAL computer — realizes this and gets emotional about it, the computer becoming more human, and winning the viewer's sympathy to a greater extent, than the human who is disconnecting it. The second reading does not consider the monoliths as a representation of a higher intelligence: they are only imaginary markers of humanity's evolution. The monolith becomes not an aid but an obstacle to development, the first result of contact with it being killing. The monolith teaches the apes to use tools not only to master nature but also to dominate and kill others, an activity in which the apes show both brutality and pleasure. Floyd's touching of the monolith leads to the *Discovery* section, where the men have been completely dehumanized in their perfection. Isolation, however, gives way to a rebirth in the last section. The view of Bowman in his bed looking at the monolith presents it as an obstacle, a perceptual block that must be transcended. The fetus moving through space is the only image in the film of a human being not dominated by things or diminished by surroundings. It is, however, also an image of solitude and powerlessness, suggesting the existence of a superior entity guiding the development of the fetus. Here the open-endedness of the film is threatened, since it may lead this second reading to the same conclusions as the first one, destroying plurality of meaning and fostering a passive human being (123–125).

This danger of becoming both the representation of passivity and the textual mechanism demanding a passive attitude links *2001* with other contemporary films. Kolker compares it to Steven Spielberg's *Close Encounters of the Third Kind* (1977) only to underline the difference between them. Kubrick's film does not try to reduce the audience to an extension of the formal parameters it uses, while *Close Encounters* does; it demands viewer attentiveness and is open, while Spielberg's produces a submissive viewer and is closed; it is speculative while Spielberg's is predetermined; and it is full of detailed images, while the images in *Close Encounters* are merely overwhelming. Kolker concludes that an open narrative is attractive but runs the risk of becoming ambiguous instead of open and of fostering passivity, in the process removing responsibility from the film's author. This is not, however, the case in *2001* (127–132).

Both the ambiguity of the film and the open-endedness proved by the plurality of meanings are marks of the difficulties with which the text presents the viewer. They are possibilities for the destruction of coherence and clarity the viewer tries to achieve through the process of visual perception. They are proofs that the inscription of the subject the text attempts is not carried out through the presentation of a completely clear and coherent final meaning. The effects of the parergon and adestination are felt in *2001*.

This idea of adestination also supports the particular kind of spatial configuration the film carries out. Space has already been discussed as part of the textual mechanisms that contribute to the creation of meaning through metaphor, but here I will briefly discuss its problematic nature in *2001*.

The production of space is one of the main activities of any narrative intention in cinema. Branigan's reflections on film narration can be further developed at this point. For Branigan, narration is a positioning of the viewer with respect to a production of space, and subjectivity is a production of space attributed to a character. This means that the text uses space to represent character, which in turn represents space (1984,

177). The presence of space is justified as an aid in the depiction of character, and this presentation of character, in turn, justifies the presence of space through subjective views that attribute space to the character's point of view. Character is, therefore, a central agent in the production of space and narrative activity. It is also an important link between the activity of telling and what is told, a relationship based on a distance that is constantly manipulated by the text. Subjectivity is a particular distance between narration and narrative (176). This distance may also be subject to the threat of adestination, thereby breaking the activity of providing coherence that subjectivity carries out.

This threat of adestination is present in *2001* in the form of an unconventional treatment of character in space. In this film characters are not the centers for whom space is built; they are placed in space as mere elements of mise-en-scène. Characters are usually surrounded by portions of setting, by an environment that dwarfs them by comparison. Characters become mere components of the perfect symmetry of the future that the text is engaged in exhibiting. Character is not the intermediary that helps narration configure the narrative, since the text consistently avoids subjective views until Bowman's last journey. Characters are seen by the viewer as objects, rather than as surrogates with whom to identify and through whom to make a coherent whole out of spatial clues.

The views we are offered of Dr. Floyd deprive him of any intentionality to master his space or to qualify it in any sense, to the extent that he is even seen asleep or exchanging conversations with members of the spaceships' crews that we do not hear because the soundtrack is filled with extradiegetic music. Bowman and Poole aboard the *Discovery* are mere extensions of the machine. The occasional subjective shots usually include one of the characters and a screen or panel of lights through which we obtain information without much filtering on the part of the humans. Even in the first section, where the theme of future has not been introduced, the apes are situated within an environment that surrounds and oppresses them. They are part of the mise-en-scène, elements that are to be interpreted within the argumentative discourse of the section. Space does not create narrative through internal subjectivity; it does not, therefore, create meaning by means of this mechanism of particularity (the subject). Metaphors are created through an external configuration that takes the character as a mere element of mise-en-scène, not as the excuse for a coherent fragmentation of space following the demands of subjectivity. It is another example of how an element of particularity — fragmentation of space following the subjective demands of character — is transformed into generality and ruled by the workings of metaphor and dissemination.

This section on the deconstructive potential of *2001* has proved the existence of alternative patterns of structure and meaning different from those the film offers at first sight. The pattern of structural logic, the possible disturbances in the apprehension of metaphors, and the ambiguity and multiplicity of the ending all reveal a text in which the weight of the processes at work is conferred on an external verification supposedly carried out by the viewer. This is accompanied by a use of textual elements that renders them mere recipients of meaning, without allowing them to suggest meaning through the creation of formal coherence, as we have just seen in the case of character. This external configuration of the text develops into instability of meaning because of the different sources of structural patterns and meaning that are made to work together.

2001 is revealed as a film that provides both plurality of meaning and ambiguity. What is most relevant in the previous analysis is the presence of a textual tendency to produce ambiguity, to abolish the code of representation and avoid the viewer's formation of a clear and definite meaning elicited by the film. The combination of the pervading attempt to prevent a stable meaning and the tendency to prevent any meaning at all seems to me an original contribution of this particular text by Kubrick. The experience the film offers the viewer becomes a purely visual experience, where the lack of narrative aids typical of classical cinema forces the audience to progress through a clearly unusual text. The spectacular nature of most visual compositions attempts to produce a different approach of the viewer to the film, a reading that follows the audience's intuitions and irrational apprehension of the evolution of perspective, shape, and color on the screen. Kubrick's acknowledged desire to create a filmic experience that demanded a different understanding from that needed in classical cinema has been fulfilled.

As was advanced in the introduction to the analysis, *2001* becomes the expression of an antinarrative strand whose basic characteristic is the presence of ambiguity. Within the discussion of the logic of theories of language — and its best representative nowadays, deconstruction — this strand represents the abolition of the code as reaction to the ideological activity perceived in any instance of communication through a code. Ambiguity means the disappearance of boundaries for meaning, the impossibility of restricting reality (possible meanings, in this case) to a limited system that would make it capable of signification. The visual experience presented to the audience by this text stresses the relevance of an option proposed by deconstructionists: the best way to avoid the strictures of a signifying code is to set free its limitless potential, so that this infinite nature ends by abolishing the code itself, rendering it incapable of signification. This is one of the possibilities within the discourse of deconstruction. The following analysis of *Barry Lyndon* will provide the option of the proper code able to signify and fix meaning — precisely what deconstruction attacks.

4: *Barry Lyndon* (1975); or, The Comfort of Tradition

THE FABULA OF BARRY LYNDON CONCERNS the rise and fall of an eighteenth-century Irishman who sets off on his adventures after a frustrated love affair with his cousin, thinking that he has killed an English officer. He joins the English army, fights in the Seven Years' War, deserts, and is forced to join the Prussian army. He later travels around the courts of Europe as an attendant to a professional gambler, which gives him the opportunity to meet and marry Lady Lyndon, who is of a much higher social class than he. In England he has a son while being forced to face both his stepson, Lord Bullingdon, who thinks that he is an opportunist, and the debts he contracts in his attempt to obtain a title. His son dies in an accident, and Barry is wounded in a duel by Bullingdon, who has decided to take measures against his stepfather. Barry, having lost a leg and been separated from his wife by the obstinate Bullingdon, returns to Ireland poor and childless. He is shown first as an inexperienced, innocent man who cannot take control of his own life and whose marriage to Lady Lyndon introduces him to a new society to which he will not be able to adapt. He is a complete failure all through the film, but his tenderness, and also his vices, reveal him as a flesh-and-blood, rounded character who contrasts with the flatness of the rest of the characters in the film. He gradually gains our sympathy to such an extent that his fall is considered by the audience a clear act of injustice.

Barry Lyndon and Parametric Narration

Within Kubrick's filmography *Barry Lyndon* represents an approximation to a narrative mode that gives more importance to textual stylistic strategies than to its contents. Parametric narration has been defined by David Bordwell as a type of telling activity that relies on the play of stylistic devices that work independently of narrative function and motivation. A parametric text will concentrate on the development of textual stylistic patterns that lack connection with the contents of the film. Parametric narration occurs when no appeal to realistic motivation can account for the appearance of stylistic features, and they have to be put down to artistic motivation (Bordwell 1988, 274–310; Thompson 1988, 245–352).

Barry Lyndon shows traces of a narrative pull that tends to disregard the contents of the film and confer saliency on the recurrence of certain stylistic strategies.

The use of shot/reverse shot sequences is strictly formalized in the scenes of the duels, in the interviews between Barry and the minister in Berlin, and particularly in the scene between Barry and Lady Lyndon at the gambling table. The strict alternation between long shots and subjective shots, close-ups, or medium shots is consistently followed by the text on the two occasions in which a duel becomes part of the fabula. Barry's meetings with the minister during his stay in Berlin are always portrayed in the same manner: instead of the usual oblique shots proper of a shot/reverse shot structure Barry's or the minister's full bodies appear in the center of the frame, shot from the front and leaving some free space on both sides of the character. The effect is the destruction of the subjectivity that such sequences might create, producing instead the stagnant impression of a film following its internal structures and disregarding the audience. The strikingly beautiful scene at the gambling table uses rhythmical cutting, whose aim is to make it possible for the viewer to perceive the characters' movements, geared to the rhythm of the extradiegetic music. Here the presentation of a beautiful image is privileged over the more narratively relevant fragment of courtship it portrays.

The appearance of a long shot of the castle in the second part of the film works as a kind of punctuation mark for long fragments of meaningful material that this shot joins together and separates from others. The use of a view of the castle with this function is a completely arbitrary choice on the part of the film. The frame distance most of the scenes exhibit is invariable, to such an extent that it turns into an intrinsic norm set by the text. The scenes usually begin with a small fragment of mise-en-scène from which the camera zooms back to reveal the whole scene through a long shot. These long shots lead us to the discovery of what is perhaps the main parametric stylistic strategy in the film: the use of reverse zoom shots to introduce scenes.

Depth of field and deep space are strategies of spatial configuration that become relevant in many scenes, in what is a logical effect of the use of zoom shots and long shots. The space created by the zoom, however, is not usually employed narratively. The text prefers to dwell on the description of visually striking compositions rather than on the exploitation of space for the movements of characters advancing the fabula. This description is helped by the inexpressive nature of the characters' acting and the use of flamboyant costumes and make-up. The lack of expression in the characters, especially Barry, seems to be a constant feature contributing to the creation of beautiful views; but it does not seem to have a narratively relevant function within the fabula we are being told. Lighting is another stylistic strategy that is consistently used to emphasize beauty. It is not a realistically motivated kind of lighting but one whose motivation is clearly artistic. Finally, extradiegetic music is transformed into a parametric strategy in its activity of linking scenes that create fragments of meaning in an utterly artificial manner. There does not seem to be any motivation for such a use of music, except artistic motivation.

The critical response to the film coincides with a parametric reading of the text. M. Crispin Miller asserts that style is what determines the apprehension of *Barry Lyndon,* our response to film style preceding the process of decoding the edited material. Style is privileged over content (1976, 1370). He thinks that this emphasis is part of a textual attempt to tease the viewer into believing that film language can create coherent meaning, which the same move proves wrong (1378–1379). For Michael Dempsey, this conception of the text implies an emphasis on description that is in part a negation of classical cinema. He therefore defines the film as experimental (49–54). Thomas Allen Nelson finds in the film a tension between objectivity and spectacle, suggesting that realism is incompatible with spectacle. For him the text employs a strategy that creates a disparity among the film's objective structure, its temporal logic, and a brilliant visual and musical form. This idea supports a reading of the text as unclassical. This rejection of classical precepts is interpreted by Nelson as a source of ambiguity. For him the clarifying function of the voice-over narrator fails to do away with all possible ambiguity, since he may understand, and explain to us, eighteenth-century mores, but he does not understand Barry's emotional complexity or moral growth, and he fails to understand the philosophic or aesthetic meaning of the film (1982, 170–171).

A deep analysis of the film, however, reveals that its narrative mode is not so clearly or exclusively parametric. I will now attempt a deconstruction of a reading of *Barry Lyndon* as a strictly parametric text. I will begin by analyzing the textual parameters in the film.

Narrative films employ a number of textual strategies to tell their stories that have their origins in photography, painting, theater, the novel, and music. Their working together is what makes of cinema such a complex artistic form and such a compendium of artistic potentialities. These textual activities are focalization, representation, narration, and extradiegetic music (Deleyto 1991). The purpose of this section of the analysis is to explain how *Barry Lyndon* is a film that is based on the inner tension among some of the textual activities that operate in it. As the analysis proceeds I will also explain what I mean by the previously mentioned textual activities and how the tensions they produce can explain the inner workings of the film.

By cinematographic focalization, critics generally understand a textual strategy that attributes the origin of space in the shots to either a character in the film (subjective focalization) or to no character in the film (objective focalization). This concept is different from the concept of focalization in literary texts, where it is understood as a selection of narrative information by Gérard Genette (1982, 49) or as a selection of the perceived narrative information by Mieke Bal (1985, 100). Although cinematic space has been traditionally said to originate in the concept of the *camera,* focalization must be understood as including other ways through which cinema may foreground the importance of a character's gaze for the construction and understanding of the meaning of a particular shot. These other strategies are framing, mise-en-scène, and camera movement (Deleyto 1991). Representation, what we actually see in a shot — a mixture of mise-en-scène elements, such as characters and acting, lighting, composition of the shot, color, costumes — is also a compendium of strategies that contribute to the telling activity of the text, since the characters' actions, dialogue, movements and arrangement within the frame, and so on provide the core of the story and develop it. In the case of *Barry Lyndon* we also find the textual activity of the voice-over narrator[1] (which makes it possible for the narrative to proceed by providing mainly expositional information, information that summarizes and links events of the fabula), and the activity of extradiegetic music.

All the textual activities contribute to the overall tension between a mode of narration close to that of classical Hollywood cinema, where the narrative attempts to depict a story line based on a cause-and-effect chain of events in the clearest possible way, on the one hand, and a mode of narration that places a great emphasis on the text as such and on its artificiality and conventionality — an attractive text that draws attention to itself — on the other.

The use of focalization in the text exemplifies this tension. The most important stylistic device of the text with respect to focalization is the reverse zoom shot. This shot gradually and slowly unfolds the space of the scene, playing with the expectation it creates in the audience about what is hidden offscreen, about what is withheld from us until the tex-

---

[1] For a full account of the role of narration in cinema, see Kozloff (1988).

tual device has finished its course. It is a descriptive method that attempts to make description attractive but cannot avoid the self-consciousness produced by the absence of narrative significance in those scenes. In a high number of these shots the space unveiled is not used narratively, and their length does not correspond with a higher narrative importance. Furthermore, their composition and beautiful photography, which make them look like paintings of the period, once again give away the text's efforts to provide a purely visual spectacle that carries small narrative weight. An example of a staged composition and picture-like beauty without much meaning can be found in the second part in a shot of Lady Lyndon and her sons Brian and Bullingdon. The reverse zoom shot unveils the space (Lady Lyndon and Bullingdon on a couch, baby Brian in his cradle); but this space is not used by the characters, who stand motionless, frozen in their expression while the voice-over narrator performs the narrating activity. It is only after the narrator has informed us of the context surrounding the shot that we understand the meaning of the visual composition offered by the text: Barry, having settled in his wife's castle, has gradually left her and their sons alone.

This kind of shot is used with a purely descriptive purpose, but this description stands out because there is no balance between the length of the material interspersed in the narrative (which stops or, at least, slows down the pace of that narrative), and the amount of new information provided by these images. Descriptive passages are too long, and the interest in what is going to follow is systematically played down by the narrator's voice-over, which usually anticipates the way in which the narrative will turn next. Also, these reverse zoom shots constantly work to make it difficult for the audience to get involved in the film. The external focalization they provide helps to present the text as an artifice, an object in itself that exists at a great distance from the viewer, in the realm of artistic excellence.

Representation enacts another inner tension that can also be seen in the previous example of description. Some shots in the film look contrived not only because of the insistence of focalization on showing them for their own sake but also because many of them are made to imitate paintings of the period. The inexpressive characters, who tend to stand still during the whole length of the shot; the soft lighting; the costumes; and the contrived composition of the shots contribute to this effect. In cinema, which is the representation of moving images, the characters' refusal to move and explore the limits of the frame creates a self-contained visual material with no reference to reality. The frame is a cinematic convention that is masked by the constant references of the elements included within it to the outside, giving the illusion that what we see on the screen is part of a whole that we do not see but that is about to be presented to us. Characters looking offscreen and offscreen sound, among other textual strategies, point beyond the limits of the frame and introduce contiguous spaces in their search for a realistic depiction of the fabula. A shot that does not point to these outside regions, whose static nature refuses to create the illusion that it is part of reality, inevitably points to itself as artifice. Representation, which usually contributes to advancing the action of the film, therefore fulfills a double task in *Barry Lyndon*.

The fabula parallels this textual tension. A low-class character, Barry, tries to ascend to a higher social class and to accommodate himself to the rigid structures of that society (its law of decorum), but he fails because of his passionate nature. In the second part of the film, in which Barry has joined a high social class by marrying Lady Lyndon, the activity of these descriptive devices is greater than in the first part, where dialogue had a more important role. This difference is indicative of the relationship between textual strategies and fabula development. The part that shows the diverse activities Barry has to carry out in his search for fortune has a quicker pace; his life at Castle Hackton allows him to enjoy his newly acquired position and his distinguished friends. These more relaxed activities fit the use of more descriptive passages. Barry's new status starts to crumble when he breaks the sacred law of polite behavior and nearly kills Lord Bullingdon, which causes his friends to ostracize him. At a textual level, it means the victory of passivity (description) over classical narration (character action), as Barry is degraded and has to go back to Ireland. In the end, the film stands out as a mainly descriptive experiment, where the action seems to be just the backbone on which the body of an unusual visual experience has been built.

To show how these tensions work in conjunction with other elements to build up a similar tension in the whole of the film, I will analyze the second part of *Barry Lyndon*. The result will be a tension between the realism, produced by the exact replicas of locales, costumes, and the rest of the visual side of the text (and of the classical narration that the text in part constructs), on the one hand, and the contrivance that arises from the use of textual devices, building up patterns based on stylistic parameters, on the other hand: a tension between what Bordwell calls classical and parametric narration. Classical narration is a type of cinematic "telling" activity where the text tries to construct a story from the basis of its characters and their actions as they develop in space and time. In this narrative mode the episodes that constitute the text are linked by means of cause-and-effect relationships, and its scenes are advanced and introduced by elements from the previous scene, creating the impression of a smooth, coherent flow of events. Parametric narration, on the other hand, does not consider events, but its formal structures, as the essential components of a film. Parametric narratives take textual stylistic parameters as the elements to be traced in their development throughout the film. The films of Bresson and Ozu are the prototypical examples of this narrative option (Bordwell 1988, 275–289).

In the second part of the film Barry marries Lady Lyndon, has a son (Brian), and turns his back on his wife once he has obtained the position he wished. Lord Bullingdon, his stepson, considers him an opportunist and profoundly hates him. Barry tries to obtain a title and in the process squanders a great part of his wife's fortune. Bullingdon finally confronts Barry, who forgets his not-very-well-assumed politeness and beats Bullingdon up in front of Barry's friends. Ostracized after this indecorous incident, Barry turns to his son, Brian, who dies shortly afterward in an accident. Barry turns to drink, while Lady Lyndon grows more and more melancholy. Bullingdon returns from voluntary exile to demand satisfaction and injures Barry in a duel. Barry, crippled, returns to Ireland, and Bullingdon becomes the head of the Lyndon family.

These fabulaic contents are divided into nine groups of scenes or sequences: 1. wedding and Barry's unfaithful conduct; 2. apparent reconciliation; 3. Bullingdon's hatred and Barry's love for Brian; 4. Barry trying to obtain a title; 5. fight with Bullingdon; 6. Barry's loneliness and love for Brian; 7. Brian's accident and its effect on Barry and Lady Lyndon; 8. Bullingdon's return and duel with Barry; 9. Barry's departure from England. The nine sequences share a number of characteristics that, because of their frequent appearance, create diverse stylistic patterns. At the level of focalization the text uses reverse zoom shots in every sequence that have a clearly descriptive purpose because they are usually accompanied by voice-over narration that actually presents the information. The use of the reverse zoom shot is so extensive that it becomes a foregrounded stylistic option; as Noël Burch says, the process of emphasizing one of the two poles of a parameter by using it extensively becomes a means of creating a stylistic structure in a text (1983, 51–69). The extensive use of reverse zoom shots when description is intended emphasizes this pole of the parameter and plays down all the other options, such as the establishing shot that introduces the locale of the action in film texts.

The stylistic option of the reverse zoom shot acquires such a status as a fixed element in the film that the text uses it on one occasion in the second part to link and contrast actions in two shots with different spatial and temporal coordinates. In sequence 1, the text cuts in the middle of a reverse zoom shot that shows Lady Lyndon, Barry, and their new-born son, Brian, to a reverse zoom shot of Barry in a brothel, pointing to the fact that Barry's life at that moment does not include his role as father and husband. The contrast between the two shots stems from the strong convention of continuity created by classical cinematographic language. Cutting between different locales is allowed as long as the second shot can be coherently read by the audience as related to the first — for example, in the case of ellipses that eliminate the action of a character going up the stairs and present the character at his destination.[2] The cut in the middle of a shot that is gradually being enlarged to another reverse zoom shot in a completely different locale does not demand from the viewer the capacity to link both locales as contiguous and create a coherent space. It demands that the viewer establish a different connection between them, a connection related to a metaphorical reading of the two shots that contrasts Barry's externally appropriate behavior as a husband with his concealed extramarital life. It is the unexpected attempt of the text to create continuity in a manner classical cinema does not accept that creates the meaning of the sequence and emphasizes the powerful workings of the reverse zoom shot in this film.

Inside these sequences, voice-over narration and extradiegetic music serve the purpose of unifying different shots; the voice or the music extend over the cutting between shots, creating stylistic and signifying units. The music usually works to mark the fact that the sequence will not finish until what the narrator has said in the sequence or its implications are shown by the text. Thus, in sequence 7 the narrator, fulfilling his task of doing away with any possibility of surprise in the film, informs us (over a shot of Brian playing croquet) that Brian will die and Barry will be childless. The same melody continues beyond the voice-

---

[2] Cutting is also possible within the same locale if characters remain, in the second shot, in the same place they occupied in the first, or if the cut takes place while the character is moving, provided that the second shot is offered to us from the same side of the 180-degree axis created by the expected progression of the action as the first one (the second shot must also maintain the screen direction of the movement that started in the first shot: if such direction was from right to left, the second shot should preserve it). Such conventions are called the continuity system of editing, whose purpose is to help the viewer construct a coherent space for action (Bordwell and Thompson 1986, 210–220).

over right up to the moment when Brian appears injured on a stretcher after he has fallen from a horse. Music provides us with the best example in the film of the text's artificiality governing the presentation of events. The scene in which Barry meets Lady Lyndon takes place in a candlelit room where the two characters are sitting around a gambling table. The movements of Barry's head and eyes and Lady Lyndon's eyes carefully follow the rhythm of the extradiegetic music in their shy attempts to make eye contact with each other. One of the most moving and beautiful scenes in the film owes its strength to the workings of a textual strategy that is clearly foregrounded.

Voice-over narration is also used by the text in a way that emphasizes one pole of the stylistic options it offers: voice-over narration always appears over shots with little narrative significance but a great capacity to describe plastic beauty; the main narrative role belongs to the narrator in these instances. When the narrator finishes and lets the characters speak, the dialogue advances the narrative. Also, voice-over narration usually provides a summary of previous events leading to that scene, thereby masking ellipses; whereas when characters' dialogue works, the time of the text coincides with that of the fabula (Bal 1985, 74).

This observation leads us to consider the workings in the text of time and its inseparable companion, space. A temporal feature that is kept stable throughout the text is its chronological order: there are frequent ellipses, but no events are rearranged in a new temporal order. One textual pattern used by the film is the alternation between groups of shots quickly edited together with spatial jumps and temporal ellipses between them and subsequent shots where the spatial and temporal coordinates are kept stable, as in shot/reverse shot sequences or, in general, in those parts where the plot is advanced by means of character action or dialogue (this is one of the features the film shares with classical narration). Those two spatiotemporal organizations are present in most sequences; the first usually accompanies voice-over narration, the second, representation.

With respect to montage, almost every one of the sequences is punctuated by an editing device: a long shot of the castle where Barry and Lady Lyndon live. This shot serves to close a sequence and announce that a new one is about to start. The arbitrariness of this option, the fact that it does not fulfill any narrative function except that of punctuation mark, and the fact that it can only be turned into a parameter by the disruption that its absence would produce make it a highly foregrounded stylistic feature. The sequences are developed and the events presented through the usual mechanism of editing, once the first introductory shot disappears.

Mise-en-scène also presents us with an element that retains a steady function all through the film. The compositions of the shots are balanced and so perfect that they give away the purpose of the text: to resemble the compositions of the paintings of the period. Every shot marks the center of the frame as the key place of the composition, following Renaissance perspective — the linear perspective in which the lines within the frame converge to a vanishing point, usually in the centre. This stylistic option is also a key concept for understanding the contrived look of the many reverse zoom shots employed by the text.

The previous textual elements have been presented as stylistic options chosen by the text to perform its telling activity. The restriction of the text to a single stylistic option in each case leads to a structured, patterned narrative in which the text contends with the fabula as the "protagonist" of the film. Burch has developed a theory, based on what he calls parameters, in his renowned *Theory of Film Practice* (1983, 51). Parameters are stylistic paradigmatic options from which the text chooses; he distinguishes, for instance, fifteen spatial and temporal ways of articulating two shots (of cutting from one shot to the next), depending on whether the space and the time are continuous in both shots or not and on the nature of their discontinuities. According to Bordwell, some narratives employ a restricted number of stylistic options or an extensive range of them and, therefore, create a stylistic game that becomes prominent in the text and sometimes outweighs the fabula in importance (1988, 285). As we have already said, this parametric narration can perform a dialectic activity and emphasize one of the two poles of a parameter by using it rarely or, perhaps, only once. I will now show how this process works in the second part of *Barry Lyndon* .

From the point of view of the fabula, this second part offers relevant information to explain Barry's life and its turning points: marriage, the death of his son, the duel in which he is injured and forced to leave what he has fought for. But the parametric narration whose existence I am trying to prove here marks another sequence as by far the most relevant. This is sequence 5, Barry's fight with Bullingdon, which will be the cause of his fall: his friends will desert him after an episode that for them is completely indecorous and will prevent him from obtaining his title; also, the attack on Bullingdon will be the cause of the duel that will confirm Barry's decay.

This scene is stylistically marked by a great number of elements, all of them involving a disruption of those commented on previously. Sequence 5 is composed of a scene in which Brian and Bullingdon are studying quietly; Brian, unable to concentrate on his work, constantly makes noises that disturb and finally anger Bullingdon. Barry comes into the room and catches Bullingdon beating his beloved son. Barry punishes Bullingdon in the next scene. In the third scene Bullingdon interrupts a concert Lady Lyndon and Reverend Runt are giving to their friends by bringing in Brian, who is wearing Bullingdon's shoes in an obvious comment that Barry and his son have stepped into his shoes. This reference is also a repetition of a line of dialogue Lord Lyndon had used in the first part, one of the obvious repetitions of dialogue lines that also point at a contrived structure at this level of dramatic content. In the end, Barry attacks his stepson. In these three scenes the voice-over narrator does not appear even once. The option of voice-over narration is accompanied in the rest of the film by images with little narrative importance; here the absence of that parametric role suggests the narrative importance of what is happening. The action is advanced by the characters, and there are no temporal or spatial discontinuities except for the usual ones marked by cutting between scenes. The stylistic option of a narrator providing a summary and masking ellipses is replaced by temporal continuity, and the sequence gets closer to fabula time than any other in the second part. Extra-diegetic music is replaced by one of the two only instances of diegetic music that appear in the second part, thus marking the temporal continuity of the scene.

The reverse zoom shot as a means of introducing the sequence or a scene has disappeared, too, and we have a panning shot from right to left in the first scene, straight establishing shot in the second scene, and panning shot from left to right in the scene of the concert. A stylistic option with such little relevance for the meaning of the text reveals more strongly the existence of an independent stylistic structure based on the text's choice to constrict itself to a single option in each stylistic paradigm. Its constant presence throughout the text has created a pattern of development purely based on stylistic features, which to a certain extent shifts the spectatorial search focus from the contents to the text as structure. The sudden alteration of such a stylistic pattern marks this sequence not only from a purely textual point of view but also draws attention to the portion of fabula that has been used as "background" for the device. The disappearance of a pattern that focuses the viewer's attention on stylistic parameters leaves the way open for a traditional apprehension of the contents of the film, foregrounding this fragment's contribution to its plot.

The presentation of events, which in the rest of the film follows the pattern of editing the shots within the sequence without much recourse to camera movement, is replaced by the use of handheld camera shots, which involve longer takes, in the scene of the fight, thereby recalling the fight in the first part. The handheld camera shots also break the stylistic pattern created throughout the film of balanced compositions in the frame: the fight is shown by means of a moving frame in which nothing is balanced or stable but everything changes constantly. The text's tendency to introduce cutting after the introductory reverse zoom shot reveals the ambiguous nature of this film. Editing within the scene is a typical device of classical Hollywood cinema, which tries to secure the viewer's complete comprehension of the scene's space by means of shot/reverse shots, eyeline matches, or matches on action. *Barry Lyndon* uses this classical technique, revealing that its attempt at a parametric narration is not completely devoid of other stylistic elements that are able to guide the viewer's attention to the fabula. The mixture of classical and parametric narration is constant throughout the film up to this sequence, where editing within the scene is partly replaced by longer takes with handheld camera. This alteration constitutes a break-down of classical editing; but it does not mean to build any anticlassical structure, since in this scene handheld camera shots follow the fabula's demand of a striking presentation of violence and not any demand of textual style. Finally, this sequence does not finish with the long shot of the castle, which has acquired the status of punctuation mark, thereby further stressing the sequence's status as disruption within a logical chain.

In sequence 6 we find another disruption emphasized by the text. As a consequence of the fight Barry is left alone, and he turns to his son, Brian, for affection. The text shows them looking at a book in a medium shot. The film's previous logic would suggest that this medium shot should be taken as the introduction to the scene and that its development would take place through a reverse zoom shot accompanied by voice-over narration. The text, however, does not use the reverse zoom shot but a cut to an extreme long shot that shows father and son in the far left corner of the frame, now occupied by a huge painting. The shot's originality with respect to the rest of the shots in the film stems from its refusal to allow the spectator to enjoy the act of description that the slow pace of the reverse zoom shot allows. The beginning of the reverse zoom shot in *Barry Lyndon* provides the viewer with a beautiful picture that points to the fact that its surroundings, which we do not yet see, contain the rest of what is going to turn out to be a remarkable artistic presentation of reality. The force of such shots therefore lies in the capacity of the text to make the viewer enjoy the process of description that is taking place. The meaning of these shots springs from the final image the text decides to offer, although most of the time such meaning can only be unambiguously elicited with the help of the voice-over narrator. Within this context the sudden cut from medium shot to extremely long shot seems a striking disruption, since it attempts to create meaning through the mere juxtaposition of two images in a purely visual manner, while at the same time refusing to use description in the process. It is this disruption of a mode of signification, together with the alteration of a stylistic pattern, that works here to emphasize Barry's loneliness and his desperate search for love in his son.

Connected with this sequence we find the only temporal disruption of the second part: a flashback to Brian's accident in sequence 7 as one of the servants relates it to Barry. This temporal disruption contrasts with the chronological order maintained in the rest of the film, which is unusual in a text that covers such a long period of time in the life of a man. This alteration adds structural prominence to the event — not dramatic prominence, because the scene would have been more striking if it had been shown directly, but a relevance that arises from the disruption of a previously established pattern.

Thus, we have seen that the textual elements of the film contain an inner tension between an attempt at classical narration and an attempt at a more self-referential narration (with a greater emphasis on the text). Stylistic parameters are kept stable until Barry's passionate disposition cannot stand that world of appearances and bursts out in the fight with Bullingdon. These disruptions are used by the narrative to show the contrast between the world of decorum in which Barry has decided to live and his real personality, which is unable to adapt to such a world and its code of behavior. The overall descriptive tendency of the text is interrupted in those instances when Barry's incapacity to act according to his new status gets him into trouble. In these cases representation takes over, and what we see in the space of the scene becomes able to create meaning, replacing extradiegetic methods of meaning-production. These disruptions reinstate character as the main protagonist of the text, even though only momentarily, and, therefore, emphasize Barry's humanity, his anger, his hopes of a better future with his son, and his despair when Brian dies.

These events are marked by the narrative as the key reasons for Barry's economic and emotional downfall. That the formal design of the film is not independent of the narrative's contents is evident in the fact that these sequences behave in a similar way to scenes in classical

Hollywood cinema: each introduces a motif that will lead the action onward by opening new lines of development. Bullingdon's hatred for Barry is introduced in the first sequence, carried on in the third, and leads to Bullingdon's fight in the fifth and the duel in the eighth. The development of the story gives a certain importance to the characters as the agents that further the narrative (typical of classical narration) and most of the parametric options fulfill tasks that lead to a clear depiction of a cause-and-effect based narrative line. *Barry Lyndon* is not, therefore, a completely parametric narrative text, since at certain moments its stylistic patterns are made to perform activities that lead to a clearer or more effective depiction of the film's line of action.

An innovative textual activity, then, has to rely on a classical frame if the text is to transmit its message to the audience.[3] But, again, the structures created by the text are also evident, and the impression it leaves with the viewer is that of a film whose concern is not so much to tell a story as to describe exhaustively the milieu in which that story takes place. The beauty of the images the text strives to achieve, and the self-conscious way in which it does this striving, draw attention to the narrative as an artificial construction. The parametric narration also stands out in such a way that it often relegates other considerations, such as story line or character development, to a secondary position, thereby inscribing this text in the Modernist tradition, which systematically takes the text as the field of development and inquiry. Finally, *Barry Lyndon* proves that it is not only in the most extreme cases of textual play or self-awareness that traces of Modernism are to be found. Certain films are capable of presenting an apparently classical narrative mode while at the same time containing a complex array of textual patterns ready to confront the rules of classicism. It is precisely in texts such as this that the study of textual stylistics is most fruitful, since it is able to unmask the apparently straightforward nature of a text and re-discover it as a richer artistic form than it seemed at first sight.

Barry Lyndon is, therefore, a mixture of parametric and classical narration. Certain parameters are invested with meaning and this seems to contradict the basic tenets of parametric narration as stated by Bord-

---

[3] An illustrative example is the work of Jean-Luc Godard. His first films retain a basically classical structure (*A Bout de Souffle* [1959], being a gangster movie, after all) that is systematically subverted. Compared to them, the films of the Dziga-Vertov group period are obscure works because they break the conventional cinematic rules without even keeping a frame of reference — for instance, a slight cause-effect relationship between scenes. Films such as *Vent d'Est* (1969) refuse to offer such a relationship.

well. For him, textual patterns that acquire saliency should never be thematized; they should be taken as such, never ascribed an allegorical meaning (1988, 282–283). Reviews and articles published at the time of the film's release, however, include abundant interpretations of stylistic elements as having fabula-related meanings. Hans Feldman sees in the textual stylization an expression of how social form may deform the social man or woman, placing them at a great distance from their primal, vital selves (1976, 17–19). This interpretation seems to be a transposition of the film's textual arrangement into the theme of the film. This piece of criticism can be used as support for the viewer's tendency to thematize structural elements. Mark Crispin Miller interprets the cut in the middle of the zoom shot as a means of identifying the two images: domestic happiness and passionate infidelity are expressions of the same desire to find warmth and comfort (1976, 1375). Michael Dempsey offers a metaphorical interpretation of the zoom shots in the text: they place human beings in timeless perspective, highlighting their temporariness (1976, 49–54).

For Norman Kagan, the contrived organization of the text by putting together two lines of similar incidents that offer commentaries on one another is a clear source of meaning (1989, 200). The reading practice fostered by an organization of the text into two parts that retain obvious parallelisms clearly depends on the thematization of stylistic patterns such as the editing of the duels or the use of lighting. Thomas Allen Nelson sees four recurring activities in the film as ways of marking parallelisms or contrasts and thereby creating meanings: duelling, wooing, card-playing, and debt-paying include in their formal order the workings of fate or chance, and each dramatizes Kubrick's everpresent conflict between human design and contingency (1982, 176). The same critic also launches a hypothesis about the meaning of reverse zoom shots — they dwarf human conflict with visual beauty (1982, 184) — and a more general interpretation of the film's consistent tendency to demand the viewer's recourse to artistic motivation: for Nelson, Barry lives in a world of art, where he does not manage to become creative; he remains an imitator throughout the film. He is entrapped by an art that he cannot master because he is not a real artist (1982, 185). Here Nelson applies his capacity to thematize form and structure to a more totalizing view of the text, an example of the extent to which a reader or a critic may feel tempted to interpret cues set by films.

The previous analysis of several elements of poetics can be focused from the point of view of the distinction between stylistic elements of generality and particularity. The zoom shot can be seen as a mixture of an element of particularity (it begins with a small component of the composition) and an element of generality (it is in part an establishing shot). This double nature can also be seen in the whole film, which is so dependent on zoom shots.

The metaphorical reading of the combination of zoom shot and editing (from placid view of Barry's family to him in brothel) provides an example. In this case the zoom shot is consistent with its being an element of generality; in the case of editing this example is creating an ellipsis (element of particularity) but also suggesting a metaphorical reading, which should be more appropriate to external, general conceptions of the text. This example hints at the double nature of *Barry Lyndon* with respect to generality/particularity: the film's stylistic patterns offer aspects of both generality and particularity, in the end usually eliciting metaphorical readings that are more consistent with a prevalence of elements of generality. I intend to use this double aspect to support a reading of the text as a mixture of parametric and classical formal systems.

The positing of *Barry Lyndon* as a mixture of parametric and classical narrative modes has a reflection in the stylistic elements included in the stock of poetics. The two components of poetics (particularity and generality) have previously been identified with the creation of formal coherence (elements of particularity) and the capacity to create metaphorical meaning together with a certain disseminative potential (elements of generality). The coexistence of parametric narration, with its emphasis on form, and classical narration, with its emphasis on meaning, also involves the coexistence of elements of particularity and generality within the same stylistic arrangement. I will now give a brief analysis of the elements of poetics that can be said to share aspects of particularity and generality, since it is my belief that the textual double nature of narration can also be proved through the analysis of style. Michel Ciment sees this double pull at work in the text but in two different strategies: mise-en-scène is interpreted as the embodiment of the eighteenth century's disciplined system, which tries to eliminate ambiguity and chance from life; on the other hand, he sees the voice-over narrator as highly ambiguous (1983). I will show how this double pull can also be perceived inside the same stylistic strategy, thereby confirming the film's intrinsic double nature with respect to narration and style.

As was seen in our analysis of shot/reverse shot sequences, *Barry Lyndon* contains cases of the structure in which the reverse shot is withheld for an unusually long time — for instance, in the introduction of the chevalier. This is an example of particularity that is distorted and transformed into an element of generality, provoking metaphorical readings. The cohesion produced by the subjective device is replaced by a distortion that links this enigmatic character with other characters presented in the same manner in other Kubrick films: Ripper in *Dr. Strangelove,* the aged Bowman in *2001.* These links suggest thematic connections with those films: for instance, these characters are all explorers, madmen who take to an extreme the hypothetical possibilities of the games in which they take part (gambling, nuclear threat, and exploring space).

Shot/reverse shots are also stylized where editing is geared to the rhythm of the extradiegetic music, as in the scene between Barry and Lady Lyndon at the gambling table. This case is, again, an element of particularity that is transformed into an element of generality, subjectivity transformed into the source of metaphorical interpretations. It suggests the artificiality of the couple's love and love etiquette; it also hints that this world relies on the law of decorum, on the external appearance and behavior of its members.

The excessively balanced compositions that constitute certain shot/reverse shot sequences in the film (the Barry-minister scenes in Berlin) do away with subjectivity (particularity), in the process suggesting metaphorical interpretations for the strategy. In this world subjectivity is replaced by the strict rules of the age's law of decorum. Shot/reverse shots in general in *Barry Lyndon* show the film's tendency to transform elements of particularity that create formal coherence into elements of generality that cue metaphorical readings. This tendency proves the general textual tendency to transform parametric patterns (particularity) into sources of meaning through metaphorical readings.

Editing is also subject to this tendency. Editing in the middle of the reverse zoom shot suggests a metaphorical interpretation, as has already been remarked. Editing is the basic tool of cinema's pull to achieve formal coherence: it allows ellipses to be created, eliminating material that is not narratively relevant. Here this formal cohesion process is transformed into metaphor, since it is made to alter an intrinsic norm the film had set: to begin each scene by using a reverse zoom shot. The usual function of editing as creator of ellipses and formal coherence, which is common to all films, is accompanied in this film by another function within a parametric pattern (even if only to break it). This is also apparent in the appearance of the castle shot that recurs at the end of each chunk of material that has been joined by music that is heard over the whole fragment. Here editing helps in the configuration of a clearly parametric stylistic arrangement, since the shot of the castle closes sequences that have been joined by purely stylistic effects.

The use of titles has a double function as expression of particularity and generality. As an element of particularity it provides formal coherence to the text by separating the two parts and giving information to the viewer about what is to come, thereby doing away with ambiguity. It is, however, also an element of generality, since it produces a certain self-consciousness, which hints at a telling activity that shapes the ideas of the film through textual elements rather than fabulaic ones.

Panning shots are a strategy whose purpose is usually to link characters or locales. In this film panning shots are transformed into marks of the alteration of a parametric norm imposed by the text and, therefore, also into contributors to the parametric narration. Panning shots are mostly related to the appearance of Bullingdon and to Barry's fall, which Bullingdon brings about. A panning shot accompanies Bullingdon's appearance at the concert, escorting his stepbrother. The panning shot in this case breaks the intrinsic pattern of introductory reverse zoom shots set by the text. Also, a panning shot introduces Bullingdon's meeting with Runt and the accountant, which marks the beginning of his counterattack against Barry.

The long shots that the film characteristically uses as the final result of reverse zoom shots become a fixed strategy in the text. This is so to the extent that a sudden break of the structure is capable of shocking the viewers and leading them to search for interpretations of the phenomenon. When the text cuts from a close-up of Barry and Brian to a long shot of them surrounded by a huge painting, the viewer is pushed to interpret it as expression of Barry's loneliness. It is not only this disruption, however, that takes on meaning in this move: the rest of the long shots also acquire meaning by contrast with the disruption. The long shots, therefore, become the expression of the strict rules of decorum that tie Barry up, as suggested by the artistic look of the compositions and by the traditional connection between art and rule that our culture has established.

Depth of field is related to the previous strategy. It has a component of particularity, since in the general code of cinema it allows the portrayal of interaction among characters and, therefore, the appearance of formal coherence. It is also an element of generality, since it helps produce metaphorical interpretations by allowing beautiful views of inexpressive characters and static nature, where the weight of the interest is the enjoyment of the beautiful visual spectacle presented by the text.

Zoom shots are the basis of the parametric structure devised by the film text. The introduction of each scene by means of a reverse zoom shot does not seem at first sight to have any purpose other than its own establishment as textual device, worth noticing for its own sake. This

parametric side of the structure can, however, be reinterpreted as possessing a meaning and a more classical effect as the expression of a
fabula-related idea. The reverse zoom shot keeps the viewer's attention
on the visual quality of what is being presented; it usually marks the
center of the perspectival composition of the final long shot, directing
our attention to the perfect balance of its components, the beautiful
colors and lighting, or the striking elegance of costume and character.
In short, the strategy of the reverse zoom shot can be interpreted as an
aid to the exaltation of the artistic beauty of the eighteenth century.
The strategy can, therefore, be understood as both an element of formal coherence and as the source of metaphorical interpretation, as an
element of particularity and generality.

Something similar can be argued about the nature of acting in the
film. The inexpressive nature of the characters,[4] especially of Barry, can
be interpreted as an element of particularity, with the purpose of emphasizing the fabula-related idea that Barry cannot adapt to his new life
or act to guide his life. As an element of generality it allows the interpretation of the text as the exaltation of the film's visual beauty, rather
than as the coherent progression of characters involved in a fabula.
Lighting in *Barry Lyndon* helps in the creation of realistic scenes, using
daylight and even candlelight, which has become one of the best-
known features of the film. Lighting is, however, also clearly made to
emphasize the beauty of the material presented. It can also be interpreted as the result of a textual effort to lend the look of sophisticated
eighteenth-century art to the scenes — an effort that is not so much
accountable through realistic as through artistic motivation. Extradiegetic music shares this double nature: it is obviously an attempt to
match the visuals with appropriate music, and therefore a realistic force,
but it is also a contributor to the emphasis on the beauty of the visuals
carried out by the text. Music is also used as a creator of textual patterns: it extends over several scenes, shaping chunks of signifying material.

The analysis of *Barry Lyndon* has revealed the text as the conjunction of classical and parametric narrative modes. Parametric patterns
have been shown to have a narrative function as elements that emphasize the key moments in the film, laying bare the fact that this parametric narration is not so parametric, after all. I will now study *Barry
Lyndon* as an attempt at parametric narration that is subverted by the
text itself: the textual patterns emphasize narratively relevant moments,

---

[4] For a study of *Barry Lyndon*'s strategies of character creation, see Falsetto
(1991, 177–220).

thereby losing the essence of what a parametric narration is supposed to be. These patterns, on the other hand, also favor the viewer's construction of metaphorical, allegorical meanings.

In the analysis of the film's textual parameters I have mentioned that several scenes in the text strike us because of their refusal to explore what is beyond the boundaries of the frame. This aspect can be linked to Peter Brunette and David Wills's application of the Derridaean concept of the parergon to the cinema (1989). As we have seen, accessory elements to a code are essential for the working of the code. The signature in a letter is something accessory (not part of the contents) that becomes essential since the purpose of a letter is to establish communication between two people (the signature allows this communication) and something whose relevance is acquired by its recurrence (a sign that only appears once cannot be codified as such a sign). *Barry Lyndon* refuses to use the effects of the parergon, of the capacity of what is outside the frame to shape a code. This text refuses to create a system or a code of signification based on the appearance of what is accessory, of what lies beyond the limits of the frame. It dismantles such a possibility by concentrating on the description of what appears inside the frame. It establishes an opposition between elements of particularity aiming at formal coherence (material outside frame, code) and elements of generality aiming at the creation of meaning through description. We can, therefore, see that the parametric narration that demands formal coherence is opposed by the text to the descriptive impulse that in the previous analysis had been proposed as an anti-classical force and, therefore, as also implicitly parametric in this particular text. It would, therefore, seem that this anti-classical force, this pull toward antinarrativity, is redirected toward the expression of narratively relevant information. The emphasis the text constantly places on the expression of beauty and its refusal to establish links of formal coherence with the adjacent elements of particularity inevitably lead the viewer to search for metaphorical meaning in the material presented and in the way the material appears before the viewer. Parametric narration acquires relevance as conveyor of contents. The film shows the double nature of its particular use of parametric narration.

Barry Lyndon is an example of the possibilities of analysis the formal approach outlined in my scheme offers to the critic. It presents us with a parametric narration that has connections with both elements of generality and of particularity. A parametric system will be founded on elements of particularity, which construct the necessary formal coherence; but these elements will have to recur to create a perceptible pattern, thereby becoming part of the elements of generality, too.

Parametric narration is, therefore, a narrative mode that mixes features of particularity and generality, building up coherent formal systems that are usually interpreted by the reader as metaphorical, allegorical constructions. So the same internal structure of parametric narration, which seems only to accept formal structures without metaphorical meaning, is immediately deconstructed when we realize that it demands a general presence all through the work, and that this presence automatically fosters the creation of allegorical interpretations, which is a feature of the elements of generality. The same repetition of the structure that constructs parametric narration simultaneously destroys its alleged exclusive faithfulness to form, since it favors the viewer's interpretation of the pattern according to the contents of the film, as we have seen.

This tendency to favor the creation of meaning has a parallel in certain pervasive textual attitudes — for instance, the configuration of knowledgeability. Almost every scene or sequence in the film contains different degrees of knowledgeability, but the text tends to place the viewer at the highest of these levels, above the characters. Thus, the text is ironic toward Nora's beauty. It tells us that Barry is deceiving Lischen and that she has had many lovers before him, thereby placing the viewer alternately above both characters. Since the text allows the viewer such a knowledgeable position, it also allows the possibility of constructing clear, definite meanings. This possibility is apparent in the workings and effects of the voice-over narration; in the comic touch of many scenes, which reveals an ironic or farcical attitude of the text; and in the many scenes where we see how one character fools another. In the Barry-Captain Quin duel our hero is fooled by Nora's family, as we later learn; Barry fools Potzdorff by making the latter believe that he is a true officer; in Berlin, Barry allies with the chevalier and lies to Potzdorff; and in the second part Barry cheats on his wife.

This same pull toward clarity and away from ambiguity can be perceived in the symmetries and parallelisms exhibited by the film. The text constantly uses the repetition of similar events, the setting up of apparently parallel elements, to elicit meanings that confirm the general evolution of the fabula. The narrative is built around certain crucial moments that become turning points for the characters. This phenomenon is particularly evident in the case of duels. Barry's father dies in a duel, and his absence will determine Barry's incapacity to face his problems with the assurance provided by paternal advice. Barry's adventures begin with his encounter with Captain Quin in another duel. This duel exemplifies Barry's tendency to defy men of a superior class. Our discovery that the duel was a stratagem set up by the family to get rid of our hero presents Barry, as always, in the hands of other people without being conscious of the fact. The final Barry-Bullingdon duel confirms Barry's fall. It shows again that Barry has not been capable of adapting to a social status in which he feels foreign, and here he is finally sent back "where he belongs" by a lord.

Barry's emotional life evolves through several milestones that the text tries to link. Barry's scenes with Nora, Lischen, and Lady Lyndon inevitably contain a certain dose of deception. In the first shy, playful relationship with his cousin, Barry is at the mercy of the whimsical girl who relishes testing his feelings. Lischen conceals the other relationships she has had, which the narrator confides to us, while Barry lies about his name and his past life in the army. This candlelit scene is a progression toward sophistication, beautiful mise-en-scène and subtle deception. The scene between Barry and Lady Lyndon is a step ahead along this line. The beauty of the scene, together with the artificiality imposed by the editing of the visuals and the rhythm of the music, marks a progression of the text's scenes of subtle deception. Barry is deceiving Lady Lyndon since his only intention is to seduce her in order to obtain a high position in society that he cannot achieve otherwise.

Candlelit scenes are associated with deception throughout the film, and the consistency with which this idea is suggested every time one of these scenes appears is a great aid to the construction of meaning. Barry tries to deceive Captain Potzdorff during a conversation rendered by means of this kind of lighting; similarly, he and the chevalier deceive innumerable gamblers at various candlelit European courts. Barry's encounter with Lady Lyndon at the gambling table bears strong resemblances to the scene in which Barry flings his glass of wine into Quin's face, a defiant gesture that will lead to the duel. In both scenes the characters are shown in a series of slow shot/reverse shot sequences that in the first case suggest Barry's true love and in the second help to mask Barry's real intentions under his naïve look. In both scenes there is a character who accompanies the object of Barry's look and reacts, allowing us to comprehend the extent of the feelings that are being shown at the table. Nora looks afraid of Barry's serious countenance, foreshadowing what is going to happen; Reverend Runt looks suspiciously at Barry, discovering Barry's attraction to his lady and her response and, at the same time, expressing the contempt and rejection of the high class towards Barry. Both scenes are crucial for the development of Barry's character and comment on one another through their similar arrangement: Barry's approach to Lady Lyndon will have a similar outcome to his relationship with Nora.

Similarly, the main male characters in these two portions of the fabula are related by the text. Quin and Bullingdon will, in the end, keep the objects of their devotion (Nora and Lady Lyndon) at the expense of Barry. They will confront Barry in duels, which Barry will inevitably lose. Both men belong to a class superior to Barry's — both are "men of property," as Quin says, which sets them off from the poor Barry.

These examples show that the film's textual effort to establish symmetries and parallelisms is an invaluable source of clarity and unambiguous meanings. The pervasiveness of the strategy, the coherence of the ideas elicited by the structures, and the suitable form in which the film has chosen to present them stress the text's desire to destroy any possible difficulty the reader might encounter in "reading" the film. This conclusion is consistent with one of the general ideas of this study: that certain Kubrick films strive to create unambiguous meanings. A parametric narration would be the rejection of content-related meaning, an open door to ambiguity (cf. *Last Year at Marienbad*, 1961), but the mixture of parametric and classical, particularity and generality, which my scheme studies, reveals *Barry Lyndon* to be a carefully orchestrated text with no concession to doubt or ambiguity.

This part of the analysis of *Barry Lyndon* is an attempt to deconstruct the notion of parametric narration. Although the film seems to be a parametric text, it discards ambiguity by bringing together and putting to work various textual codes. The mixture of parametric and classical narration, together with the double side that parametric narration has in this text, produces a film in which the textual patterns are invested with meaning thanks to the general, external position suggested by its stylistic structures, which allow an allegorical interpretation of textual mechanisms.

It therefore seems not only that a certain dose of classicism helps in the appearance of unambiguous meaning, but that a clearly unclassical narrative mode such as parametric narration can also acquire classical features and evolve into clarity and lack of ambiguity if the text is apprehended from an external position of the viewer, fostered by the elements of generality. This claim can be linked to the idea that spectacle is, after all, an element of classicism, where it is a major contributor to the configuration of the text. In *Barry Lyndon* the purpose of parametric narration is to emphasize the spectacular quality of settings and characters, and this emphasis seems to encourage a metaphorical/allegorical reading of the text: beauty as the reflection of the law of decorum that surrounds and constrains Barry.

If we search through the critical literature devoted to this film we will find interpretations that reveal a similar underlying conception. Some studies show the capacity of cinematic language to be unambiguous. William Stephenson sees in *Barry Lyndon* not a description of the past but an experiment in cinematic form with the purpose of allowing us to see how film can suggest the deceptive distance of history, how the superficial view offered by history usually conceals the real passions, desires, and hatreds of the age (1981, 258–259). From this conclusion it may be inferred that the film is both an analysis/questioning of this historical distance and an exploration of the communicative potential of language. This interpretation indicates that the film is capable of eliciting unambiguous meanings. Nelson also sees in the film a clear statement about Barry's development from imitator to creator. Barry's experience of his son's death and his encounter with Bullingdon take him back to the real world; he leaves the artistic world, where people only behave decorously, and is then capable of moral choice. The film opposes human qualities such as choice to art and beauty (1982, 192).

Penelope Houston (1976) sees a tension in the film: abstraction and distance are counterbalanced by the film's beautiful form, which keeps the viewer's attention and prevents a perception of the text as experimental. She understands the film as an opposition between experimentalism and beauty; since experimentalism is opposed to classicism, beauty (spectacle) is linked to classicism. This is clear support for the idea that the film mixes experimentalism (parametric narration) and classicism and for the idea that spectacle is part of the classical code. The remarks on the film by Herb Lightman in *American Cinematographer* (1976) reinforce this thesis: beauty can be obtained from the faithful rendition of reality. Realism is not incompatible with a beautiful view of reality; beauty is compatible with lack of ambiguity.

Poststructuralisms and *Barry Lyndon*: The Originality of the Film

The privileging of beautiful views in *Barry Lyndon* may be the source of spectacle with antinarrative effects, as part of a scheme of parametric narration that attempts to avoid thematization. The presentation of strikingly beautiful views that consistently refuse to let the audience understand their relevance and meaning is foregrounded as mere formal device. This parametric quality is accompanied by a textual refusal to allow the viewer an easy interpretation of the formal pattern, or to offer a ready-made thematization of the structure.

At the same time, this emphasis on spectacle may also be the source of narrativity, since it may be transformed by the viewer, through a metaphorical reading, into an element that helps in the interpretation of the film as a battle between art and passion, between the eighteenth-century society of decorum and Barry. This is a position of the reader-decoder that is explained by the external placement of the viewer produced by certain narrative modes, a process accounted for in my scheme.

Barry Lyndon creates a subject who must feel himself as external to the text to grasp all the connections and meanings suggested by structure and style independently of the fabula. The zoom shots and the beautifully striking and balanced shots demand a subject who identifies with the text as a whole, not just with certain characters or elements of the story. The enjoyment of specific elements of the film leads to an appreciation of the beauty of the views, of the appropriateness and subtlety of the conjunction of music and visual spectacle, and of the faithful reconstruction of the period's costumes, settings, and behavior. Such an appreciation may, however, block the audience's response to the obviously unusual narrative mode that the film offers. The slow rhythm, the cold relationships established among the characters, and the character's inexpressive nature reveal the film as at least a strange narrative within the classical canon. These deviations shift the emphasis of the film from the depiction of drama to the enjoyment of spectacularly beautiful views.

The text's change from drama to spectacle is apparent in the use of reverse zoom shots, which emphasize the final combination of color and shade and composition and perspective. The use of inexpressive acting has been discussed as contributor to the spectacular nature of the text. Also, the film's attempt to remain faithful to the painterly nature of its images lays bare, in its consistency, that the depiction of character relationships and fabula in general is secondary for *Barry Lyndon*.

In what ways does this spectacular nature affect point of view, since the perception from an external position involves a shift of point of view? It transforms closeness into distance, emphasizing the externality of focalization. The film creates subjectivity through editing, camera movements, dialogue, mise-en-scène, and voice-over narration. We have already mentioned examples, however, in which these mechanisms are made subservient to the rendition of beauty. Editing is sometimes made to work to the rhythm of the extradiegetic music. Camera movements are rare in the film but they cannot avoid helping in the coherent portrayal of the painterly world of the text. Dialogue is so scarce that it acquires a great potential to signify. It shows how Barry's diction and intonation sound artificial in the new world of nobility he has joined. The use of dialogue by the rest of the characters, however, reveals that they take great care and interest in modulating their voices to utter soft, agreeable collections of sounds. Mise-en-scène and voice-over narration work together to elicit from the viewer a reading practice that will pay more attention to the appreciation of beautiful compositions than to the construction of the fabula. Mise-en-scène tries to make each shot resemble eighteenth-century paintings, while voice-over usually antici- pates the development of events, shifting the audience's attention from drama to the appreciation of beauty. Through these strategies the film's point of view gradually shifts from internal to external.

What ideas about the process of film perception, or understanding reality in general, does this film suggest? Following the assumption that the text is metafictional, we have reached the conclusion that the de- scription of beauty is opposed to narrative progression — at least theo- retically, because in practice this description is turned into a narrative force by suggesting (through composition, character movement, and camera movement) notions of eighteenth-century behavior. The text's descriptive tendency, together with its preference for scenes and slow- downs, is not an obstacle for narration; the experiment, therefore, proves that a certain emphasis on the physicality of the material pre- sented to the viewer may be useful to achieve a narrative, and also proves that the iconic side of cinema does not always evolve into non- narrative spectacle.

On the other hand, and as has already been mentioned, this empha- sis on the physicality of the image may destroy the system of the narra- tive, which is a proof that the text may have a political meaning: if physicality produces antinarrativity, then it has a political effect. By drawing attention to itself as language the cinematic sign lays bare its mimetic rendition of reality, therefore foregrounding the difference between art and reality.

Returning now to the use of iconicity with a narrative effect, the reading practice imposed by externality and the elements of generality in *Barry Lyndon* establishes a position for the viewer that is similar to that created by what Colin MacCabe calls a metalanguage (1981, 3– 15). The viewer is offered all the tools needed to interpret the film from an external position. This positioning of the subject implies an ideological process, since it forces the viewer to adopt an attitude of de- coder of a macro-scheme hidden in the text's stylistic strategies. The externality inherent in the process, however, produces an awareness in the viewer that avoids the powerful effect of ideology, which is always based on its invisibility. On the other hand, the importance conferred on the icon (as part of the language that makes cinema possible) lays bare the materiality of the text, thereby preventing the fetishization that can transform art into a blind acceptance and expression of the ideology contained in the text.

To disentangle the analysis of the film and study the real effect of the double possibility offered by the icon (narrativity and antinarrativity) the present analysis has resorted to the tools provided by deconstruction. It has deconstructed the strategy of parametric narration, whose reliance on repetition constitutes both its basis and the possibility for its dismantling. Certain ideas provided by deconstruction are useful in explaining the concept of generality. The notion of the parergon says that what is offered to the viewer is constituted by what is not offered, which frames what is offered. The zoom shot is an example: the reverse zoom shot, by expanding the frame, gives meaning to the small portion that appeared at the beginning. The metaphorical/allegorical meaning a viewer may feel tempted to give to a certain element will depend on the rest of the film, on the consistency of meaning that a certain interpretation may find in the whole of the text. These two examples of the capacity to invest material with meaning, to elicit metaphors, in the film are examples of the workings of elements of generality that can be explained through the capacity of the parergon to shape a code.

The power of the context of the code that deconstruction lays bare is also perceptible in the scheme outlined in this work. Unity is produced by generality, not by particularity, since generality provides a more external view from which to apprehend the context of the cinematographic signs. Does the film prove that the unity proper to externality cannot be caused by elements of particularity? I think it does, since the allegorical interpretation of the text creates a unity of meaning. This interpretation would not be possible without the external view offered by the elements of generality, a view that is not offered by the elements of particularity. The formal coherence produced by particularity does not necessarily amount to a rich web of signification.

These postmodernist notions have shaped a certain type of text. But on what grounds does *Barry Lyndon* claim its originality? *Barry Lyndon* rejects the idea of originality as it has traditionally been understood by criticism. It is a text that does not use the elements of particularity to create an inexplicable effect that will later be clarified by the rest of the text. It is, rather, the elements of generality that prevail and produce a coherent meaning from an external position that creates a coherent metaphorical/allegorical reading but does not turn any trace of irrationality into the main original aspect of the film. This is consistent with the text's attempts to eschew ambiguity.

A brief look at the connections that may be established between *Barry Lyndon* and various postmodernist topics has again confirmed the text's privileging of clarity and lack of ambiguity. A textual variable in the film exemplifies this tendency: the spatial configuration of the scenes. An analysis of the process of spatial construction at work in the film will help us defend the idea that such a construction creates clarity. The film sets up expectations about its spatial configuration that are consistently met by the text; the viewer is not let down through the reading of the dynamics of space fostered by the film itself.

E. H. Gombrich has dealt with this process of artistic apprehension in his renowned *Art and Illusion: A Study in the Psychology of Pictorial Representation* (1984). Gombrich stresses the relative nature of art's relationship with reality. Art is made possible by the viewer's capacity to perceive relationships in the face of change: if a certain artistic tendency decides to use specific techniques and codes to denote a specific aspect of reality, the viewers will only understand it if they have learned to identify such a code with the appropriate aspect of reality. It is not the expression of faithful relationships between sign and reality that constitutes a code but the agreement to refer to reality in a codified manner that people can identify.

Artists use their knowledge of things in the creation of the work of art. They try to accommodate reality within a previously acquired frame of reference. Art is, therefore, an appropriation of the real thing by the artist, who uses stereotypes, assumptions about the real shape and color of things, etc. as aids in his creative activity. This previous knowledge is organized into schemata that are set against the new information in order to process it with the help of already assimilated material. These schemata are also used by the consumers of art, who have to resort to their knowledge of reality, artistic conventions, perspective, etc. in the process of apprehending a work of art. It is a process that involves the setting up of hypotheses and the testing of their appropriateness by means of a dynamics of trial and error (1984, 63–90).

Gombrich interprets the Greek revolution in art as an evolution from an art that believes in essences to one that relies on relationships. It meant the discarding of a conception of art that possessed the mythical power of creating, of making what was represented. The new Greek art replaced making with the matching of reality, the imitation of reality through the use and modification of canons and rules of pictorial art. It meant the introduction of the idea of art as the expression of an illusion, of a dream that does not necessarily have to conform with reality and that demands certain canons and rules in order to exist (1984, 116–145).

The existence of canons, stereotypes as artistic norms, and of perception schemata shape the activity of the perceiver. What the subject perceives depends to a large extent on what one expects to find. The knowledge we have of reality and art conditions and guides our apprehension of artistic renderings. Our expectations are key elements when we come to interpret a work of art. Also, our capacity to infer is crucial in perception: we are often asked to complete an image on our own, based on our knowledge of reality. Art relies on our ability to clarify and complete what the artist has left indistinct; the viewer's desire for consistency will transform anything according to the context in which it appears. The ambiguity that is intrinsic to many artistic norms — the depiction of perspective, for instance — will have to be solved by the subject (1984, 181–287).

Barry Lyndon creates internal laws about the ways in which the configuration of space is carried out. The text is gradually revealed to be faithful to these laws. It does what Gombrich says a tradition or artistic background does: it gives the viewer a stock of canons and schemata to be applied in the apprehension of stimuli. The film is, therefore, revolutionary in its awareness of the way art, and the apprehension of art, work, implicitly supporting the idea that the role of the viewer/decoder is essential to the construction and development of art. The film is an explanation of the ways in which films may contribute to the evolution of art in those cinematic aspects that are most proximate to pictorial art. The configuration of space, the composition of the shot, the use of color, and the effects of plastic beauty are relevant to this study. *Barry Lyndon* shows an awareness of film's capacity to study and advance the medium's potentiality to express ideas by means of what we call mise-en-scène in cinema. The film is an exercise in this capacity to create canons, to foster and elicit schemata, which shows the effectiveness of that side of cinema that is most closely related to pictorial art.

What canons does the film establish, and what schemata does it help elicit? They are related to the creation of depth and perspective, a typical feature of painting that in this film is introduced and transformed into one more sign. This creation of space proves that the text aims at clarity by exploring the ways of creating perspective and by repeating their structures.

Barry Lyndon employs overlapping to create depth and perspective. The superposition of elements of mise-en-scène or characters in the same frame help the viewer identify the object or person partially concealed by proximate elements as more distant from the foreground.

This is such a common method of signaling depth that it becomes difficult to appreciate. The film's tendency to favor static compositions and characters, however, emphasizes camera and character movement when such movement appears. In one of the first scenes in the film Barry and his mother walk together outside their house while the narrator tells us how the family was left without the husband and father. The character movement has no purpose except the description of the beautiful Irish countryside that the camera movement following the characters allows. This camera movement offers the viewer cues about the perspectival relationships among the elements in the scene as trees go past from right to left in the foreground and the characters' movement reveals the walls and hills behind them. The accessory nature of the whole scene manages to draw attention to the mechanisms at work in the depiction of the striking view created by the film; and within these mechanisms the expression of perspective is a key factor, since the text so clearly follows patterns of pictorial art. While it is true that all films resort to compositions that use perspective as an organizing strategy, the tendency of *Barry Lyndon* constantly to emphasize the pictorial quality of its shots points to its particularly self-conscious nature in this respect.

Perspective can also be achieved by means of atmospheric elements. In the scene with Barry and his mother the view is partly obtained by the presence of clouds, creating a certain quality of lighting that is merely to be put down to the natural elements configuring a realistic composition. The same thing happens later when we see Barry riding away to Dublin: dark clouds foreboding a storm surround Barry, establishing cues about the distance he is traversing, about the point in the background from which he has come, and contributing to the general emphasis on mise-en-scène. A similar technique of suggesting perspective is used in the scene showing Barry leading the cows in the Lischen episode, where the colors of the sunset create different areas indicating different degrees of depth.

Another common procedure to suggest depth and perspective, and also related to pictorial art, is the arrangement of compositions in which components of landscape create a receding center where the lines of perspective are made to converge. In the scene where Barry sees Nora home, they walk along two lines of trees that frame the composition and point to the background, where perspective leads our eyes into the distance. In the first duel scene the trees on both sides of the frame, which disclose a clearing where the two duelists stand, recede toward the center pointing to a lake in the background. In the Lischen episode we see Barry lead the cows along a path toward the sunset. The composition marks the importance of the center by means of fences on the sides of the path. The first view we get of Berlin resembles a painting so much that its similarity with paintings of the period has been remarked. The road, the hedges, the trees, and the arrangement of the houses in the distance create a pictorial perspective consistent with the text's general purpose of emphasizing visual beauty.

This same technique of establishing receding lines of perspective can also make use of characters as centers of the composition. In the scene of the announcement of the Nora-Quin marriage the center of the frame is occupied by Barry, who refuses to share in the toast for the couple. He appears flooded in light, which makes his inexpressive face stand out. The use of perspective helps the text express his reaction. In the scene that follows, Barry and Captain Grogan are transformed into the center of perspective by the lines that form the path along which they are approaching the foreground of the frame. Later, a scene shows Barry's cousin convincing Barry's mother that her son has to go to Dublin after killing Quin in a duel. The scene privileges Barry, who is placed in the center of the composition, in the most evenly lit area, configuring a strikingly beautiful view of the three people sitting at the table, illuminated by a soft, orangeish side light.

Finally, the establishment of perspectival cues is also carried out by the use of light and shadow. This strategy paradigmatically combines the creation of depth and the presentation of spectacular views. A spectacular composition appears in the night-watch scene. Barry appears in the center of the frame wearing the English army's uniform; he is doing the night-watch by the fire, leaning wearily over his rifle. The light produced by the fire illuminates the center of the composition occupied by Barry. The center of perspective is, therefore, the lighted area surrounded by the darkness of night. The scene reminds us of paintings of the period that made use of the same motif and employed similar colors and shades. The creation of perspective is accompanied by an obvious attempt to suggest connections between these compositions and the painting tradition of the eighteenth century. The candlelit scenes have achieved deserved popularity among cinema fans because of the subtlety and warmth they connote. The use of candles divides the the frame into areas of light and, where light recedes, growing darkness. This division sets a center to which all the lines in the shot are directed: the lighted area. Grogan and Barry in the army camp's tent introduce this kind of shot, which also appears during the meeting with Lischen, in the scenes at the gambling table, and in the second part in scenes of seduction.

At the same time, I think the text clearly ascribes meanings to these methods of creating space in an attempt to adhere to the canons of eighteenth-century painting. The use of landscape and of dark colors and the rendering of grass by means of brownish tones aided by lighting all emphasize the side of cinema that most approximates the codes and nature of painting. They claim for cinema the capacity to create the same canons painting does: the capacity to create meaning by setting up codes and eliciting schemata from the viewers. In this case the text is trying to copy the compositions and methods of constructing perspective employed by traditional painting, more specifically by eighteenth-century painting.

This meaning is also created by the use of the zoom shot. Zoom shots frequently emphasize the center of perspective: it is another proof that the creation of perspective is a key factor in the meaning creation process of the film. The center of perspective is sometimes gradually focused by means of a zoom shot. Our first view of Lady Lyndon is constructed as a lateral camera movement that describes the garden where Barry and the chevalier spend the afternoon; this camera movement discovers a group of people in the background, and a zoom shot takes us closer to them while the voice-over narration informs us that the group is the Lyndon family and that Barry is about to attempt to seduce Lady Lyndon. Most commonly the center of perspective is marked by a zoom shot that moves back to place the object or character in context. This is a constant tendency throughout the film, as has already been discussed.

Some of these compositions are surprising not only because of their privileging of beauty but also for their emphasis on symmetrical compositions. The scene in which Barry's mother convinces her son that he must obtain a title to secure his position is a good example. The scene begins with a close-up of the mother; the reverse zoom discloses that she is talking to Barry and that they are on a bridge over a lake near the house; Lady Lyndon is in the lake, rowing a boat with her sons and Reverend Runt. The reverse zoom shot transforms the close-up into a long shot in which the bridge is reflected on the lake, creating a symmetrical composition in the middle of the frame; the boat is seen through one of the bridge's arches, emphasizing the symmetry and marking another center of attention within the enlarged shot. The most characteristic stylistic option in the film is, therefore, a great aid to the general textual strategy of constructing perspective in a pictorial manner and of emphasizing such a construction. Furthermore, the zoom shot is a formal strategy that in this film becomes reconciliatory of the classical privileging of perspective and of self-consciousness. Zoom shots self-consciously transform mise-en-scène as particularity into mise-en-scène as generality, and since the final purpose of this trans-

formation is the privileging of perspective the move means a reconciliation of classical and self-conscious modes of narration.

The consistency acquired by the recurrence of zoom shots is bound
to make any variation look extraordinary. The setting up of perspectival
cues by means of zoom shots is extraordinarily altered by the alternative
use of editing. As we have mentioned, after Barry beats up Bullingdon
and is ostracized by his noble friends he finds refuge in his son, Brian.
This search for tenderness, and Barry's growing loneliness, are expressed by means of a long shot in which the center of attention is not
Barry or his son but a huge painting that appears on the wall behind
them. The frame is orientated to place the painting in the central position, turning it into the centre of perspective. This long shot appears
after a close-up that shows Barry and his son looking at a book and
talking. The change from close-up to long shot does not use the zoom
but a cut that relegates the two characters to a corner, the main space
now being occupied by the painting in a clear reference to the overwhelming nature of that society's rules and to the connections established by the film between those rules and pictorial art. The rendering
of perspective is, therefore, also part of the meaningful intrinsic code
set by the film, which has been shown to be based on the use of zoom
shots and their variations.

The previous examples are proof of the signification pull at work in
the film, which ascribes meaning to each instance of perspective. Other
alterations of the structure of perspective also become meaningful. The
rejection of character movement where realistic motivation clearly demands it and the displacement of the centrality of character in perspective are particularly relevant in the last moments of the narrative. After
Barry has been wounded and his leg amputated he has to leave England
never to see Lady Lyndon again, as the narrator says. This information
is delivered as we see Barry leave the inn where he has recovered from
the effects of the duel and walk toward a carriage on the left. As he is
entering the carriage the frame freezes, and over this view of the crippled Barry leaving for good we hear the narrator's voice announcing his
final defeat. The use of the freeze frame is a rejection of character
movement as marker of the center of perspective. The text now focuses
on the static figure of our fallen hero: the view is enlarged, rejecting
perspective as a means of leading the viewer's apprehension in favor of
an emphasis on the patterns of light and color. The signifying force of
this strategy is clear because it involves the breakdown of an established
pattern. It suggests that this world of law and decorum to which Barry
has not been able to accustom himself has finally managed to deprive
him of the force that propelled him into such a class: his activity, his

capacity to act and change things, no matter how naïve or unfair his actions might have been. The device also carries connotations that have been acquired by its appearance in certain cinematic styles. The freeze frame inevitably conjures up connections with the French New Wave, particularly with François Truffaut's *Les quatre cents coups* (1959). The feeling of helplessness and open-ended narrative suggested by Truffaut's use of the device is also present in *Barry Lyndon*. The capacity for signification of this stylistic strategy is clear, and the alteration of perspectival models set by the film is part of this capacity.

The final scene of the film is also an alteration with respect to the text's attitude to perspective. After Lady Lyndon hesitates and signs the order to pay Barry his annual stipend in Ireland, the text cuts to a long shot in which Lady Lyndon is overwhelmed by a huge painting that covers the background wall. This scene, which is similar to the one with Barry and Brian, is a rejection of the centrality of human beings in perspectival constructions; here they are replaced by a work of art. The meaning of the scene is obvious: again, art, associated by the film with the laws of decorum, has triumphed over human feelings and desires, leaving only the coldness distilled by formal perfection. The alteration of perspective by placing a painting in the center of the composition is made to signify.

As a conclusion to this section, it may be said that the film attempts to move from ways of reading typical of film to those of painting, with the purpose of finally combining both methods in an enrichment of the cinematic medium. It is this aspect that constitutes the film's originality: the emphasis given to a specific element of film and to its capacity to signify. The originality of *Barry Lyndon* consists not in creating narrative disturbances, fostering antinarrative tendencies, and accommodating them as the most original part of the text but in the elaboration of a code of signification based on an aspect of cinema: its connections with pictorial art. The antinarrativity that might be present through the self-conscious working of the reverse zoom shot, which transforms mise-en-scène from particular views into long shots (from particularity into generality), becomes in fact an aid to the classical construction of perspective. The film presents us with an overall tendency to privilege clarity and avoid ambiguity.

Barry Lyndon introduces generality as the creator of clear and definite meanings by reconciling two narrative modes that seem irreconcilable, classical and parametric, and by reconciling the classical code of the pictorial basis of cinema with the self-consciousness of the zoom shot in the construction of perspective. The film becomes an expression of an extreme faith in the capacity of the code to signify, a code that is able to accommodate seemingly antinarrative forces and present them as the essential core of the classical mode. *Barry Lyndon* represents the traditional view of the linguistic system as capable of creating clear and definite meanings; it represents the rejection of a limitless system that allows infinite readings and finally evolves into the abolition of the system itself. In short, this film stands for the favorite prey of deconstructionists, who are fond of theorizing about the ideological potential inherent in a concept of language that promises the capacity to provide a definite relationship with reality. So far, two positions toward language have been explored — which, by the way, are taken to be polar opposites, to the extent that the rejection of one of them seems to justify the adoption of the other. In the analysis of *Full Metal Jacket* we will be offered another possibility, which might help the critic free her/himself from the constrictions of a conception of language that, as exemplified by deconstructionists, constantly moves from one extreme to its opposite.

5: *Full Metal Jacket* (1987): One Possible Answer

*F*ULL *METAL JACKET* DEALS WITH THE EXPERIENCES of a group of soldiers in the Vietnam War. The film is divided into two parts. The first deals with the training the recruits have to go through on Parris Island. Their drill instructor, Hartman, tries to create efficient killing machines through constant abuse. One of the soldiers, Joker, becomes our guide when his voice makes us share his thoughts. Pyle, an overweight recruit, fails to meet Hartman's demands and ends up shooting the instructor, only to commit suicide shortly afterward in the final scene at the camp. The second part takes us to Vietnam, where the Tet offensive forces Joker partially to abandon his task as a journalist for *Stars and Stripes* and join his friend Cowboy's squad. In their ramblings through Hue they lose their way and are set upon by a sniper who kills three of the men, Cowboy among them. Joker discovers that the sniper is a Vietnamese girl. He kills the dying enemy to save her the pain of a slow death, and the film ends as Joker joins the rest of the soldiers, who sing the Mickey Mouse song. He confides to us that he has learned to survive in the war and that that is the only thing that matters; he is alive and not afraid.

Repetition

Critics agree that repetition is a key strategy used by the film to shape its meaning. The first and second parts are made to interact in ways that affect the level of the fabula — the level of cinematographic properties and composition of the shot, mise-en-scène, and verbal language. Gilbert Adair asserts that the division of the text into two parts inevitably invites the viewer to understand them as the two panels of a diptych, suggesting their complementary nature (1989, 171). Michael Pursell is more specific, mentioning examples of the interaction between the first and the second part. For him the slow motion deaths of Doc Jay and the sniper match the slow-motion views of the squad stumbling in the mud in the first part. The sniper also recalls Hand Job, since both deaths are shown through point-of-view shots from the ground. The final scene's Mickey Mouse song reminds us of the reference Hartman makes before Pyle's death: "What is all this Mickey

Mouse here?" Pursell even sees connections between the "Head" where Pyle dies and Joker's "dead" head at the end of the film (1988, 223) in a convincing proof of the tendency to elicit meaning created in the viewer by the technique of repetition.

The first section of my study of *Full Metal Jacket* is devoted to the analysis of repetitions, which become meaningful by establishing comparisons and contrasts between elements of the text. The first object of this section's analysis will be those textual parameters that fall under the category of mise-en-scène.

Settings are an obvious source of repetitions, which, in turn, suggest contrasts. The military base in the first part is characterized by outdoor spaces arranged in straight paths along which the soldiers run and by series of obstacles that in their cold symmetry present an almost insurmountable hostility. The huge room where the soldiers sleep has polished, shining walls and floor, the result of intense three-point lighting. Together with the lavatory they are the only two indoor spaces in which the text allows us to observe the characters. In these rooms the beds and the toilets are aligned on both sides, leaving an empty corridor in the middle. The angle from which the text presents these rooms preserves this perfect arrangement, using it as an aid for the construction of perspective. We can say that in general the first part of the film makes an explicit attempt to build ordered, symmetrical spaces in a metaphorical reference to the strict logic of authority that governs the boot camp. The only intrusions of disorder and dirt are the two slow-motion views of the soldiers charging an imaginary enemy, one of which shows the platoon wading through mud to help Pyle. They are foreshadowings of the final effect that the logic of authority will have on them: Pyle will die because of the "help" of his friends, who beat him into insanity in their attempt to make him improve his military performance, and the rest of the platoon will become disorganized in the battle in Vietnam. Pyle's death is the only event that alters the balance of the clean closed spaces, as Adair asserts (1989, 179). Hartman's blood and Pyle's brains are the only examples of human "flesh and blood" that break the perfection of the setting, marking the inadequacy of the inhuman ideological code Hartman has tried to teach to his men.

The second part represents the antithesis of the setting of the first part. Vietnam is a mixture of American-like colorful iconography and burning rubble where nothing seems to follow an arrangement of any kind. The tent where the soldiers sleep tries to maintain the perspectival perfection of the room in the first part, but here the light is so dim that nothing can shine; and it is the flickering light that first warns the soldiers of the North Vietnamese offensive, putting an end to the text's rendering of ordered authority. From then on the men wander without a clear direction. Tanks crossing the setting, burning buildings, and piles of corpses are the environment through which the soldiers reach the sniper's stronghold. The platoon's problems begin when they are forced to enter unknown, disordered, and imperfect urban landscape; a huge hole in a wall is the cause of Cowboy's death; and Joker remains alive because he finds shelter behind a pillar that the sniper's fire almost reduces to nothing. Setting has changed from the knowable but tough order of the boot camp to the unknown disorder of actual war, where the men find death or salvation in spontaneous appearances of elements of setting that nobody can control. The inside of the sniper's building is a mess of oriental furniture that has succumbed to the sophisticated American weapons — a clear reference to the role played by the Americans in the war, and exemplified by the platoon in its final action.

Interesting uses of repetition are found in the text's handling of costume and of the actors' physical appearance. The credit-title sequence includes the shaving of the soldiers' heads, suggesting the power of the military and of war to wipe out all traces of individuality and difference among the men. The different styles, colors, and lengths of the soldiers' hair are quickly destroyed and replaced by almost identical skulls, while they are forced to dress in identical suits. The second part allows the men to become differentiated, since they wear their own hairstyles and decorate their helmets in various ways, making reference to the difference between what was demanded from them in the boot camp and the real necessities imposed by a war. While the training works to eliminate individuality and form a hard group, war demands the capacity to take individual decisions. The ideology behind boot camp, that the group (nation) is the seed of victory and safety, is replaced by a more realistic experience in which the individual is shown to be alone even in the company of others and where the ideological constructs of army or nation do not help the soldiers to remain alive. Once this is made clear, war becomes a mere attempt to kill in order not to be killed, no matter who gets killed or how.

The expression and movement of the actors are key mise-en-scène elements that the textual strategy of repetition puts to work. In the first part the characters follow straight lines in their formation-like movements; the second part presents them following random paths, once they are left to their own devices. Their facial and corporal expression in the first part is always geared by Hartman's command: they are tense and martial in their responses. In the second part the men's faces relax but still preserve the aura of violence the first part has produced in them. Their reactions to the dangers of real fire are more human than the pure aggression shown in boot camp. The demand made by Hartman on the soldiers is quickly revealed to be almost impossible to meet. Hartman and the Marine Corps wanted men whose killing instincts were pure, soldiers who would not hesitate at the moment of shooting an enemy. Hartman wants to erase from the soldier's minds all feelings of sympathy that may endanger their lives in combat. Such purity is, however, replaced by the men's most human feeling of fear of dying and by Joker's sympathy for the dying sniper, situations that clearly depend on the actors' capacity to express themselves through facial and corporal gesture. The element of mise-en-scène that demands the most participation from flesh-and-blood characters, and not from other textual elements where no people intervene, is precisely the one that most clearly indicates the growing experience of humanity undergone by the soldiers.

Cinematographic properties are other textual elements that may shape structures of repetition and contrast. Strategies of framing reserve to camera movements the task of creating patterns of repetition. Tracking shots accompany the soldiers in both parts, stressing the contrast between the organization of the first and the disorder of the second. The camera movements that portray the course of the training follow straight lines of progression along paths or corridors or follow the men along the obstacles in the training field. In Vietnam these tracking shots follow the soldiers in combat: their trajectory is not straight but accompanies the men's attempts to avoid enemy fire or to find shelter behind tanks or buildings. The level of the camera is much lower, since the men have to crawl or crouch; the frame, therefore, includes the men in a closer connection with the ground.

This change of level carries metaphorical connotations: the soldiers are closer to the ground because they cannot take refuge in the rules of the organized military; but they are closer to their origin, to the nature that bore them and threatens to reclaim them prematurely. They have lost the rules of social institutions that oppress them and have gained an unconscious awareness of their nature as animals who fight for self-preservation. The shot in which Cowboy lies dying while his friends try to assist him is reminiscent of the apes' shots in the first section of *2001*.[1] Here human beings are shown as still animals who in their de-

---

[1] Certain critics have noticed the presence in this scene of a building in the background that resembles the monolith in *2001* (Castro 1994, 126–127). Is the mise-en-scène to be understood as another warning to humankind, as a

fenselessness seeks comfort in the group; the resemblance of these shots suggests that the human race may have developed more complex systems of organization, but they do not necessarily mean an improvement in human nature. Low speed of motion links the two scenes of the wild group in the mud in the first part with Doc Jay's and Eight-ball's deaths and even with the view of the sniper's appearance and death. The contrast is evident from the moment we realize how the views of the group in the first part are replaced by views of isolated people dying. The meaning suggested by this contrast makes clear that the return to the most basic human nature does not prevent isolation, solitude, or death.

The perfect perspective created by the organization of beds or toilets in the barracks and is congruent with the first part's world of order is also the object of contrast. Traditional perspective is deleted from the second part. The settings where the climaxes of the two parts take place (the lavatory and the sniper's building) are set apart by the use of point-of-view shots. The subjective shots from Pyle's point of view in the lavatory preserve perspectival coherence, while the zoom shots from the sniper's position crush the planes of depth and gradually destroy perspective. The order that is threatened in the lavatory sequence, but that nevertheless still exists, is not even contemplated in the second part, where the screen is filled by close-ups of Doc Jay and Eight-ball being slowly killed. In the second part's zoom shots there is no possibility of order because there is nothing to order: there is not a variety of elements on the screen that are arranged in space; there is only one element (isolated dying bodies), which in its proximity states the crude reality caused by the order and perfect perspective of the first part. Gilbert Adair seems to coincide with this reading in an argument where he mixes camera movements and perspective. For him, camera movements cease only to create symmetries, which inevitably lead the viewer to scan the center of the screen: a dead center in its lack both of action and of compassion (1989, 176).

Sound is a communicative channel in cinema that provides a great amount of information. Part of its relevance lies in the importance the text gives to dialogue. The contents of dialogue are susceptible of expressing the effects of repetition. Dialogues express recurrent meanings, usually through recurrent diction. It is a language of bigotry, which reveals prejudices against all kinds of social, cultural, or sexual difference from the norm of the white American. The language of abuse destroys

---

sign that the symbol of perfect intelligence has been replaced by chaos and irrationality in Vietnam?

the personal identity of the soldiers. It appears in the sniper's sequence: Animal Mother answers "fuck 'er" to Joker's demand for an opinion about what they should do with her. This kind of language turns war into a matter of sexual difference, too, where the soldiers try to eliminate their most feminine side. This process is evident in the language used by Hartman and his men. "Eskimo pussy is mighty cold," "Your rifle is the only pussy you people are going to get," or "Today you are no longer maggots, today you are Marines" are only a few examples of the instructor's verbal diarrhea that proves that he understands training as the process of ridiculing and finally killing the most feminine aspects of his men's personalities.[2] Hartman's language despises blacks, homosexuals, women, people from certain states, the physically handicapped, and, in general, anybody or anything that may be taken as a mark of difference.

Hartman's language contains so many swear words that it creates in the viewer the fear that he is about to destabilize the basis on which culture is founded. Cultural precepts are founded on a certain respect for difference; Hartman's language, however, destroys these foundations, or at least almost seems to be close to doing so. This kind of language makes its way into the other Marines, as we see in the second part of the text: Joker's last speech is an example.

Language is used to evoke and inscribe American clichés into the text. The teenage ideology that considers becoming a male heartbreaker something desirable is present in the film. When Joker and Rafterman find Cowboy in the second part, one of Cowboy's mates says "we are life-takers and heartbreakers"; and after Rafterman has killed the sniper and has overcome his awe of battle he also calls himself a heartbreaker. The use of this cliché, typical of American pop songs, associates love with violence and competition among teenage boys: the fight becomes the locus where the male gains access to the woman precisely by killing the woman in himself. Joker also uses several quotations from the films of John Wayne, a mythical figure associated with the defense of violence as a suitable method of establishing a civilized state, as represented by his part in John Ford's *The Man Who Shot Lib-*

---

[2] Tania Modleski sees in this attempt to destroy femininity one of the objectives of war: to subjugate femininity and keep it at a distance. She mentions the notion that sexuality manifested in violence is the expression of a fear of dissolution with a woman that propels men into a homosocial relation with other men (1991, 62).

erty Valance (1962).³ He stands for the myth of the frontier, where such irreconcilable notions as violence and law are compatible. The colonel who interrogates Joker next to the lime-covered dead exemplifies the application of this myth to the circumstance of Vietnam: we are killing the Vietnamese because by doing it we bring freedom to them. "Inside every Gook there's an American trying to get out."

Language may also suggest a return to childhood. The Mickey Mouse song takes the soldiers back to American youth associations, where the individuals find a safe haven to protect them from the hardships of maturation. Childhood is the age when the subject can still feel that one can have everything, without renouncing anything. The intrusion of this kind of language at the end of the film fits the process of reconciliation of opposites that informs the text. The difficulties Joker has in accepting the military code, and later the realities of combat, seem to have been overcome in his last speech, where he has learned to reconcile the act of killing with his own self-esteem: he kills to survive, and that is the only thing that matters. A similarly childish enthusiasm to that present in the Mickey Mouse song lies in the demand for action expressed by the typical war tough guy. Rafterman wants to pretend that he is a tough soldier, and he adopts the diction of the veteran. "I want to get into the bush and get some trigger time, Joker," he says, asking for dangerous activity in an attitude prototypically associated with American youth.

The expression of the men's opinions about the war finds a channel in language. At Hand-Job's funeral his comrades gather around the corpse and utter brief remarks:

> T.H.E. Rock: You're going home now.
> Crazy Earl: Semper fi.
> Eight-ball: Go easy, bros.
> Animal Mother: Better you than me.
> Rafterman: At least you can say they died for a good cause.
> Animal Mother: What cause was that?

Some express feelings of comradeship, while Animal Mother expresses his satisfaction in being alive, since this is all that matters in Vietnam. There is no cause that can justify the slaughter in which they are involved. Some of the men are more conscious of this than others, who still believe there is a reason for the American intervention that they can use to justify their personal plights.

---

³ For more information on John Wayne, see Virginia Wright Wexman (1993, 113–129).

In the television interviews the soldiers express their difficulty in reconciling language and reality. War is indescribable because it does not fit their mental schemes. Animal Mother ends his explanation of what they do in battle by saying: "we basically blow the place to hell." After an attempt to say what they do with exact words, he gives up and uses this sentence, which seems to compress what he "really" feels he is doing, leaving aside the subtleties of language he had attempted before. War can only be expressed by means of this destructive vocabulary, as if war destroyed the human capacity to dominate reality through language. Cowboy finds nothing better to say than a complaint that there are no horses in Vietnam: he has assumed his role as a representative of a certain part of America — Texas — and says what a Texan is supposed to miss in such a remote country. His remark also shows the Americans' tendency to judge Vietnam according to their national parameters; they are unable to open their eyes and see that they are in a country that cannot be explained through an ideology designed to understand the United States. Eight-ball shows a high degree of irony when he says: "We take our freedom and give it to the Gookers. They don't want it, they'd rather be alive than free, I guess. Poor damn bastards!" He takes the idea of freedom as the aim of American involvement and twists it to show its utter illogicality. Joker is difficult to read, since there is no clear division between what he says in earnest and what he says ironically: "I wanted to meet interesting people from a different culture, and kill them. I want to be the first kid on the block to get a confirmed kill." He seems to adopt an ironic stance, but the last sentence sounds like the expression of his most intimate desires. Joker's status as ambiguous figure is reinforced by this remark.

An effective use of dialogue structure consists of the elaboration of sentences that use repetition to create striking verbal compositions. It is, in fact, the use of repetition, so consistently evident at a visual level, that is translated to verbal language. Rhyming sentences become slogans in boot camp and in codes of behavior throughout the film. "This is my rifle, this is my gun / This is for fighting, this is for fun" connects violence and sex, suggesting that they share the same sources. "I love working for Uncle Sam / Lets me know just who I am" represents an acknowledgment of how dominated by the country's system the soldiers are, and how the war is a vehicle for representing such subjugation. "Put a nigger behind the trigger," says Eight-ball when he is picked to explore a potentially dangerous area — constitutes an example of his awareness of racial discrimination in military life, which is an extension of discrimination in civilian life. Racial bigotry is recognized and accepted, since he does not hesitate to obey Cowboy's order to explore the sniper's area. "Hard core, man, fuckin' hard core" is the verbal description of Joker's decision to kill the sniper. It is a self-contained expression of Joker's process of subjectivity. He is trapped by his "hard-core" — his intimate feelings turned cold and ruthless — which has helped him get to the end of the war alive and in one piece.

Rafterman's reply, "When the shit gets tough, they call mother green and the killing machine," encapsulates the workings of rhyming structures. It joins an attractive form with certainly disagreeable contents. Another boot-camp song exemplifies this:

> I don't want no teenage queen,
> I just want my M-14,
> If I die in the combat zone,
> Pack me up and ship me home,
> Pin my medals upon my chest,
> Tell my mom I've done my best.

The chant is a rejection of sexuality in favor of war and killings, nationalistic pride taken to an extreme. The form of dialogue and chants seems more important than its contents. The rhyming patterns or structural perfection become enough justification for its use, disregarding the contents, which are usually offensive. The communal repetition of chants or stereotyped sentences links the individual to the group; he is searching desperately for comfort, regardless of the ideology such a search may force the soldier to accept.

Repetition also works by creating compounds of verbal language that become prayers for this new religion of violence:

> Today is Christmas! There will be a magic show at zero-nine-thirty! Chaplain Charlie will tell you about how the free world will conquer Communism with the aid of God and a few Marines! God has a hard-on for Marines because we kill everything we see! He plays his games, we play ours! To show our appreciation for so much power, we keep heaven packed with fresh souls! God was here before the Marine Corps! So you can give your heart to Jesus, but your ass belongs to the Corps! Do you ladies understand?

Hartman adopts the tone of a priest in indoctrinating his men. The mixture of religious references and obscenities shows, on the one hand, the tendency to present American interventions as religious crusades and, on the other, the presence of a sense of community that the military command tries to foster in the soldiers.

This new religion attempts to create superior men who accept killing as their code. It demands a particular purity:

If your killer instincts are not clean and strong you will hesitate at the moment of truth. You will not kill, you will become dead Marines. And then you will be in a world of shit, because Marines are not allowed to die without permission.

The demand for purity, even this kind of purity, reveals the military's creation of men who feel different from others. The same superior nature is attributed to the enemy: "These people we waste here today are the best human beings we'll ever know. After we rotate back to the world we are gonna miss not having anybody who's worth shooting," says one of Cowboy's buddies shortly after Joker and Cowboy meet in Vietnam.

The men use a coded vocabulary in combat that sets them off from those who have not experienced the hardships of the war. For Touchdown, "we are expecting rain" means that they are expecting an air attack. Rafterman wants to get "some trigger time," meaning some experience in real combat. For Payback, Joker does not have the "stare" that Marines get after they have been in the "shit" for too long. "VC," "NVA," "grunt," and "Gook" are words used by the combat veterans to set themselves apart from the newcomers. This vocabulary turns the war into a kind of religious experience where through pain and danger the soldier improves his nature, finally becoming acceptable for the standards of violence, of Vietnam.

The contents and the structure of dialogue interrelate in the film's soundtrack. The use of popular songs is a rich source of meaning since they are the expression of a direct contact with the people and therefore contain a great part of the ideology that power tries to spread to justify violence. Moreover, they envelop contents in attractive forms, which makes them good examples of ideological vehicles. The song that accompanies the title sequence is "Hello Vietnam." "Goodbye sweetheart, hello Vietnam," "it involves us one and all," and "there is a battle to be won" are lines that summarize the predominant ideology that American youths must renounce the comfort of love at home to fight for a cause that is their cause. The rhythm and tone are those of a country song, the quintessentially American kind of music that expresses the most American feelings about frontier life. Country music preserves the ideology of the traditional West's values and ideas, where violence is used to impose the law. The song defends America's intervention in the war, sanctioning the process of homogenization illustrated by the shaving of the men's heads. It also makes reference to the well-known image of Elvis Presley being shaved before joining the army. The relationship suggested contrasts the positive connotations of patriotism and egalitarianism of Presley's image with the negative view of men being shaved into a single prototype.

The first scene in Vietnam is introduced as Nancy Sinatra's "These Boots Were Made for Walkin'" sounds in the background. "One of these days these boots are gonna walk all over you" goes the song. America is walking over the Vietnamese, not only physically but also culturally. The Vietnam city resembles typical American streets. The colorful advertising walls reveal how the Vietnamese have been colonized to the last detail. The song's lines also foreshadow the development of the second part if we put them together with the trick played by the prostitute and her pimp on Joker and Rafterman, where they steal Rafterman's camera: the Vietnamese boot is going to slaughter Cowboy's platoon. This prostitute seems to forecast how a female Vietnamese character will become a threat to the soldiers at the end of this section: she "walks all over" Cowboy's platoon.

The Joker-Cowboy reunion evolves while "Woolly Bully" sounds in the background. This is the scene where the most American clichés crop up, where men are qualified as "life-takers" and "heartbreakers," linking violence and the terminology of pop music. Through this strategy the film reveals the process of coming to terms with the war by taking it as an extension of the teenage activity of seduction so valorized in American culture. Joker impersonates John Wayne, the best representative of the frontier life. A soldier makes the speech about the enemy's value.

"Surfing Bird" accompanies the killing of two Vietnamese at the hands of an American soldier. In the course of a raid Cowboy and his comrades are seen facing enemy fire until one of the men kills two Vietnamese. The song bursts onto the soundtrack as the soldier's face beams with joy. This explosion of music and happiness confers on war the look of Americanness necessary to be acceptable, according to the clichés presented before. It transforms the episode into one more instance of spectacular action, the gaiety of the music drawing the audience to identify with the soldier and share his joy. The final song, the Rolling Stones' "Paint It Black," does away with such optimism, suggesting that the degradation of Joker's personality as a requirement of such a cultural construction does not inspire hope for the future:

> I have to turn my head until my darkness goes . . .
> I look inside myself and see my heart is black . . .
> Maybe I'll fade away and not have to face the facts
> It's not easy when your whole world is black . . .
> Paint it black! . . . Paint it black! . . . Paint it black!

The rhythmic patterns of popular music are based on repetition of lines and chords, shaping an attractive rhythm that envelops contents that also tend to recur in the various songs on the soundtrack. Repetition produces a spectacular form that is enjoyed independently of the ideas the accompanying lyrics may express. The importance of both the contents and the form of dialogue is evident by now, to the extent that we can consider them one of the main themes of the film. *Full Metal Jacket* explores the power of language to shape a system of signs based on repetition as difference, in a word, the power to create a symbolic system that sets its laws on the men. The development of this system throughout the film leads us to agree with Michael Pursell that the physical aggression depicted in the last section is first hinted at in the symbolic universe of thought and language (1988, 224).

Elements of style suggest connections between events, which mark them as repetitions producing parallelisms or contrasts. The first and second parts suggest the parallel development of Hartman and Joker. Joker manages to "mature" and achieve a hard heart during the second part — just what Hartman wanted for him. Joker, despite his awareness of the "duality of man" — as he says — will have to adapt and be content to be alive after all he has to go through. Hartman's death at the end of the first part parallels Joker's internal death in the course of the war: both are "shot in the heart," since Joker's process of maturation involves his killing of a person. The expression of his sympathy is paradoxically transformed into the very act that Hartman trained him to perform.

The credit-title sequence's music is set against the final "Paint It Black." The naïve satisfaction about war of the first song is replaced by the pessimism of the Stones' song. After the process of the film the Vietnam War cannot be viewed so naïvely, since it has become an expression of man's constant impulse to survive by killing. The two scenes of soldiers running across the pond in the first part are made to contrast. The first shows them covered in mud and helping Pyle as he falls; the second presents them all running in perfect coordinated movements. They have learned to be killers and only care for themselves. The training of the first part, however, is completely reversed in the second: they do not follow strict rules, and they do care about one another. Animal Mother goes out to defend Eight-ball, who is in danger in the sniper sequence.

Pyle is equated to the Vietnamese girl who dies in the second part. Pyle is the scapegoat of the first part, the man who dies as a culmination of the process of dehumanization effected by the Marines; the girl is the culmination of the huge strategy spread over Vietnam. Both deaths reveal the inconsistency of the systems to which they belong: the army and the Vietnam War. They are, therefore, killed as part of the plan to conceal the failure of such systems. Pyle is shot in the lavatory, where the title "Head" is on the door; the sniper dies from Joker's shot in her head. Both suggest that death in this context is the result of the destruction of the soldier's mental capacity to confront the ideological process at work in a war. Moreover, the sniper is compared with the Vietnamese prostitute who appeared at the beginning of the second section. The young sniper represents the Other, difference from the American soldiers: she is nonwhite, a woman, and a Communist. She is the greatest opposite the men can find, and she has managed to kill part of the squad, avenging the status of the prostitute who in the first scene of this part had tried to sell herself — an act that expressed the subjugation she and the other Vietnamese were suffering at the hands of the Americans.

Mickey Mouse appears in the form of speech in Pyle's death scene, as a toy in the newspaper office, and as a song in the final scene. It represents the soldiers' attempt to return to lost childhood as a shelter against the demands of the military. It progresses from Hartman's reference, which disparages the image ("what is all this Mickey Mouse shit?"), to the final communal song. Mickey Mouse encapsulates the myth of eternal youth fostered by American culture as a weapon against the demands of adult life. The final song adds connotations of desire to belong to a group that can in part comfort the soldiers. Besides, Mickey Mouse is a Hollywood product — perhaps a reference to other Vietnam movies, whose effect has usually been to support the American intervention. It also suggests that an ideology that incorporates national chauvinism, racism, and sexism in the media and in culture can be essential for the construction of popular support for war, understood as domination of Third World nations (Klein 1990, 33).

The two examples of soldiers' addresses to television cameras are made to contrast, too. The first presents the soldiers taking refuge behind a low wall. They address the camera in turn, assigning themselves various roles as if they were taking part in "Vietnam, the Movie!" The fiction they choose is a Western, where the "Gooks" play the Indians. The soldiers are taken as a group. In the second example they are taken individually, and the homogeneity of the previous address is broken. Here some soldiers are serious about their answers, showing awareness of the facts and meaning of the war. Others are trapped in the fiction about wars in general, as when Cowboy says that this is what he thought a war was really like. It is real for him because it conforms with previous clichés about war; it fits the fiction about war he had in his

mind. Others are able to show a double attitude that includes awareness of the real effect of American intervention and the realization that
only by killing will they escape that hell alive. Joker and Eight-ball are
the best representatives of this second trend. The comparison between
group address and individual address suggests that awareness can only
grow in the realm of the individual, since masses or groups are easily
handled by cultural products and weapons such as television, newspa-
pers, and popular culture in general.

The view of the soldiers around the dying sniper contrasts with a
previous scene where they had gathered around Hand Job and Touchdown. Whereas in the case of Hand Job opinions about war differed,
here all agree on their hatred of the girl except Joker, who kills her in a
final gesture of humanity. Joker's position is here revealed to have been
constructed by the film so that his definite step toward maturity is,
paradoxically, an act of killing. The logic of events that had taken the
soldiers through experiences that involved dehumanization culminates
in a killing. Joker's last speech is set in contrast with his voice-over
speeches of the first part. His calm tone shows the progression from the
mere awareness of the training process to the acceptance of a situation
in which he has had to repress part of his human impulses to stay alive.

Repetition is, therefore, a productive textual strategy that can be
seen to pervade the most essential parts of *Full Metal Jacket*. This section will now introduce several ideas about the strategy of repetition in
art that will be likely to influence the elaboration of a conclusion. Bruce
Kawin distinguishes two kinds of repetition, both of which can be applicable here. One kind of repetition works to emphasize and build
meaning. It is based on a conception of art that uses repetition with
variation as source of meaning:

> Artists who repeat something now to make you remember something
> then and set you up for something that is coming later; who build one
> use of a word on top of another; who draw contrasts and assume you
> will remember how a word or image was used last and will draw con-
> clusions from the difference of context; who emphasize. Their art is
> primarily one of repetition with variation (1989, 34–35).

He understands emphasis, however, as the mark that gives away the inadequacy of repetition to convey truthful contact with experience. We
can only try to emphasize until emphasis itself manages to communicate. Repetition is understood as emphasis that may transcend language
(1989, 50).

Repetition builds up meaning. In *Full Metal Jacket* this process of
meaning creation allows the viewer to apprehend the text. Repetitions

are also used by characters, however, and they become method and expression of their adoption of external clichés as a way of shaping their identity. Repetition, therefore, contributes to separating the characters from their reality, and in a similar way the text may be said to create a fiction of Vietnam through repetition, a fiction that may separate the viewer from the truth. The self-conscious commentary suggested by the soldiers' address to the camera and their comic staging of a Western points to the capacity of cinema to distort the reality it tries to convey, to distance the subject from the object of scrutiny.

A second kind of repetition can have the power to abolish time, to transport humankind to perfect communion with nature and its repetitive cycles. It can lead humankind to apprehend the reality of things. Repetition confers reality on events; events repeat themselves because they belong to an archetype: the exemplary event. Repetition, in this mythical sense, acts as the great unifier of nature, identity, and time:

> Eliade's belief that repetition alone confers reality upon events supports my suspicion not only that repetition is the great unifier, both in art and in nature, in identity and in time, but also that it is that tool, in a more aesthetic context, whose activity can lead to the annihilation of boredom, to the vitality of language, to the increasing intensity of time and image, through its fundamental sympathy with the rhythms of our desires, of our existence (Kawin 1989, 94).

To what extent can it be said that repetition unifies identity in *Full Metal Jacket*? In my opinion it can only unify the identity of the spectator as external agent who watches all the information and is asked to elicit meaning from the comparisons and contrasts set by actions or stylistic elements that repeat themselves.

This leads us back to the issue of identity and subjectivity in the film as linked to repetition. Repetition produces in the viewer the impression that the pleasure of knowing something is surpassed by the pleasure of recognizing something that has been experienced or known before. Why? Because what the subject enjoys is the confirmation of expectations, the fulfillment of what one is capable of anticipating. This is so because the subject creates schemata, rules that help one understand reality. Recognizing something is the confirmation that our rules, our systems of understanding reality, are useful; hence the pleasure. Pleasure is, therefore, the discovery that the subject can handle reality. This also means that knowing is, in fact, more possible when we learn things that are closer to our nature, to our inner subjectivity. Knowledge is, therefore, in part an expression of our subjectivity: we cannot know anything other than ourselves, recognize ourselves in reality, and shape reality to our whim. Therefore, such reality will be as mediated and unreliable as our internal prejudices make it. This is similar to what repetition can do: it can emphasize, but its success at transcending language is questionable.

Repetition is, therefore, an expression of this pull toward coherent subjectivity, which finds a way toward that coherence by apprehending and interpreting repetitions. Coherence is aimed at, but this does not mean that coherence may produce a more faithful, closer rendition of reality. In any case, this process involves a great deal of externality, since the viewers' apprehension of repetitions and contrasts depends on their awareness of the text as a whole, and a general view can only be obtained if the viewers are forced by the text to place themselves outside the flow of events, in a position from which they can perceive similarities and differences.

Subjectivity

The film presents subjectivity as a threat to the system of formal design that mise-en-scène tries to establish. Form is given the capacity to express the meanings supported by the military command: nationalistic bigotry, sexual annihilation, and destruction of identity. The text is unanimously understood as the expression of the process of negation of character psychology by the Marine Corps, denying any introspection in the characters' lives (Adair 1989, 175). Form gives away the true dimension of bigotry in the boot camp. When Hartman says that he is hard but is fair because he does not look down on, among others, "niggers," the way in which this is said shatters that meaning and reveals him, and by extension the whole military command on Parris Island, as a bigoted liar.

The tracking shots from the front of the marching soldiers create a pattern of perfect design. They emphasize the ordered, square-like formation of the men at the same time as they reject subjectivity, since they show us a group from which it is difficult to isolate individuals. The film leads us to identify with the men as a group, allowing the audience a panoramic point of view from which we perceive the various ideologies without committing ourselves to any of them. For Gerry Reaves the film tends to make us identify with Joker, but this tendency is subverted when he stops being likeable (1988, 232–236). Thomas Doherty thinks the film lacks stylistic features devoted to the presentation of subjectivity, shaping a distancing point of view that adds an antiseptic quality to the text (1988, 27). Terrence Rafferty thinks this distance is set by the film to establish a control on the process of creation of identity and, therefore, meaning (1987, 259). In my opinion the perfectly symmetrical views offered by the previously mentioned shots suggest the perfection provided by distance, which the film links to the realm of concealed brutality. Within this context isolation-identification-subjectivity and Joker's calm voice-over narration mean a threat to the formal strategy of the film. Joker acts as an observer for us, an observer who gradually reveals his subjectivity, his imperfection, his potentiality to distort reality for us.

The rifle-prayer is preceded by a shot of a perfect perspective across the recruits' beds. The idea of joining such a shot of a perfect perspective with the obscene prayer attacks the traditional, pro-establishment relationship of art to religion, which has traditionally employed classical norms of artistic representation to exalt religious iconography. Accordingly, the prayer does not express sympathy or love or learning or beauty, only death and madness. The classical forms that produced effective communication to foster humanism are here used to depict the end of such humanism, criticizing its innermost mechanisms. "This is my rifle, this is my gun" links violence and sexuality: the origin of death and desire is the same, as is also the origin of art and communication. The song is also presented in a tracking shot from the front, which emphasizes form rather than subjectivity. So desire and violence are similar to language and form: all of them try to reach their object of desire or their enemy — their signified — while, at the same time, their not reaching it allows them to go on existing.

Therefore, violence is represented by an army that fights to the death in Vietnam but only does so because fighting keeps it alive; but it never reaches its signified, which would be an objective reason for fighting. So violence, like art, exists precisely because of the absence of such an objective reason for it to exist. In this context, the rise of Joker as consciousness and subjectivity is a rebellious activity, one that contradicts the internal workings of art and war because it realizes that both are just a set of relationships with no reference to reality.

Humor lays bare the existence of a concealed brutality that form tries to control. Humor is present in the montage sequences that show us the physical training in the camp fields. The camera constantly focuses on Pyle's inability to perform the drills properly. Slapstick comedy makes its way into the text when Pyle repeatedly tries to climb on top of a log and slips to the ground. The viewer cannot avoid smiling at his utter clumsiness, which is presented in a slightly comic way. The humor in these scenes is, however, the wrong kind of humor. The scenes seem to be a subversion of classical films where montage sequences, including a character's humorous process of learning, advance the action. This process of development is subverted here and turned into one of degradation, of stripping the individual of human qualities and dignity. But humor still plays an important role. Humor is subverted because although it might help us cope with the harsh reality of Pyle's degradation at Hartman's hands, it is surrounded by so much verbal violence that it reminds us that we are laughing for the wrong reasons, that we are participating in the ridiculing of Pyle. Humor reveals an underlying human tendency to fight for self-preservation even at the cost of the integrity of others, a tendency that its form tries to control.[4]

Joker's subjectivity emerges in the tone and vocabulary he uses when instructing Pyle. His tone is soft and calm, his diction is not offensive, in a strong contrast to the dialogue we have been offered so far. The jelly doughnut scene again introduces the issue of imperfection as related to subjectivity. All the soldiers stand still, like robots, while Pyle is humiliated by Hartman. The soldiers' conforming to the rules turns them into anonymous people, while Pyle's imperfection singles him out and allows us to share his subjective perception of the scene. Subjectivity is linked to imperfection and is again qualified as disturbing or threatening.

In the beating scene, Joker's consciousness becomes not only threatening to the establishment of perfect form in the film but also threatening to the viewer's inference process, since he becomes more ambiguous: his taking part in the chastisement of Pyle provides a hint at the change Joker may have undergone. This is later suggested in the lavatory scene. Joker and Cowboy are seen cleaning the latrine, polishing the shining floor. The cleanliness of the locale points to the spotless nature of the context-form that surrounds the men, while Joker's dialogue — "I want to slip my tubesteak into your sister" — suggests the growing change that is suggested to the audience about Joker's personality: he is adopting a diction and assuming a sexual bigotry that resemble Hartman's. Pyle's death also takes place in the latrine, an expression of how formal pattern may want to reach and organize even the basest, and at the same time the most human, necessities of the men. The antiseptic atmosphere suggests that nothing imperfect could take place there. Pyle's brains splattered over the wall reveal how too much perfection leads to irrationality and death. Pyle's death is the

---

[4] See Freud's theory of humor. For him, humor is a triumph of narcissism, where the ego refuses to be distressed by the provocations of reality, to let itself be compelled to suffer: the ego avoids such suffering through humor. It is also the triumph of the pleasure principle through the action of the superego, for which the ego appears as small and all its interests trivial (1990, 426–433). Ridiculing Pyle produces comfort and is an aid to self-preservation.

victory of the military's mechanism of imposing homogeneity and norms over Pyle's weak personality-subjectivity.

The second part shows Joker's battle against the reality of war, and how his subjectivity constantly clashes with those attempts to present the war as something rational and coherent. He clashes with the newspaper's editor and also with the colonel next to the lime-covered dead. In the latter scene he has to justify to the colonel his wearing both a helmet with "Born to kill" written on it and a peace-symbol button. He explains it as the proof of "the duality of man, sir, the Jungian thing." The remark exemplifies his internal fight, but at the same time it is ironically mentioning the ideological attitude America tries to produce among the soldiers: we are killing to bring peace. The colonel's inability to accept and understand this suggests his unawareness, which even reaches the most visible aspects of the ideology he is supposed to support. This scene also introduces a certain distrust of Joker's privileged subjectivity. The voice-over that accompanies the views of corpses communally buried is quickly identified as belonging to Joker. He says: "The dead know only one thing: it's better to be alive." The utterly obvious idea expressed, together with the tone of importance given to it by Joker, seems to suggest an irony of the text on him. Perhaps Joker is not as aware as he thinks he is, and his perception of reality is shallow, after all.

Another significant clash with the crude reality of war is Joker's killing of the Vietnamese girl. His decision to spare her the suffering of a slow death goes against the wishes of the other soldiers, who would prefer a more painful end for her, and against Hartman's teachings, since it is not a productive killing. The interesting thing is that this partial rejection of the military code constitutes Joker's surrender to Hartman's ideas. Killing when one has to, and before the enemy shoots you, was Hartman's code. Here Joker's sympathy leads him to kill the sniper, who is no longer a threat to him any longer; but his act, at this point in the narrative, makes him join those who are content with the ideology of the military command, which, paradoxically, holds that one must never feel sympathy for the enemy.

Even though the film presents Joker's decision as his final realization that humanity is possible even in war, one should not forget that the sniper's death is also the completion of the ideological circle represented by Hartman. I think the end of Joker's evolution in the film is ambiguous and contradictory: he feels that he has become more human after showing sympathy for the sniper, but he also feels that he has become part of the military mechanism that has forced him to renounce his humanist ideals and kill while at the same time feeling safe to do so.

Joker's final words confirm that he has accepted the world of war, since
he has learned to survive and overcome fear, which is what the military
code demanded of him. I do not think that one can fail to have mixed
feelings about the ending of the film, and that these feelings are the result of the ambiguity of this section.

Joker usually resorts to verbal language to express his disgust with
what he sees. His language has, however, become in part that of Hartman, and he shows traces of sharing the desire to take part in combat.
His interview for television reveals contradictory statements that may be
perceived as irony or may be understood as the expression of the contradictions inherent to the Vietnam War. He says he wanted to know
the Southeast jewel, meet its people, "and kill them." Are we to think
he is joking again, or is moral ambiguity the only way to survive in a
world with a double morality? Is Joker's ambiguity a challenge for the
construction of subjectivity that is taking place around him at the same
time? Ambiguity challenges the forms of art that construct subjectivity.
Irony works by saying something that you do not mean and that is un-
true, but here the irony is revealed to express something that will be
true: he will kill the sniper. The film is dismantling the traditional concept of irony since it is here injected with too much reality. The film
brings in too much realism and makes it impossible to portray irony,
just as the war does not allow irony because it is too cruel. Irony demands a certain distance from the reality with which the text is dealing,
to allow the viewer to understand both the "real" thing and the product of irony; if reality is too proximate, however, there is no room for
distance, making irony impossible. In a similar way only external focalization can produce an effective rendering of subjectivity; if subjectivity
is too closely allied with the character the impression of subjectivity is,
paradoxically, lost.[5] The film is saying that the experience of war does
not allow the distance necessary for irony or effective subjectivity. The
proximity produced by the iconic language of cinema is used by the
film to express how the presence of real danger and killing does not allow the soldiers the necessary distance to fight reality through irony or
to develop an effective individual subjectivity: they are forced to identify with the crude reality of the war, within which the ideology of the
military command is best at finding comfort and learning to accept
danger. This is suggested by the scene's growing ambiguity, which ap-

---

[5] See Deleyto's "Focalization in Film Narrative" (1991) where he studies filmic focalization and concludes, among other things, that stylistic strategies
that closely link the rendition of subjectivity to the point of view of a character usually make it difficult for the viewer to identify with such a character.

pears because the text poses difficulties in deciding between the two options: irony or faithful account of Joker's feelings.

In Vietnam the strict code of behavior is not provided by the military command, expressed in a formalized mise-en-scène, as in the first part. Here the constriction is imposed by the soldiers' assumption of ideologies and cultural artifacts that preserve an idea of Vietnam as the new territory to be freed and an idea of the Americans as satisfied with their petty cultural background, which seems to be reduced to clichés about the conduct of youths, the feigned bravery and sexually "correct" conduct of men. This is clearly seen in the scene of Joker's reunion with Cowboy. The iconography of modern American popular culture sanctions the act of killing, since it inscribes the soldiers into the predominant world of images, where they are taken as "heartbreakers." They have built the image of the enemy as equal to the soldiers, since they share the same hardships and dangers.

The sequence continues, and we reach the scene where a soldier kills two Vietnamese accompanied by a textual explosion of joy expressed through music. This music links the three following scenes: it bleeds over an image of the soldier happy at his deed and over views of an offensive — helicopters taking off, tanks firing. The camera tracks from these machines to show us that Cowboy's comrades have found refuge behind a low wall. At this point a television camera begins to record them, and they address it, turning the situation into the construction of a Western, a mythical account of the American desire to reconcile violence and law. Joker wants to be John Wayne, Eight-ball a horse, and they will let the "Gooks" play the Indians. The scene is interesting because of its self-consciousness. Each soldier speaks to the camera in turn, just as it focuses on him. The camera governs their construction of the myth, and the film suggests that television, since it provided the news about the war, was the means of communication that most contributed to this construction. But not only does the diegetic television camera move and govern the men's dialogue, the extra-diegetic camera that produces *Full Metal Jacket* for us also moves, following the television crew. The text is, therefore, aware of its status as construction, rendering reality in a specific manner that is not free from becoming partial and mythical, since viewers may find in the text justification for the events portrayed. The film acknowledges its awareness of belonging to the class of Vietnam movies, where a certain mystification can be found in most members of the genre, and acknowledges that even the mere fact of trying to tell the story of such an emotionally charged event as Vietnam may be interpreted as support for the war.

If we look at other Vietnam films, it is not difficult to find narratives that, despite their crude descriptions of the degradation of human beings at war, seem finally to defend the idea that America's intervention was necessary and that it was only some degenerate members of the military who caused the atrocities that Americans cannot accept nowadays. Oliver Stone's *Platoon* (1986) and Brian de Palma's *Casualties of War* (1989) still offered this vision in the 1980s. *Platoon* presents the war as almost a religious martyrdom, and *Casualties of War* suggests that, even though part of the American army was rotten and willing to massacre even their Vietnamese allies, there were other soldiers, here represented by the main character, played by Michael J. Fox, who believed in the cause that took them to Vietnam and even reacted against the repulsive behavior of their comrades, thereby in part cleansing the army and justifying the intervention. *Full Metal Jacket* shows its awareness that cultural products such as cinema can easily support the reality they depict, even though they may apparently be criticizing it. Kubrick's film is different from other Vietnam movies in that it acknowledges the risk that a film may be accepted by audiences as what it is not, since audiences are used to accepting the manipulating power of mass media and cinema is no less a manipulating medium in this respect. The film's consciousness of its own status as cultural artifact sets it off from the other examples of mainstream Vietnam cinema.

At Hand Job and Touchdown's farewell meeting the soldiers show their differing acceptance of the clichés that are being forced on them. While some soldiers say their comrades died for a good cause, others doubt it. Rafterman says that they died for "freedom," to which Animal Mother retorts that he is not killing for any word, and that if he had to choose, his word would be "poontang." Animal Mother realizes that the ideology of the fight's cause is a construction to force the men into battle. He acknowledges the power of language to dominate the soldiers. His reaction, however, is to ally with the fight and, consequently, accept that his terminology for the war only expresses destruction and chaos. His is a subjectivity whose awareness might challenge the dominant discourse, but he has already assumed that his only chance of surviving involves accepting his situation and becoming a good killer, something Joker will only do at the end of the text.

The smugness of these clichés is, however, destroyed by the attack on the sniper. The sniper is revealed not to be a violent enemy equal to us, as was suggested in Cowboy's reunion scene, but a weak Vietnamese girl on her own. The sniper's identity destroys the myth of the Western, since the code of honor based on sameness cannot be applied here. The enemy is different; it is weak and a woman. The myth of justifiable violence is shattered here, as the privileged subjectivity given to the sniper during most of the sequence had anticipated. The point-of-view zoom shots that showed how the sniper aimed at the defenseless soldiers again present subjectivity as a threat to the power of form and conceptions of truth as something whole and apprehensible. Also, the zoom shot has brought us a close view of the crude war, again wiping out any possibility for irony or independent subjectivity on the part of the viewer: the audience is also made a participant in the surrender to the principle of reality.

The communal subjectivity imposed by the war and revealed in the group of men watching the sniper together is revealed to be an expression of the incapacity to think individually, something Joker shatters with his decision to kill her. The trap of the notion of subjectivity designed by the text is that the expression of one's point of view has to be carried out by breaking the communal subjectivity set by the text. Such an action would seem to free the individual from the constrictions of dominant discourse, but we have seen that this action placed at the end of the text means precisely Joker's acceptance of such a discourse.

Joker ends up by surrendering to the reality of the war as he joins in the Mickey Mouse song. The youth clichés that have created the form of this second part are seen to triumph over Joker's individuality. Joker's threatening subjectivity is finally engulfed by the cultural background of the United States, which has led the country to the war in the first place. This background regains its predominance and emphasizes its shortcomings (its dubious contents), but, as opposed to an individual's subjectivity, this background is shown to be able to communicate, to establish links among people, fostering a feeling of belonging to a common place. The clarity and capacity to communicate is born out of the one-sided nature of this background. Subtlety of subjective views is not productive in communication — one-sided nature and broad categorization are always better. This is, in fact, an implicit criticism of cultural products in general.[6]

Kawin's idea of repetition as unifier of identity is again relevant here. In this film the creation of the system of military rules in the first part, and of American cultural background in the second, are based on repetitions of textual elements. In this sense the text works to unify the identity of those individuals identified with such rules. Joker's identity is fractured, and he is, therefore, not the object of repetitions as much

---

[6] See my "John Ford's *Seven Women*: The Workings of Mise-en-Scène and the Subversive Text"(1992a) for an analysis of a text that also teaches us how directness and clarity are always better ideological tools than subtlety.

as the systems are. His constant variation of point of view keeps him away from the play of repetition. The fact that Joker is finally engulfed by such systems does not mean that the text accepts such a process without criticism. The film is charged with a heavy component of satirical venom. It criticizes the mental system that uses American nationalism, religion, and sexual bigotry as weapons to justify America's intervention in Vietnam. The excuse that America is there to free the Vietnamese is attacked in Eight-ball's answer to the television camera: he supposes the Vietnamese would rather be alive than free. Joker uses sarcasm in his remark that he wanted to meet the Vietnamese and kill them, that he wants to be the first kid on his block to get a confirmed kill. The final Mickey Mouse song also replaces the Marines' Hymn in a satirical comment on the childishness of the reasons that have led the Americans to this war.

In this section we have seen how the form-subjectivity dichotomy is staged to present the destabilizing potential of subjectivity. The process of transformation of subjectivity from a menacing force into the expression of surrender and acceptance of the reality of war is the object of satirical criticism by the film.

Full Metal Jacket and Sexual Difference

Sexuality is a key issue in *Full Metal Jacket*, since the text contains numerous references of all kinds to it. Sexuality and sexual difference are present in the language used by the military command and the soldiers, as has already been remarked. The textual choice of a woman to play the part of the sniper constitutes a striking novelty in the context to which the film belongs. The Vietnam genre and the reconciliatory paradigms of the Western and the war film rarely include a female enemy, and certainly not usually one who fights single-handed as the sniper does. Both the nature of language and the presence of an isolated female enemy draw attention to the film's concern with the formation of sexual roles and with the relevance of such roles in the world of the text. The process undergone in the boot camp is an attempt to foster the soldiers' masculinity by rejecting their feminine side, revealing that these qualities are not inherent in the human being but are socially produced (Klein 1990, 30). Besides, the dynamics of training for combat or combat itself invariably portray a life of pain and danger that the soldiers' code forces them to endure. The acceptance of suffering by a group exclusively composed of men seems to link sexual difference and the issue of war, where it is not difficult to see the relevance of masochism and the sexual implications it carries. This section of the book will be concerned with the film as an expression of different versions of masochism as formulated by several authors. This study will allow us to perceive meanings suggested by the depiction of sexual difference that will move my analysis in new directions.

Full Metal Jacket presents us with the process of construction of sexual difference and, more specifically, the construction of male sexuality. This process is carried out by making the characters fit stereotypes, clichés, about America and about what being an American soldier is like.

Such assumption of images resembles Kaja Silverman's account of socialization. According to Silverman, the construction of subjects in society depends on their assimilation and acceptance of an image of themselves. This image is nonexistent until it is formed by fantasies, by the views subjects create about themselves. Following Althusserian concepts, she asserts that the workings of ideology rely on the subject's acceptance of a fantastic image and on the subject's acceptance that the reality offered is the only possible reality, that it cannot be any different from what it is. The creation of a social agreement about laws and customs depends on the extent to which the members of a group share the same imaginary world. Therefore, the link between the subject and the symbolic is constituted by this set of fantastic, imaginary identifications. It is only through these identifications that the subject can enter the world of the law represented by the Name-of-the-Father (1992, 15–51).

This powerful set of imaginary relations is what Silverman calls the "dominant fiction." This fiction ascribes to the male the role of master, providing him with a position from which to exert power. This is the case in *Full Metal Jacket,* where the soldiers are given a position of power that is linked to sexual dominance, clichés of American prepotency, and the use of language as a weapon. The language of abuse that spreads from Hartman to the whole of his platoon excludes all types of sexuality other than male-dominated heterosexuality. The treatment of the few women who appear in the film, the prostitutes and the sniper (all of them Vietnamese), clearly places them in a position of inferiority with respect to the men.

The American prepotency that pervades the film is expressed by stereotyped images that relate it to the issue of male/female relationships. The American soldiers use Vietnamese prostitutes whose imperfect English is constantly ridiculed. The subjugation of the country is dislocated and presented as the oppression suffered by the prostitutes, the film suggesting that for the American ideology of the soldiers the occupation of a country possesses undertones of violent sexual mas-

tery.[7] The soldiers call themselves "heartbreakers," making reference to
the clichéd lyrics of pop music songs where the male hero invariably
controls the feelings of his "sweet-heart" to his own advantage.
Moreover, the soldiers' recurrent use of the term "fuck" in the context
of combat makes the word acquire the meaning of "to kill," as in the
sniper scene. Sex and death are here clearly interrelated in the expression of American prepotency, this use of language being consistent
throughout the text. Language is turned into a weapon whose use
Hartman teaches the rest of his men. Joker, the newspaper's editor, and
the platoon in Vietnam all share this bigoted and misogynist language
of abuse. Its use becomes a stereotype to which the soldiers gradually
accommodate themselves, seeing themselves reflected in a linguistic
system that places them above everybody and everything.

For Silverman, the laws imposed through the general acceptance of
imaginary identifications by the members of a community clash with
the laws of nature that rule social life. The law of kinship, for instance,
contradicts the general law. The general law states that all members of
the community must abide by the same rules; the law of kinship, however, exempts the male from giving away the power he has traditionally
possessed in primitive forms of social life. In a word, the law of kinship
exempts the male from castration. The dominant fiction accepted by
the community resolves this contradiction by denying male castration
through the imaginary equivalence of penis and phallus: the male is
consistently given the most powerful position in the community merely
because of his being male. This equivalence is based on an illusory fantasy (that the penis is the phallus), and it is precisely this imaginary nature that gives away the fact that man is also castrated. The resolution
of the contradiction in the fantastic dominant fiction does not resolve
the real status of man as also subjected to the dictates of the law.

---

[7] Michael Selig (1993, 1–18) interprets the film as an attempt to attack the
notion of the female since it poses a threat of castration or dissolution for the
male hero. This seems to be a recurrent notion in Vietnam films, and we only
have to turn to Brian de Palma's *Casualties of War* (1989) to find a similar
narrative in this respect. Here the members of a patrol kidnap, rape, and finally kill a Vietnamese girl as a reprisal for a previous Vietnamese ambush in
which some of their buddies had died. In Michael Cimino's *The Deer Hunter*
(1978) the threat of homosexuality that haunts the main character and is
somehow posed by the feminized nature of one of his friends, is resolved
through the experience of Vietnam, where the main character proves his masculinity in the face of danger and his feminized friend dies. The war is turned
into the arena where the threat of feminization is finally overcome.

This construction of the male by equating penis and phallus reveals the attempt to conceal male castration. The same process is apparent in the development of the soldiers in *Full Metal Jacket*. The men are gradually taught to eliminate all traces of femininity in themselves to become killing machines. For Michael Pursell the film consists of the gradual expunging of women psychologically from the context of the war. Good values are associated with men and manly actions, while negative values are ascribed a feminine origin or nature. The universe in which the men are forced to live is based on gynophobia (1988, 221–222). Paula Willoquet-Maricondi sees in battle a fight within the self, where the men are themselves oppressed. Self and enemy are the same, and all wars are suicides, confirming the relevance of the sexual politics of masochism. The enemy within the self is that part that does not conform to the definition of masculinity associated with war and the Western hero. The film shapes this internal feminine enemy as a sniper who must be wiped out (1994, 12–13).

The attempt to eliminate femininity from the men to make masculinity appear rests on the assumption that sexual difference is governed by systems of opposition: that the opposite of feminine is masculine and vice-versa. This assumption would first reveal that, following this same system of oppositions, the attempt to destroy feminine traces would be in fact an attempt to conceal the existence of femininity (the threat of castration) in men, since something that does not exist in the first place does not have to be fought. Moreover, the existence of systems of opposition has been offered an alternative in Jane Flax's ideas. They reveal the tactics of making something appear by eliminating its opposite irrelevant in the context of sexual difference.

Men are, in fact, castrated in the film because they do not possess the phallus: they are oppressed. They have been deprived of their humanity and have been transformed into war machines who are not allowed to think. They are castrated because they are not aware of the position in which they have been placed. They do not realize that they are being made to accommodate themselves to an imaginary world that makes their oppression possible. Although Joker shows a more rebellious and ambiguous attitude, in general all the men fall prey to the textual construction of a dominant fiction where they are made to accept as positive and privileged a life of pain and danger. As Paula Willoquet-Maricondi says, this construction of a sexual role is a strategy of patriarchy that affects both men and women, and in this film it is shown to operate first on men (1994, 18). The lyrics of the introductory song in the second part, "These Boots Were Made for Walkin'," suggest the sadomasochism the war involves, as Thomas Doherty has pointed out (1988, 28). The men are teased into that situation by the identification the film establishes between war and the phallus (power), and by the identification of the phallus with the men (penises), forcing the men to accept the identification on which they have been made to depend by annihilating their feminine side: they have been made to depend on the images of masculinity they have been given and forced to assume.

Therefore, the identification process through which the soldiers adopt the dominant fiction outlined by the text leads them to accept positions that are clearly masochistic. I would now like to dwell on the notion of masochism, since it can help us appreciate the film from new perspectives. Masochism for Freud is a perversion that shares the characteristics of all perversions: eroticism displaced from coitus to foreplay, and erotic function extended beyond the physical areas that are commonly reserved for sexual union. Freud distinguishes three kinds of masochism: erotogenic, feminine, and moral. Erotogenic masochism provides the corporeal basis both for feminine and moral masochism and is defined by Freud as "pleasure in pain." "Erotogenic" is linked by Freud with "zone," designating a part of the body at which sexual excitation concentrates. Feminine masochism means desire for the father and identification with the mother; it implies that the male is castrated. Moral masochism implies a great desire for punishment, which leads the subject to transgress the law and accept the pain returned for such a transgression with pleasure. For Theodor Reik, masochism's emphasis is on the enjoyment of those preparations necessary for sexual climax, on the rituals that usually accompany it but that in masochism replace it. This preparation is meant to accumulate tension that will be liberated at the climax; in masochism, however, the subject's only enjoyment comes from this building up of tension. According to Silverman, perversions in general, and masochism in particular, are disruptive forces that may shatter traditional accounts of gender. They do not contemplate any function, biological or social, for sexuality, and they subvert the binary oppositions on which social order rests. In the case of masochism the border between pleasure and pain is deleted; and in a way the separation between masculine and feminine disappears, too, since masochists adopts feminine positions independently of their biological sex (1992, 185–213).

From this point of view a masochistic position would attempt to destroy masculinity, which would bring about the shattering of social order. In *Full Metal Jacket*, however, what we find is a textual tendency to deny the men's femininity rather than to affirm it. The film tries to show how the war represses all the men's desires that are felt to be deviant, such as the desire to sympathize with the weak and not kill. The men are forced to endure the pain and in this sense to repress their most human feelings, which does not seem at first sight to be a revolutionary kind of masochism.

Joker's subjectivity shows a certain balance between his sympathy for the American military's ideology and his sympathy for those Vietnamese who suffer the pain inflicted by the Americans — the sniper scene is a climactic one in this sense. What the film wants to present as Joker's scattered moments of humanity and potential rebellion against the norm of the war can be reinterpreted as only a strategy to reconcile violence and human feelings, if we follow Silverman's account of what she calls reflexive masochism. For her, reflexive masochism means the subject's identification with the one who suffers pain but also with the one who inflicts it. She analyzes T. E. Lawrence's life as reflected in his writings and explains it as a constant desire to identify with the peoples he encountered, to adopt the customs and even the dress of the Arabs. She explains this desire as the result of the sublimation of Lawrence's homosexuality, which transports the desire from the bodies to the ideals those bodies represented: Arab independence. At the same time, the ego is exalted through this identification with the ideal, and Lawrence feels himself to be the representative of the Arab fight. For Silverman this type of masochism allows Lawrence to justify his desire to dominate, which could not be explained or accepted by the sexual politics of feminine masochism. This masochism produces the belief that the one who suffers most is entitled to become the leader; it allows the possibility of remaining masculine and virile while at the same time exerting one's power over those one wishes to dominate, thereby becoming a justification for an imperialist attitude (1992, 299–338).

For Silverman, Lawrence's writings have to be taken as partly fantastic, since they represent an attempt to accommodate his mental schemes to his desires and to the facts. The fantastic nature of his writings makes them appropriate for a study of the alterations in the personal dominant fiction that a certain individual may create for his own purposes. The contradiction between his attraction to the Arabs and his desire to dominate them led Lawrence to build up a system of ideas to justify his deeds.

The concept of reflexive masochism has also been hinted at as one of the components of the film that links it to Christian imagery and ideology. Pursell suggests that certain sexual language used in the text evokes the sadistic/masochistic necrophilia of Christianity (1988, 224). If we apply the notion of reflexive masochism to a figure such as Joker, we would be led to accept that the film is sanctioning Joker's behavior.

The film is setting an ambiguous relationship between Joker and the enemy, a relationship of hatred imposed by the military life, but also of sympathy when he faces the sniper and decides to help her die painlessly. This ambiguous attitude is also present at times in the rest of the soldiers: when Joker and Cowboy reunite in Vietnam, a speech by one of the members of Cowboy's platoon refers to the Vietnamese as the best human beings they will ever know. This comradeship with the enemy, because the Vietnamese suffer the same privations and pain they do, would seem to allow the Americans to feel more superior to the enemy the more pain they are forced to endure. Comradeship would allow the appearance of the desire to subjugate. Joker's position would then be that of the main killer, since he is the most ambiguous toward the Vietnamese and the war. This would explain Joker's final killing in the sniper scene.

The film would, therefore, ultimately approve of Joker's acceptance of the military code; it would unveil Joker not as a rebel but as an example of the process undergone by all the other soldiers. The sadomasochism at work in boot camp and in Vietnam teaches the soldiers to feel superior to the Vietnamese, against whom they have the right to use force. *Full Metal Jacket,* therefore, seems to follow mental patterns that can be explained according to Silverman's account of reflexive masochism, but it does not show the potential of masochism to disrupt schemes of sexual binary oppositions. It instead reinforces these sexual oppositions, since the reflexive masochism the film exhibits is the expression of perfect virility and the rejection of feminine attitudes. In this sense the ideas suggested by reflexive masochism support Susan Jeffords's reading of the film as shutting down ambiguity. For her, the text rejects all ambiguity about the position of masculinity and femininity: it formulates a clear rejection of the feminine and assertion of the masculine (1989, 173–176).

Feminine masochism would entail identification with the mother and desire for the father. *Full Metal Jacket,* however, attempts to eliminate the feminine side of the soldiers. For Willoquet-Maricondi, certain accounts of sexuality link the child to the mother, from whom the male child has to separate to find his masculinity. This separation takes place in the film through a ritual of humiliation, self-mutilation or mutilation by others, which attempts to transform the soldiers' identities. The act of killing the female sniper is a step further in Joker's self-mutilation and, therefore, in his process of masculinization (1994, 15–17). Masochism finds pleasure in the postponement of pleasure: the film postpones the introduction of the woman that reveals the process of sexual definition-by-opposition at work in the text. This discovery is not pleasurable but a killing, prolonging the pain for Joker and at the same time allowing his acceptance of the imperialist attitude implicit in reflexive masochism, as the final communal Mickey Mouse song reveals.

The previous explanation proposes a system of masochism at work in the text, but a masochism that does not try to subvert preestablished forms of sexual definition. Femininity is destroyed in the hope that masculinity will appear in the process, implicitly accepting a traditional model of sexual definition based on the binary opposition male-female. The fact that the enemy is finally revealed to be a woman, however, brings new significance to the film. Lawrence's masochism is explained by Silverman as the result of his identification with the male Arabs, which produces a homosexual desire to be sublimated by the tactic of becoming sufferer and, therefore, leader. In *Full Metal Jacket* the enemy is throughout taken to be masculine; but the only active enemy we ever see is the sniper, who is revealed to be a woman. This suggests that the possibility for homosexuality and its displacement does not exist any more for Joker, since the enemy is feminine. Therefore, the identification becomes now an identification with the feminine, as in feminine masochism, and it is, therefore, in the appearance of the woman sniper where the seed for subversion lies: Joker is made to identify with the feminine, breaking the boundaries between masculinity and femininity. The presence of a man who is led to identify himself with a position of femininity breaks the traditional system of binary sexual definition, since now a mixture of masculine-feminine enters the opposition male-female, introducing a menacing novelty. So, although the film apparently privileges masculinity by destroying any trace of femininity in the soldiers, in fact the logic of reflexive masochism inherent in the imperialist narrative reveals how the hero is made to identify with what he is apparently trying to destroy. This new possibility presents the narrative as potentially subversive.

Tania Modleski follows Gilles Deleuze's account of masochism in her discussion of *Full Metal Jacket*. For Deleuze, masochism may place the mother as the pain-inflicting agent, leaving to the father the place of object being beaten. For Modleski this type of masochism aims at ridiculing the concept of authority by giving it to a woman. In *Full Metal Jacket* the move of replacing the hard drill instructor Hartman, an enemy wrapped as a figure of authority, by a young Vietnamese girl shows the ridiculousness of war. In the process the text uses woman to attack the idea of war, and Modleski sees in Deleuze's notion of masochism a manipulation of men to place woman as master and despot, which she finds completely unfair (1991, 61–75). What I find interesting in this explanation of the film is the shifting of positions of father

and mother, and most specifically the placement of the father as the
passive receiver of pain, adopting what in Freudian accounts of masochism would be a feminine position. Deleuze's masochism as explained
by Modleski offers us another example of a possible change of sexual
positions.

We can, therefore, see that the text can be analyzed from different
points of view that entertain different possibilities for the male hero's
identification tendencies. The hero may be interpreted as trying to eschew femininity throughout most of the film; from the moment we
learn that the enemy is feminine, however, the same logic of reflexive
masochism leads the hero to accept the feminine and identify with it. If
we have different available possibilities (masculine or feminine) we will
have to discard the notion that only one identification is possible. The
theoretical possibility of different positions, together with the unac-
ceptability of one immutable position, is hinted at by Joker's subjectivity in the film. Joker rejects the process of sexual construction as
opposition that follows the line of traditional accounts of sexual definition. He rejects it through his use of language and through his ambiguous nature, which introduces the possibility the reconciliation of
dualities such as war and the peace symbol.

These two ways of challenging definition by opposition work by
showing the constructed nature of reality. The conversations held at
the newspaper office reveal the manipulation of war carried out by language; the massive collection of mental as well as physical war images
the soldiers are made to share and identify with show how the reality of
war is created by agents such as the drill instructor, by popular culture
emerging in songs, or by communal exercises of identity affirmation.
This artificial nature makes it easy to understand that there may be possible positions for the subject other than those two poles presented in
American international politics and, by extension, in traditional sexual
definition by opposition. The subject may oscillate between positions
that the text marks as male and female. In the imagery created and accepted by the soldiers bigotry is characterized as male, understanding
and sympathy as female; aggressiveness is male, meekness female. Joker
seems to identify with both sets of images, thereby opening a way out
of systems of oppositions.[8]

The previous account presupposes a notion of sexual identity and
identification that allows different, and changeable positions for the

---

[8] Theorizations of sexual systems that reject the traditional binary one based
on opposition have been proposed by D. N. Rodowick (1982, 1991) Jane
Flax (1990) and Elizabeth Cowie (1984).

subject. This notion contradicts accounts of identification tendencies that have traditionally been informed by Laura Mulvey's influential essay "Visual Pleasure and Narrative Cinema" (1989). Mulvey's thesis is that classical cinema invariably offers positions of subjects for male spectators while it reserves for female spectators the place of object. She asserts that in the process of viewing spectators repress their exhibitionism and project the repressed desire to the actor or actress. The pleasurable structures of looking are two: scopophilic or voyeuristic, where the spectator finds pleasure in using another person as object of sexual stimulation through sight, and narcissistic, where pleasure is produced through the identification with the image. These structures cannot work at the same time, and they are gender-distinctive, since the male look is privileged in films.

Woman is usually presented as icon, as deprived of narrative relevance, as arresting the development of the narrative. Man is in control of the fantasy, holding the look and possessing both an object of identification (male hero) and an object of scopophilic activity (the woman). Woman introduces sexual difference into the experience of viewing, implying a threat of castration that the male unconscious can fight by means of fetishistic scopophilia and sadistic voyeurism. The first consists in transforming woman into a fetish so that she becomes reassuring rather than dangerous; the second works by demystifying woman, investigating her, and punishing her (1989, 14–38).

Mulvey's account of the process of viewing, as well as of the possibilities for identification, relies on a system of sexual definition that operates by defining maleness through opposition to femaleness and vice versa. It is this logic of definition that D. N. Rodowick criticizes in his *The Difficulty of Difference* (1991). Rodowick analyzes film theory and its appropriation of Freud's writings to study the possibility that Freud's work can propose a model beyond binary oppositions (1991, 4). In an earlier article also entitled "The Difficulty of Difference" (1982) he had already discussed Mulvey's essay. There he saw a lack in that part of Mulvey's scheme that probed the ways in which the spectator can see a way out of castration anxiety. Mulvey proposed an active way (sadism), but she refused to offer the corresponding way out, which would be masochism, associated with passivity and fetishistic scopophilia. To Rodowick this absence seemed to be a move to avoid associating with the male gaze the contradictory methods of sadism and masochism. The male gaze cannot be sadistic and masochistic at the same time if it is to be consistent with the rest of Mulvey's argument, where males are aggressors and females recipients of aggression. This lack also meant for Rodowick that the male gaze could not be consid-

ered passive; it had to be always allied with active drives, which in Rodowick's opinion did not conform to reality (1982, 4–15).

In the later book Rodowick pursues his critique of Mulvey. Since
she considers the look to be active, identification with the male hero
can only exist if associated with a sense of omnipotence and control of
the narrative. Identification with a passive male character is not possible, and females only appear as objects of the male active look, never as
subjects: women as subjects have no place in Mulvey's scheme. Rodowick uses Freud's "Instincts and their Vicissitudes" to support his
new proposal. Freud says that the polarities of mental life are subject-
object, pleasure-unpleasure, and active-passive. He warns that the relations of activity and passivity must not be confused with the relation of
the subject and the object. The life of the ego (subject) is formed by a
mixture of active and passive relations. In Freud the drives are taken to
be active and passive by turns, rather than being immutable (1991, 4–
17).

Rodowick asserts that Mulvey, for all her alleged attempts to present
sexual difference as constructed, in fact sees in film an artistic form
through which a real understanding of the psychic development of individuals can be achieved, one through which "concealed elements of
'authentic' feminine experience are to be found" (1991, 46). For Rodowick, this view does not coincide with Freud's efforts to question the
relationship of sexual identity to biological difference. Mulvey's arguments implicitly assume that in film theory masculine and feminine
identifications are associated with male and female spectators and that
"the position of the female spectator can be defined ontologically in
opposition to that of the male" (1991, 67).

Rodowick resorts to the notion of bisexuality because it allows a
notion of identification as not immutable or fixed but changeable. Bisexuality means that both positions defined in relation to difference are
available for the subject. Rodowick jumps from the concept of female
spectatorship to that of feminine identification, which is less linked to
ontogenetic notions of femaleness and which leads him to the analysis
of Freud's "A Child is Being Beaten" as an example of multiple,
changeable identification. Freud's essay deals with a fantasy told by several of his patients, the purpose of which was to obtain sexual pleasure,
and which he interprets as a narrative explaining the process of castration and the appearance of sexual difference. There are three possible
accounts of the fantasy, and in each of them the patient produces a
teller who sees the beating, a subject who inflicts pain, and an object
who suffers it. For Rodowick the interesting aspect is that the fantasy
allows a complex and fluid spectatorial activity that includes "transac-

tions between activity-passivity, sadism-masochism, and masculine and feminine identifications in both men and women" (1991, 82). The fantasy allows identification with the position occupied by a male or female character independently of the biological sex of the spectator. Rodowick still sees problems for female subjects here, however, since female sexuality and desire are understood to be passive, while male desire is understood to be active from an ontological position.

Therefore, although Rodowick still criticizes the part of Freud's writings that allows an explanation of fluid identification, he finds strong support in his reading of "A Child is Being Beaten" for a critique of positions that approximate identification to biological sex. Psychoanalytic studies include the possibility of multiple, changeable identification, which inevitably modifies conceptions of sexual difference based on binary oppositions such as Mulvey's.

Full Metal Jacket allows the hero to entertain both possibilities as a soldier in Vietnam: being a man and destroying/being a woman and feeling sympathy. This possibility of changeable, multiple positions of identification poses a problem for traditional forms of sexual definition based on opposition. We have seen that the film is strongly dependent on this traditional account of sexual roles, since the soldiers are forced to develop their feeling of belonging to the community of men through the assimilation of stereotyped images of masculinity. This process of masculinization uses the concept of femininity as the pole to be derided to affirm its opposite.

The film, however, shows that the events that exemplify both possibilities result in killings. Pyle is the victim of Hartman's attempt to masculinize him along with the rest of the soldiers, revealing the inadequacy of the system of degradation of the feminine applied by the drill instructor to the men. The second part of the film introduces the presence of a female enemy, with whom the politics of reflexive masochism that pervade the film should lead Joker to identify. The sniper, however — the cause of Joker's identification with the female — also dies at the hands of the hero, at the hands of the military code that informs the life of the soldiers in Vietnam. Not only does the woman die, but the act of killing her is considered by the film as the climactic moment in Joker's process of becoming a soldier, a member of the community to which he belongs, during the Mickey Mouse song.

It therefore seems that the presentation of both possibilities is only an illusion of subversiveness, since the text manages to reconcile both of them as part of the usual process of maturation of the soldier, which leads him to accept his position in the military and in Vietnam, as the final song reveals. The discovery that the enemy is feminine suggests the identification of Joker with the woman, but his act of killing her means the victory of American masculinity over Vietnamese femininity. The fact that Joker kills her to spare her the pain of a slow death reconciles the act of killing with America's constant justification for its presence in Vietnam: it intervened to help the Vietnamese. The text offers the possibility for the subject to shift, but the positions remain unchanging: male is presented as destructive, female as sympathetic. So the constructions of femininity and masculinity themselves remain constant.[9]

Rodowick understands "A Child is Being Beaten" as a detailed account of the struggle between the individual and the law of the father that tries to install the rule of the phallus. The different possible narratives within the fantasy invariably entertain the possibility of escaping the dictates of the phallus at one stage or another: "The utopia expressed in phantasy life, regardless of the sexual identification of the subject, is for a sexual world ungoverned by the constraints of phallic desire" (1991, 84). This escape is always rendered utopian, since the aim of the fantasy is, in the end, to express the law that the subject feels to be external.

For Rodowick the role of criticism is to explain and articulate the utopian function of fantasy. Narratives are always the conjunction of desire and its interdiction. They move on in the hope of escaping subjugation to the law but always know from the beginning that such an escape is impossible. He sees such a struggle represented in the repetitions contained by a narrative:

> I argued in the last chapter that the "narrative" structure of phantasy is fundamentally paradoxical — the simultaneous expression and prohibition of desire. An impossible process, the nature and forms of repetition in phantasy represent an expressly ideological conflict in the attempt to represent a mostly inchoate desire that is utopian in the sense of its effort to dream possibilities of identity, sexuality, and pleasure unconstrained by norms of phallic division (1991, 96).

The very insistence and repetitiveness of phallic division is an indication of the impossibility of finding an appropriate or convincing escape toward bisexuality in the symbolic. Repetition is, therefore, the mark of the inadequacy of the representation of a sexuality that pre-

---

[9] This conclusion seems to coincide with other analyses of Kubrick's work. The idea that the film supports the traditional construction of masculinity and femininity matches Gregg Jenkins's analysis of Kubrick's adaptations to film of literary texts: he concludes that Kubrick tends to simplify the narratives and steer their moral slant toward conventionality (1994).

tends to be organized around the phallus when, in fact, it is multiple, because repetition is the mark of desire but also the mark of its repression, of the repression of the force that liberates from the tyranny of the phallus.

Repetitions in *Full Metal Jacket* are an attempt to express this contradictory view of sexuality. The film's organization tries to offer a view of how a sexuality based on the phallus — that of the soldiers — is altered and turned into the object of the attack carried out by the Vietnamese girl. The repetitions of language, which consistently try to define woman and Vietnam by opposition to masculinity and the American view of foreign countries, reveal how that reality which is defined through opposition to the phallus is finally unveiled as also oppressive for the soldiers, and, paradoxically, at the hands of their most radically opposite: a Vietnamese woman. There is a certain expression of the pull between phallic identity and a more liberated identity ungoverned by the phallus. The authority of the male is questioned, and a more bisexual view is outlined by Joker's presence. In the end, however, a phallic division is reestablished first through the female oppressing the male, while the sniper kills, and then through the male oppressing the female in Joker's killing of the sniper.

The film might be understood as an expression of the utopian fantasy described by Rodowick. The transformation of males from privileged into oppressed — into objects of masochism — seems to be part of this reluctance to allow the phallus to govern the forces of identification in the text and to present as true the equation of phallus and penis. Here the males are powerless, while the female "has" the phallus. The move of passing power on to the female, however, reestablishes the phallic division of identity: the privileged pole, the powerful side of the binary opposition, is the female, but sexual definition is still based on the opposition to the opposite pole. Woman has the phallus while she kills the soldiers, but then the men are defined by opposition to her, without abandoning the system of binary oppositions on which the process of masculinization was previously based. Repetition is, therefore, shown, as Rodowick says, as only the mark of the phallic division-unconstriction from the phallus struggle, but not as the expression of its resolution. Repetition can, therefore, also have a function of inscription into phallic identity and symbolic patterns.

Repetition can be interpreted as the confirmation that our rules, our projections onto the external world, are correct — repetition as expression of ourselves, as has already been pointed out. This is related to the process explained in traditional accounts of formation of sexual difference. The subject reacts to the encounter with the other by projecting onto that other and, in discovering one's split nature, by defining one-self by opposition. So, it is in fact the use the subject makes of subjectivity that produces sexual definition by opposition. Therefore, both processes of acquiring knowledge and facing reality are similar. This idea is a partial conclusion to my discussion of *Full Metal Jacket,* where repetition and sexual definition are taken as proof of the film's pervasive attempt to apply schemata to reality to shape it, to pattern it to explain and understand it. The process of apprehension of reality undergone by Joker and the presentation of his consciousness to the viewer are carried out through a complex web of patterns that make the audience elicit meaning. The similarity of the processes of meaning-making and formation of sexual identity supports a reading of the text as tending toward clarity and the rejection of ambiguity, once we have seen how the film in the end reinforces traditional, unambiguous notions of sexual definition.

The link established by Rodowick between desire and utopian narratives leads him to discuss a model of textual analysis that fits his purposes. He begins by adopting Bellour's model of film analysis, based on repetitions that resolve themselves toward a dialectical compromise. Bellour studies sets of pairs that repeat themselves in film, the figures of filmic language being characterized by their repetition with a difference. Rodowick quickly sees in Bellour's model, however, a kind of analysis that is based on a logic of identity where the processes of the text are assumed also to take place in the spectator, since the processes of repetitively comprehending what is external to the subject to acquire psychically an identity are directly equated to the logic of meaning-creation through repetition in film texts. Rodowick thinks that textual analysis should base itself not on this logic of identity but on "a logic of difference where the reader confronts the text from 'outside the institution'" (1991, 125–126). The power of desire in film, together with the instruments of its analysis, are born out of the pursuit of an object that never stops moving away from apprehension. Textual analysis is a compromise between the norms imposed on the text and the text itself. "Any claims made for textual analysis as a theory-building activity are not based on a logic of identity, but rather of reading as difference" (1991, 128–129). Rodowick asserts that criticism must never confuse identity and identification. Sexual identity is unknown to processes of identification; the self is never singular, and its internal divisions and contradictions can be quite complex. All processes of identification are also complex structures where multiple subjective relations may coexist in contradictory ways that are different from binary oppositions. Similarly, all processes of textual apprehension should be undertaken from a position that allows the perception of contradictory identifications: from a position of externality.

To conclude, I should now like to return to the division of textual elements into elements of particularity and generality, which in the first part of this book were also distributed in pairs of opposites. The study of such pairs has already revealed a complex web of repetitions, marks of desire that according to Rodowick reveal the fight between phallic division and a more changeable concept of sexual identification. Repetitions in Kubrick's cinema are usually meant to create meaning: patterns and structures are the marks revealing sexual fight. This fact shows that meaning — the result of patterns — is an agent in this sexual fight, at least as far as Kubrick's cinema is concerned. This takes us back to the issue of externality as essential to a textual analysis that aspires to account for the struggle between phallic division and more bisexual accounts. Externality is essential to the apprehension of patterns, to the formation of meaning on the part of the viewer.

So Rodowick's ideas about sexual identity being fought in utopian texts, which should demand an external approach on the part of the viewer, coincide with the ideas proposed in the first part of this study. In *Full Metal Jacket* we can perceive the double function of repetition: it can be the mark of the fight between diverse conceptions of sexual identity, and it can also be the force that forms a sexual identity based on phallic division and resulting in symbolic organization, patterning, and meaning-creation. Repetition entertains the utopian fantasy proposed by Rodowick, but at the same time is the basis of symbolization, as has traditionally been expressed in structuralism. In a similar way, the notion of externality also has a double function. It may help the apprehension of changeable, contradictory positions of identification, thereby allowing the utopia of unconstriction from the phallus, but it is also an essential element in the configuration of identity, which is inevitably bound to symbolic, phallic norms. Similarly, for Terrence Rafferty, Joker becomes an observer who provides the viewer with a place of traditional identification but who also becomes a figure external to the other characters, a figure whose activity of observing makes the configuration of the others' identity possible (1987, 257).

For Kaja Silverman, identity depends on the subject's awareness that he is the object of someone else's look (1992, 125–156). In psychoanalysis identity springs out of the internalization of images that are at first external to the subject: the recognition of what exists outside as different from oneself triggers the formation of one's conscious identity. The process of formation of identity, which involves the entrance into the symbolic, the acceptance of the rules of the phallus that will divide and force the subject to accept a defined sexual position, is also clearly informed by the workings of externality. Externality, therefore, becomes a key factor of textual configuration and manipulation, since through it we can make meaning but also apprehend the potential destructive subversion inherent in the text. It becomes an ally of repetition, which is, in turn, also ambivalent: it can form structures of meaning, and it can be the mark of the utopian escape from the constrictions of phallic division. The concept of externality allows us to perceive the different implications of texts, as the case of *Full Metal Jacket* makes clear.

The analysis of the film has revealed, first of all, a structure of repetition as the element that secures intelligibility and a unified subjectivity on the part of the audience. This textual design shares a common attitude with generality in its demand from the audience of constant comparison of fragments of the film. *Full Metal Jacket* has also been studied as a good example of the classical tendency to present the reconciliation of opposites. The study of sexual difference has added to such a conclusion the notion that the ending chosen by the film may also be a hint of such a reconciliatory tendency. An ending that shows that the text is following sexual models based on systems of opposition qualifies the film as certainly traditional and conservative in this respect. The previous exposition of different alternatives for identification and sexual definition, however, — coherent with modern theories proposed by Cowie, Flax, and, mainly, Rodowick — provides the text with an original contribution within Kubrick's filmography and within the context of modern cinema: a system of textual strategies that maps out a set of alternative sexual positions that in turn becomes the expression of a new attitude with respect to the dichotomy presented by deconstruction.

Returning once more to the context outlined in the introduction to the analysis of the three films by Kubrick, *Full Metal Jacket* stands for an original alternative to the system of polar opposites favored by deconstruction. Neither the presentation of an omnipotent code, as *Barry Lyndon* suggested, nor the defense of the abolition of the system, as we found in *2001,* are contemplated here. Neither the exclusive forces of generality as producer of a single meaning (*Barry Lyndon*) nor generality as exclusive producer of multiplicity of meaning (*2001*) are present in *Full Metal Jacket.* Rather, we find a text that exemplifies both sides of generality/externality: it entertains the possibility of fixed meaning represented as a fixed sexual position and also the possibility of multiple meanings in sexual positions. We are presented with a system of alternative endings, several options for identification that contest the privileged one proposed by the ending.

The contribution of *Full Metal Jacket* becomes more relevant when we realize that the film introduces these alternatives within a limited, comprehensible set of differences and contrasting ideas that gives them an additional value, since it is not the rejection of sexual identification or definition that is defended, but the creation of different ways of sexual definition that may challenge the dominant one. The offer of alternatives is a positive and original attitude on the part of the film, coherently with its position toward sexual difference, as has been explained in the analysis. *Full Metal Jacket* rejects the unity of meaning of *Barry Lyndon* together with the multiplicity of *2001*, and chooses to present a limited number of possibilities for signification. This limited nature allows the text to become more communicative than *Barry Lyndon* and *2001* with respect to the alternatives it presents. Similarly to the workings of a verbal language, a limited number of options turns them into the expression of graspable concepts, whereas the existence of only one option (*Barry Lyndon*) or of too many in an uncodified system (*2001*) make the presentation of alternatives in such a way that they can be coherently exposed and communicated to an audience impossible. It is in this context — the positing of a way out of the systematic movement between two polar opposites typical of the logic of deconstruction — that *Full Metal Jacket* should be finally placed.

Conclusion

THIS STUDY HAS ANALYZED THE MOST basic components of Stanley
Kubrick's cinema. It has used this analysis as raw material on which
to build theoretical considerations which provide a new perspective on
the understanding and study of cinema.

The first step in this process was an exhaustive cataloguing of elements of style in Kubrick's films. We saw that Kubrick uses style in
both traditional and modern ways, usually offering altered versions of
highly codified patterns that he combines with traditional applications
of those codified structures. These stylistic variations usually serve a
specific purpose: to emphasize relevant portions of the fabula. Moreover, stylistic options show a tendency to distort subjectivity in order to
foreground its external nature, which coincides with the ever-present
relish for the use of strategies that draw attention to their artificial
status.

Kubrick's films were studied as examples of texts that constantly try
to set out structures based on symmetries and parallelisms in order to
suggest meanings. This attempt is one of the defining strategies of a
cinema that also relies on the traditional canonical story format, the disregard of realistically motivated events, and on a pervading self-
consciousness that finds its favorite field in the creation of space.

The externality produced by style was connected to another relevant
characteristic of Kubrick's poetics: the capacity to emphasize the iconicity of cinematographic language. The notion of autofocalization,
understood as the power of the icon to focalize itself, provided a concept that was able to contain the two notions of externality and emphasis on the icon. These two aspects of style favor the appearance of
metaphorical structures, which were also carefully explored. Out of this
analysis of metaphors, the importance of the signifying options offered
by the conjunction of the potentiality of the icon and that of the rhetorical structures that the icon itself could create was recognized, which
led us to the definition of cinematographic language as a combination
of icons and rhetorical structures.

The capacity of the icon to produce a logic of its own was also analyzed. Kubrick's films contain a powerful tendency to create a logic
based on the foregrounding of the iconicity of cinema through certain
rhetorical structures. The logic of spectacle produced by this tendency

results in the capacity of these texts to disseminate meaning, to destroy the meaning that seemed to be privileged by the film. A logic of spectacle is based on the tendency of the text to highlight a certain iconic element (lighting, performance, setting, etc.), which relegates the supposedly privileged meaning of the film to a secondary place. A new meaning is, therefore, suggested by a purely textual logic that subverts the original intention of the film.

Since this emphasis on the icon was highly indebted to the externality produced by cinematographic language,[1] all the rhetorical structures that shared such an external nature were revealed as producers of iconicity, while at the same time also establishing the basis for metaphors. Consequently, those structures that did not foster externality were analyzed as more closely allied with the expression of formal coherence, unaltered by the disruptive effect of the icon. These two types of formal structures were called elements of generality (those that produce iconicity) and particularity (those that produce formal coherence), and a scheme was proposed that in my opinion was capable of reconciling formalism and poststructuralism in a single model of analysis. It was, therefore, suggested that the scheme is capable of encompassing critical tendencies that disregard textual form as an ideological weapon and those that believe that texts can carry ideological connotations to be explored by the critic.

The scheme of generality/particularity showed that a study of cinema both as structure (formalism) and as ideological construct (poststructuralism) are possible, since the scheme presupposed the existence of a possible external position, shaped through form, from which the constructedness — that is the ideological potential — of films could be perceived and therefore also resisted.

The second part of the book was an attempt to apply the possibilities offered by the scheme of generality/particularity to a specific example of postmodernist thought: deconstruction. Deconstruction's tendency to theorize by adhering to systems of binary oppositions, where the validity of one pole is supported by the argument that its opposite pole is not valid, was criticized. This tendency was more closely analyzed in the case of deconstruction's discussion of the creation of meaning and the capacity of languages to offer clear meanings. Ac-

---

[1] Cinematographic language creates textual structures that are ultimately external, since the mechanisms of representation are based on the presence of an element external to the world of the diegesis: the camera. For a discussion of focalization as a key aspect of externality, see Deleyto (1991).

cording to deconstruction, the creation of clear meanings is impossible because languages can only refer to their signifiers.

This part included an analysis of three Kubrick films that offer three distinct perspectives on the signifying possibilities of languages. We saw that these films privilege the presence of the elements of generality, and that these elements of generality present us with a way out of the dead end at which deconstruction had placed language. Generality appeared as the creator of ambiguity and plurality of meaning in *2001* and as a contributor to the expression of clear, definite meaning in *Barry Lyndon*. The two polar positions with respect to the shaping of meaning were resolved through the conclusions provided by the analysis of *Full Metal Jacket*. This film exemplifies the potential of externality, since it provides (in the terms set by the film, which revolves around the issue of sexual definition) the two possibilities of fixed and multiple sexual positions. The film provided a resolution to the polarity that did not involve a radical movement away from an idea in order to affirm its opposite but an attempt to include the two concepts outlined in *2001* and *Barry Lyndon*. *Full Metal Jacket* set a limited range of possible meanings, thereby favoring the functioning of the code and rejecting deconstruction's concept of the infinite play of signifiers that led to the collapse of the capacity of language to signify.

Thus, the analysis of the films in terms of the generality/particularity scheme led us to find an example of language organization where concepts do not rely on their belonging to a pattern of binary opposites and where a limited range of possibilities was offered to the decoder, enabling such a decoder to inhabit a realm of definite, and therefore accessible, options. This second part of the book has proved the value of the notions of generality/particularity. But what is the relevance of the specific postmodernist idea chosen in the analysis (deconstruction's concern with the production of meaning) with respect to the notions that formed the first part of the study? In what way does the possibility opened by generality in the analysis of the three films contribute to the study of style and narrative organization undertaken there? Generality suggests an alternative to the attempts to subvert the code that have been outlined by postmodernism, an alternative that offers a range of options that is larger than the dead end of binary oppositions and, at the same time, restricted enough to enable the subject to understand the range and work within it, avoiding the nihilistic position offered by the postmodernist proposal of an unlimited range of options. The possibility of a limited set of options that surpasses the previous binary opposition may be felt, on the one hand, to be just a strategy to tame the subversive potential of postmodernism by bringing it back to the realm of the comprehensible and acceptable. On the other hand, it may be understood as an improvement brought about by postmodernism, which is now able to propose a step forward in its original presuppositions. It may also mean a progression in the context of the traditional oscillation between positions that were presented as opposites and that constantly led us from one pole to the other in a closed circuit that had become sterile.

It seems to me that the idea of a signifying realm where different options may coexist in the terms outlined by generality is a useful critical concept. It is a concept that can include the workings and effects of textual practices that were analyzed in the first part of the book and that are, in fact, part of the set of structures usually associated with postmodernist art. The self-conscious nature of Kubrick's texts, their tendency to impress the viewer with displays of the materiality of cinematographic language, and their permanent use of patterns of repetition that suggest parallelisms and contrasts have been presented as marks of the textual tensions between traditional modes of filmmaking and the more modern, eclectic ones represented by Kubrick. These tensions appeared in the shape of confrontations where the disruptions from the classical norm were usually accommodated by the text so that they became aids in the creation of meanings. The inclusive concept proposed by *Full Metal Jacket* provides this textual practice so common in Kubrick with a critical area where it can be analyzed. Self-consciousness, which is most powerful and pervading in the emphasis of the icon and in the creation of repetitions, is turned into a narrative element by Kubrick's films, but I do not think that the subversive capacity of these textual forces can be overlooked just because they are quickly accommodated and absorbed. They become marks of the potential instability that pervades all texts, an instability that is mastered to shape a coherent meaning. I think that the previous analysis has revealed that these elements of unrest are marks of the fight between two kinds of narration, a fight that is resolved by what we can now propose, following *Full Metal Jacket,* as a third type of narration that is neither the classical nor the art-cinema, self-conscious one but a mixture of the two. The self-consciousness that most potently appears in the cases of emphasis on the icon and of repetition, and that is quickly integrated by the narrative dynamics of the text, produces a communicative activity that may guide the viewer's decoding process through alternative paths that can at the same time be made compatible. So the viewer may be lured by the power of self-conscious strategies, such as striking visual compositions or obvious patterns of repetition, to relegate the cause-effect chain of events to a secondary place. Or, alternatively, the viewer may quickly interpret the relevance of those self-conscious moments as part of a traditional classical narrative, paying more attention to the metaphorical meanings suggested by the striking views of outer space or of painting-like compositions, for instance. Or, finally, the viewer may share an identification with both of the options just outlined, achieving a balance between a reading that abandons itself to the joy of the "endless play of signifiers" and one that searches the text for links in the chain of events presented in a classical fashion. The viewer may maintain a reading attitude that, while responding to the power of spectacle, redirects that joy to the analysis of the relevance of spectacle together with the relevance of the more classical backbone of the text. The viewer may be placed in an external position of apprehension of all the elements of the text, the self-conscious as well as the classical ones. Self-consciousness, the emphasis on the icon (the materiality of the sign), and the ambivalence of repetition find, in the concept outlined in the analysis of *Full Metal Jacket,* a critical realm where their functioning, as well as the effects they produce, can be included in the form of a clear representation accessible to the decoder of the text.

The external position is produced by the capacity of the elements of generality to both shape meaning through metaphor and introduce the possibility of dissemination, of the breakdown of the communicative system. The new narrative mode that Kubrick's films propose is based on the construction of this external viewer, a viewer who is constantly asked to analyze and interpret metaphors, to provide explanations for self-conscious turns of the narrative, etc. At the same time, this new mode allows various positions for this decoder, who at times, depending on the narrative fragment, is abandoned to the logic of spectacle, while other times is prefigured as a typically classical and naïve viewer. This availability of different reading positions, which go beyond the traditional classical cinema-art cinema polar opposition, is a central characteristic of Kubrick's cinema.

In the preceding study postmodernist techniques and effects are understood by means of an analysis that considers them as formal devices. The emphasis on the icon is interpreted through the formal option of autofocalization, while the overt patterning of fabula and style is studied through a close analysis of their components: mise-èn-scene, lighting, costume, composition of the shot, editing, and sound. Therefore, the possibility of various alternatives of meaning and of positioning the viewer also offers the possibility of reconciliation of postmodernist narrative tendencies and a formalist analysis, a reconciliation that, in its capacity to study both the effects of postmodernist concepts and formal structures on meaning and viewer's attitudes, opens the way for options of meaning which may offer a new and more fruitful perspective on postmodernisms. The concept outlined by *Full Metal Jacket*, which shapes a realm of study for those stylistic strategies, is capable of including the effects of such postmodernist strategies and of placing them, together with notions of formal coherence, through the scheme of generality/particularity.

The same principle of creation of a limited set of alternative meanings or viewer positions can be applied to the formalism/poststructuralisms dichotomy through the scheme of generality/particularity. The scheme allows a mixture of both tendencies in a realm of availability that counteracts the nihilistic conclusions of postmodernism with respect to the role of language. It is not accurate to say, if we recall John M. Ellis, that everything that exists is a fact of language. There is a connection between language and reality, reality shapes language to a certain extent, and an analysis of this connection may provide a middle way that results in an escape from the nihilism of postmodernist thought.

It is not that the critical panorama should be restricted to the play of two polar opposites called formalism, with the negative connotations of manipulation and ideological oppression that have been ascribed to it in its capacity to shape our relation to reality (a capacity that stems from its connection with such a reality),[2] and poststructuralisms, invested with an aura of liberating ideology that is based on a distrust of language and leads to bleak statements about the impossibility of achieving knowledge of reality. The use of the scheme of generality/particularity and the conclusions reached in the analysis of *Full Metal Jacket* with respect to language allow us to propose a third possibility for critical development: one where the distrust of language is still present and is accepted through an external analysis provided by generality but where such an external position also contributes to the study of the formal structures that shape meaning and that approximate the decoder to reality.

For example, *Full Metal Jacket* presents us with the possibility of subversion through masochism, but this is a possibility that in the critical scheme set by Kaja Silverman is reversed so that a more conformist rejection of femininity and affirmation of masculinity appear in the end. The external position for analysis that is here represented by Silverman's ideas had been anticipated by the formal analysis of repetition

---

[2] This idea pervades the writings of, for instance, Marxist critics, who claim that formalism fails to take the historical context in which a text is produced and consumed into account. See Eagleton (1976, 1986).

and subjectivity that preceded the discussion of sexual difference. The formal approaches had already coincided in the text's tendency toward coherence, reconciliation, and acceptance of the reality of war as presented by the film. This is precisely what the analysis of sexual difference also suggests: the soldiers are finally led to affirm their own masculinity while destroying its opposite, which is what the war is really about. The fact that the possibility for subversion offered by masochism is finally dismissed does not mean that it is not present in the text, since it is a valuable tool for studying the evolution in the presentation of sexual difference. Subversion and conformity are combined in the text, and the position of externality necessary to carry out the study that will lead us to perceive both is a guarantee that both share a similar importance as textual elements. The position of externality fostered by the film is evident in the self-conscious use of repetition, subjectivity, the connections of the film with other cinematographic genres, and the introduction of the issue of sexual difference. This position allows a study of the mechanisms set by war to convince the soldiers of the necessity of a confrontation, while it also allows a study of the possibility for subversion inherent in such an ideology. Both are encompassed by a wider concept governed by the rules of generality/particularity.

The study of the mechanisms of the text has provided an analysis of the ways in which an ideology of violence is set and maintained, which equips us to understand this position better in reality. On the other hand, the study of the possibility offered by the system of sexual difference, which might lead to the abolition of such an ideology of violence, has also incorporated this issue of sexual difference into the "reality" of the film, into our apprehension of the film.

The analysis of Kubrick's poetics and the development of the concept of generality/particularity has revealed the relevance of externality. Within externality the role of autofocalization and, in general, of structures that produce spectacle is also important. Spectacle is present in the three examples that have been chosen as objects of analysis: in *2001*, views of space, perfect geometry inside spaceships, and music; in *Barry Lyndon*, beautifully arranged and lit compositions, together with the perfect combination of painting-like shots and the music that accompanies them; and in *Full Metal Jacket*, slow-motion displays of violence, outbursts of music that accompany characters' moods, and eerie or colorful settings. Spectacle seems to appear together with the three narrative options that have been studied. It is not, therefore, a strategy that exclusively supports subversive narrative modes, but it seems just one more mechanism within the strategies of mainstream cinema. Kubrick's cinema is, therefore, revealed as a neoclassical narrative mode where spectacle is acknowledged as a major force of classicism.

This acknowledgment, together with the exploitation of spectacle, defines an important part of the cinema that has been produced in the 1980s and 1990s. The cinema of, for example, John Carpenter takes spectacle as a force of mainstream cinema whose main aim is either to provide narratives that audiences can easily follow or merely to entertain through a striking display of technical visual devices. Spectacle for its own sake has become a major ingredient of current cinema, and Kubrick's films represent such a change from the aesthetic values of the 1950s, 1960s, and 1970s, a change he had already anticipated in *2001* in 1968 and in *Barry Lyndon* in 1975. It is precisely when such a notion of spectacle became central in Hollywood cinema — the 1980s — that Kubrick seems to have used it to provide us with a narrative, *Full Metal Jacket* (1987), that encompasses the more subversive kind of spectacle of *2001* and the more conservative kind of *Barry Lyndon*, turning spectacle into one more among the plurality of narrative options present in the film.

Works Consulted

Adair, Gilbert 1989. *Hollywood's Vietnam: From* The Green Berets *to* Full Metal Jacket. London: Heinemann.

Austen, David 1968. "*2001: A Space Odyssey,*" *Films and Filming* 14.1, 24–27.

Bal, Mieke 1985. *Narratology: Introduction to the Theory of Narrative.* Toronto: Toronto UP.

Barthes, Roland 1975. *The Pleasure of the Text.* Trans. Richard Miller. New York: Hill & Wang.

——1980. *S/Z.* Trans. Nicolás Rosa. Madrid: Siglo XXI.

——1989a. "Introduction to the Structural Analysis of Narratives" (1966). Trans. Stephen Heath. In Barthes 1989c, 251–295.

——1989b. "The Third Meaning" (1970). Trans. Stephen Heath. In Barthes 1989c, 317–333.

——1989c. *Barthes: Selected Writings.* Glasgow: Fontana.

Bordwell, David 1988 (1985). *Narration in the Fiction Film.* London: Routledge.

——1989. *Making Meaning: Inference and Rhetoric in the Interpretation of Cinema.* Cambridge: Harvard UP.

Branigan, Edward 1984. *Point of View in the Cinema: A Theory of Narration and Subjectivity in Classical Film.* Berlin: Mouton.

——1992. *Narrative Comprehension and Film.* London: Routledge.

Brooks, Peter 1984. *Reading for the Plot.* Oxford: Clarendon Press.

Brunette, Peter, and David Wills 1989. *Screen/play: Derrida and Film Theory.* Princeton: Princeton UP.

Burch, Noël 1979. *To the Distant Observer: Form and Meaning in the Japanese Cinema.* Berkeley: U of California P.

——1983 (1969). *Theory of Film Practice.* Trans. Helen R. Lane. London: Secker & Warburg.

Carroll, Noël 1988. *Mystifying Movies: Fads and Fallacies in Contemporary Film Theory.* New York: Columbia UP.

Castro, Antonio 1994. *Rebelde sin causa/La chaqueta metálica.* Barcelona: Dirigido.

Chatman, Seymour 1978. *Story and Discourse: Narrative Structure in Fiction and Film*. Ithaca, NY: Cornell UP.

——1981. "What Novels Can Do That Films Can't (and Vice Versa)." In Mitchell 117–136.

Ciment, Michel 1983 (1980). *Kubrick*. Trans. Gilbert Adair. London: Collins.

Cohan, Steven, and Linda M. Shires 1988. *Telling Stories: A Theoretical Analysis of Narrative Fiction*. New York & London: Routledge.

Cook, David A. 1990 (1981). *A History of Narrative Film*. New York: Norton.

Cowie, Elizabeth 1984. "Fantasia," *m/f*, 9, 70–105.

Dayan, Daniel 1974. "The Tutor-Code of Classical Cinema," *Film Quarterly*, 28.1, 22–31.

Deleyto, Celestino 1991. "Focalization in Film Narrative," *Atlantis*, 13 (November), 159–177.

——, ed. 1992. *Flashbacks: Re-Reading the Classical Hollywood Cinema*. Zaragoza: Servicio de Publicaciones Universidad de Zaragoza.

——1993. "The Focalizer Focalized in King Vidor's *The Crowd*," *Miscelánea*, 14, 27–40.

Dempsey, Michael 1976. "*Barry Lyndon*," *Film Quarterly*, 30.1, 49–54.

Dittmar, Linda, and Gene Michaud, eds. 1990. *From Hanoi to Hollywood: The Vietnam War in American Film*. New Brunswick, NJ: Rutgers UP.

Doherty, Thomas 1988. "Full Metal Genre: Stanley Kubrick's Vietnam Combat Movie," *Film Quarterly*, 42.2, 24–30.

Dyer, Richard 1986 (1979). *Stars*. London: BFI.

Eagleton, Terry 1976. *Marxism and Literary Criticism*. London: Methuen.

——1986. *Criticism and Ideology: A Study in Marxist Literary Theory*. London: Verso.

Ellis, John M. 1989. *Against Deconstruction*. Princeton: Princeton UP.

Falsetto, Mario 1991. "Narrative Style and Meaning in the Films of Stanley Kubrick." Dissertation. New York University.

——1994. *Stanley Kubrick: A Narrative and Stylistic Analysis*. Westport, CT: Praeger.

Feldmann, Hans 1976. "Kubrick and His Discontents," *Film Quarterly*, 30.1, 12–19.

Flax, Jane 1990. *Thinking Fragments: Psychoanalysis, Feminism, and Postmodernism in the Contemporary West*. Berkeley: U of California P.

Freud, Sigmund 1990. "Humour" (1927). Repr. In his *Art and Literature,* vol. 14. Harmondsworth: Penguin. 426–433.

García Mainar, Luis Miguel 1991. "Kubrick's *Doctor Strangelove:* The Logic of Spectacle," *Miscelánea,* 14, 93–106.

——1992a. "John Ford's *Seven Women:* The Workings of Mise-en-Scène and the Subversive Text." In Deleyto, ed., 77–96.

——1992b. "*La naranja mecánica* o el código sin contexto," *Atlantis,* 14 (May-November), 63–80.

——1993a. "Focalisation and 'Slant' in Kubrick's *Paths of Glory,*" XV Congreso de AEDEAN, Logroño, 439–444.

——1993b. "Auto-focalisation in Film Narrative," *Atlantis,* 15 (May-November), 153–167.

——1994. "Kubrick's *Dr. Strangelove:* Desire and the Fragmentation of Character," *Revista Alicantina de Estudios Ingleses,* no.7 (November), 67–82.

Gelmis, Joseph 1970. *The Film Director as Superstar.* London: Secker & Warburg.

Genette, Gérard 1980 (1972). *Narrative Discourse: An Essay in Method.* Trans. Jane E. Lewin. Ithaca, NY: Cornell UP.

Gombrich, E. H. 1984 (1960). *Art and Illusion: A Study in the Psychology of Pictorial Representation.* Princeton: Princeton UP.

Heath, Stephen 1981. *Questions of Cinema.* London: Macmillan.

Houston, Penelope 1976. "*Barry Lyndon,*" *Sight and Sound,* 45 (Spring), 77–80.

Hutcheon, Linda 1985. *A Theory of Parody: The Teachings of Twentieth Century Art Forms.* London: Methuen.

——1991 (1980). *Narcissistic Narrative: The Metafictional Paradox.* London: Routledge.

Jeffords, Susan 1989. *The Remasculinisation of America.* Bloomington: Indiana UP.

Jenkins, Gregg 1994. *A Rhetorical Approach to Adaptation: Three Films by Stanley Kubrick.* Dissertation, Pennsylvania State University.

Kagan, Norman 1989 (1972). *The Cinema of Stanley Kubrick.* New York: Continuum.

Kawin, Bruce F. 1989 (1972). *Telling It Again and Again: Repetition in Literature and Film.* Colorado: UP of Colorado.

Klein, Michael 1990. "Historical Memory, Film, and the Vietnam Era," in Dittmar and Michaud, 19–40.

Kolker, Robert Philip 1988 (1980). *A Cinema of Loneliness: Penn, Kubrick, Scorsese, Spielberg, Altman*. New York & Oxford: Oxford UP.

Lightman, Herb 1976. "Photographing Stanley Kubrick's *Barry Lyndon*," *American Cinematographer*, (March), 269–275, 320–321, 338–340.

Lodge, David, ed. 1988. *Modern Criticism and Theory*. London: Longman.

MacCabe, Colin 1981 (1979). *James Joyce and the Revolution of the Word*. London: Macmillan.

McKee, Mel 1969. "*2001*: Out of the Silent Planet." *Sight and Sound*, 38 (Autumn), 204–207.

Mamber, Stephen 1990. "Parody, Intertextuality, Signature: Kubrick, De Palma, and Scorsese," *Quarterly Review of Film and Video*, 12.1–2, 29–35.

Metz, Christian 1974. *Film Language: A Semiotics of the Cinema*. Trans. Michael Taylor. New York: Oxford UP.

——1979 (1977). *El significante imaginario*. Trans. Josep Elías. Barcelona: Gustavo Gili.

Miller, Mark Crispin 1976. "Kubrick's Anti-Reading of *The Luck of Barry Lyndon*." *Modern Language Notes*, 91.6, 1360–1379.

Mitchell, W. J. T. ed. 1981. *On Narrative*. Chicago: U of Chicago P.

Modleski, Tania 1991. *Feminism without Women: Culture and Criticism in a "Postfeminist" Age*. New York & London: Routledge.

Monaco, James 1981 (1977). *How to Read a Film*. Oxford: Oxford UP.

Mulvey, Laura 1989. "Visual Pleasure and Narrative Cinema" (1975). In *Visual and Other Pleasures*. Bloomington: Indiana UP, 14–38.

Nelson, Thomas Allen 1982. *Kubrick: Inside a Film Artist's Maze*. Bloomington: Indiana UP.

Nichols, Bill 1981. *Ideology and the Image: Social Representation in the Cinema and Other Media*. Bloomington: Indiana UP.

Oudart, Jean-Pierre 1977–1978. "Cinema and Suture," *Screen*, 18 (Winter), 35–47.

Phillips, Gene D. 1975. *Stanley Kubrick: A Film Odyssey*. New York: Popular Library.

Pursell, Michael 1988. "*Full Metal Jacket*: The Unravelling of Patriarchy," *Literature/Film Quarterly*, 16.4, 218–224.

Rafferty, Terrence 1987. "Remote Control," *Sight and Sound*, 56 (Autumn), 256–259.

Reaves, Gerry 1988. "From Hasford's *The Short Timers* to Kubrick's *Full Metal Jacket*: The Fracturing of Identification," *Literature/Film Quarterly*, 16.4, 232–237.

Rodowick, D. N. 1982. "The Difficulty of Difference," *Wide Angle,* 5.1, 4–15.

——1991. *The Difficulty of Difference: Psychoanalysis, Sexual Difference and Film Theory.* New York & London: Routledge.

Rother, Rainer 1989. "Das Kunstwerk al Konstruktionsaufgabe," *Merkur: Deutsche Zeitschrift für europäisches Denken,* 43.5 (May), 384–396.

Selig, Michael 1993. "Genre, Gender, and the Discourse of War: The A/historical and Vietnam Films," *Screen,* 34 (Spring), 1–57.

Silverman, Kaja 1992. *Male Subjectivity at the Margins.* New York & London: Routledge.

Sontag, Susan 1964. "Against Interpretation," in her *Against Interpretation.* New York: Delta, 3–14.

Staiger, Janet 1992. *Interpreting Films: Studies in the Historical Reception of American Cinema.* Princeton: Princeton UP.

Stephenson, William 1981. "The Perception of 'History' in Kubrick's *Barry Lyndon,*" *Literature/Film Quarterly,* 9.4, 251–259.

Sternberg, Meir 1978. *Expositional Modes and Temporal Ordering in Fiction.* Baltimore: Johns Hopkins UP.

Thompson, Kristin 1981. *Eisenstein's Ivan the Terrible: A Neoformalist Analysis.* Princeton: Princeton UP.

——1988. *Breaking the Glass Armour: Neoformalist Film Analysis.* Princeton: Princeton UP.

Todorov, Tzvetan 1982 (1977). *Theories of the Symbol.* Trans. Catherine Porter. New York: Cornell UP.

Waugh, Patricia 1984. *Metafiction: The Theory and Practice of Self-Conscious Fiction.* London: Methuen.

Walker, Alexander 1972. *Stanley Kubrick Directs.* London: Davis-Poynter.

Wexman, Virginia Wright 1993. *Creating the Couple: Love, Marriage, and Hollywood Performance.* Princeton: Princeton UP.

Whittock, Trevor 1990. *Metaphor and Film.* Cambridge: Cambridge UP.

Willoquet-Maricondi, Paula 1994. "Full-Metal-Jacketing, or Masculinity in the Making," *Cinema Journal,* 33 (Winter), 5–21.

Wollen, Peter 1972 (1969). *Signs and Meaning in the Cinema.* Bloomington: Indiana UP.

Worton, Michael, and Judith Still, eds. 1990. *Intertextuality: Theories and Practices.* Manchester: Manchester UP.

Youngblood, Gene 1970. *Expanded Cinema.* London: Studio Vista.

Index